WOMEN'S TRAVEL LITERATURE FROM TRAVELERS' TALES

100 Places Every Woman Should Go

100 Places in France Every Woman Should Go

100 Places in Italy Every Woman Should Go

100 Places in the USA Every Woman Should Go

50 Places in Rome, Florence & Venice Every Woman Should Go

Best Women's Travel Writing series

Gutsy Women

Gutsy Mamas

Her Fork in the Road

Kite Strings of the Southern Cross

A Mile in Her Boots

Sand in Her Bra

More Sand in My Bra

A Mother's World

Safety and Security for Women Who Travel

The Thong Also Rises

Unbeaten Tracks in Japan

Whose Panties Are These?

Wild With Child

A Woman's Asia

A Woman's Europe

A Woman's Passion for Travel

A Woman's Path

A Woman's World

A Woman's World Again

Women in the Wild

THE BEST WOMEN'S TRAVEL WRITING

Volume 10

TRUE STORES
FROM AROUND THE WORLD

TRAVELERS' TALES

THE BEST
WOMEN'S TRAVEL
WRITING

Volume 10

TRUE STORES
FROM AROUND THE WORLD

Edited by
LAVINIA SPALDING

Travelers' Tales
An imprint of Solas House, Inc.
Palo Alto

Travelers' Tales and Solas House are trademarks of Solas House, Inc., 2320 Bowdoin Street, Palo Alto, California 94306. www.travelerstales.com

Credits and copyright notices for the individual articles in this collection are given starting on page 302.

Art Direction: Kimberly Coombs
Cover Photograph: top image (Thai sculpture detail) ©tHaNtHiMa LiM (Shutterstock); bottom image (hanging bridge) ©thebezz (Shutterstock)
Editor Photograph: Lou Lesko
Interior Design and Page Layout: Scribe, Inc.
Production Director: Susan Brady

ISBN: 978-1-60952-098-4
ISSN: 1553-054X
E-ISBN: 978-1-60952-091-5

First Edition
Printed in the United States
10 9 8 7 6 5 4 3 2

Tell me, what is it you plan to do
with your one wild and precious life?

— MARY OLIVER

For two of my favorite adventurers:

my late Auntie Ruth, who taught me to read when I was five and who learned to land a plane when she was in her seventies

and

my Goddaughter, Margaret Burke: You're only five now, but I can already see a lifetime of adventure in you.

Table of Contents

Introduction

My best friend and I rarely call each other. Not because we don't enjoy talking; we just prefer to catch up in person, ideally over frosty drinks in a foreign land. But before our recent trip to Nicaragua, I texted her, "Are we taking backpacks or rolling bags?" and my phone rang.

"*Rolling bags?*" she asked, her voice high with alarm and disdain. "What have you done with my best friend?"

It was a good question.

Erin and I became friends thirty years ago, in a clear-cut case of teenage supply and demand: she had a car; I needed a ride. But before long, we discovered we were our happiest selves in that car, cruising the streets and cul-de-sacs of our small town, windows rolled down, heat cranked up, and some terrible music blasting from the stereo. In moments of abject boredom, we'd race along a stretch of road with an incline steep enough that if she floored it going up, we caught air on the way down. Other nights we sped in circles around the highway on-off ramp. We never cared where we went—all that mattered was movement.

Over the years we began inching out, driving to the next town over, and the next town after that. Soon we graduated to a cross-country road trip, then our first international border, Mexico, where we drank cheap tequila and haggled for trinkets in clumsy Spanish. In college we backpacked through Europe for three months. Later we lived in South Korea and vacationed in Thailand, Saipan, and Bali. We spent a month in Australia, where we met Erin's future husband, and we married her off on a beach in Costa Rica. Four years ago, we celebrated our fortieth birthdays together in Cuba.

And not once, in all those years, had I proposed swapping backpacks for rolling bags. What changed? What *had* I done with her best friend? Was it a symptom of middle age? Did it have to do with the fact that I was recently married and trying to start a family? I'd been working insane hours to meet deadlines—could I blame fatigue? One final ignominious thought terrified me: *Were my adventuring days over?*

In Nicaragua, Erin and I backpacked, ate street food, stayed in hostels, took "chicken buses" (retired American school buses, brightly painted and squeezed tight with locals) and *lanchas* (small, crowded boats cheerfully described as "unstable" by one helpful official). All the other backpackers we met—mostly ten to twenty years younger—were hiking volcanoes, clearly *the* thing to do in Nicaragua. We'd considered doing it too, but then we weren't feeling especially motivated, and we hadn't packed the right shoes, and we'd hiked volcanoes before. We'd also gone skydiving, hang gliding, trapezing, rappelling, ziplining, canyoneering, rafting, snorkeling, and scuba diving—not to mention participated in countless other adrenaline-buzzing activities, like the time in Korea we ran a high-speed relay race using an enormous slithering live eel as a baton. We reckoned our resumé of shared adventures gave us a pass this time. So we decided to skip the volcano boarding, too.

Instead, we walked miles each day in 95-degree heat and 85-percent humidity—blistered and sunburned and bugbitten—traipsing through museums, cathedrals, parks, and plazas, braking only for the occasional Tonya beer or *jamaica* (hibiscus) juice. In Granada we rented bicycles (I fell off mine), and in the evening we sang karaoke in a tiny bar filed with locals who treated us like American pop stars. We visited the markets in Masaya, still haggling in clumsy Spanish, and devoured heaping plates of *vigorón* (yuca root, coleslaw, plantains, and *chicharrones*). We toured the island of Ometepe, lingering in Ojo de Agua, Eye of the Water, a mineral pool the attendant swore would make us younger.

For our final two days I'd booked us into Surfing Turtle Lodge, an eco-hostel that Lonely Planet described as a "utopian beach paradise." The reviewer wrote that we might stay "like forever." We wouldn't, of course—our jobs wouldn't allow it. Two days would have to suffice. But even two hours sounded dreamy: it was off the grid, on a secluded stretch of island, 100 percent solar powered. Its main tourist draws were surfing and turtles, but since we wouldn't be surfing (the current was too strong), and no baby turtles were hatching (wrong season), we'd be left with nothing to do but sit on the beach and let our blisters heal. I was enforcing a 48-hour time-out.

To get there, we hired a taxi from Leon, a canoe across a river, and a tiny horse cart through the jungle. When we finally arrived at the remote hostel, a British kid in a tank top that read, "*¿Porque no?*" gave us a tour, starting with the outside bar, which had swings instead of stools and served two-for-one Nica Libres all day long. A sign read: "Happy Hour is <u>Every</u> Hour." As we settled in and met the other guests—all beautiful, tan, barely clothed twenty-somethings draped across couches and hammocks and beach chairs—I realized the Lonely Planet reviewer wasn't being hyperbolic about guests staying "like forever." The first three we talked to had been there three weeks, six months, and seven months, respectively.

Déjà vu hit. Erin and I had once made a habit of lingering in spots like this—sunny hostels in Greece, Thailand, Bali, Australia. We'd arrive intending to stay a night, and weeks later still be installed poolside or surfside. We could do that then; time was elastic and languid, belonged only to us. Now

there's less lollygagging. Travel obliges us to pay closer attention, squeeze more from each moment. Plus, we have careers
and husbands and homes to return to now. But truthfully,
these days we'd also go stir-crazy, staying still that long.

Our first night at Surfing Turtle, one of the owners, Aldo,
joined us for a beer. He was closer in age to us than to his
guests, and I confessed that although I loved his place, I was
feeling self-conscious—after all, we were decades older than
the others.

"Age doesn't matter," he said.

Cliché, I thought.

Aldo leaned forward. "I'm going to tell you a story," he
said, "about Barbara."

He used to lead adventure tours, and Barbara joined one of
his trips through Costa Rica, Nicaragua, Honduras, and Guatemala. A dozen travelers made up the group, all young, fit
backpackers except Barbara, a tiny octogenarian who arrived
hauling a gigantic flowered rolling bag behind her.

Erin shot me a grin, which I ignored.

"Central America is a hard place to travel," Aldo said,
"with its cobbled and uneven roads, but there was Barbara
every day, dragging this huge bag behind her, bump bump
bump bump, everyone offering to help—but she always
waved us off, insisting she was fine."

Aldo regaled us with story after story about Barbara: how
she misplaced her passport and emptied her suitcase onto the
airport floor in Costa Rica, flinging clothes everywhere until
she located it; how she refused a short flight from Nicaragua
to Honduras in favor of a two-day haul on multiple chicken
buses because she knew she'd get a seat (and how she then
sat comfortably while the others stood, hanging on for life,
sardined and cursing her name); how one afternoon Aldo discovered her clutching a coconut she'd found on the ground

and hacking at it with a knife, and when he asked what she was doing, she answered, "I need mixer for my rum!"

"Barbara was awesome," Aldo said. "In fact, she's the only person I remember from that group. So you see, age *really* doesn't matter."

This time it didn't sound like a cliché.

Over the next two days while Erin and I read in hammocks and got massages, the twenty-somethings surfed, played volleyball in thong bikinis and—like backpacker versions of Midas—turned everything they touched into drinking games. They tried to recruit us, and though we declined, we liked being asked.

Our last night at Surfing Turtle, rain brought out the wildlife. As we walked to the bar in the dark, dozens of baseball-sized moon crabs scuttled across our path, and we screamed and ran, laughing hysterically. Later we huddled under a mosquito net reading by the light of our phones, like kids at camp with flashlights under covers. I felt young and—so what if we hadn't volcano-boarded or surfed or even played hula-hooping drinking games?—like we were having a great adventure.

I've been traveling for more than twenty years now, and the thrill of being on the road has always been wed, for me, to the thrill of never knowing what a day might involve, knowing only that I'd say yes. But lately when I travel, I struggle to reconcile my aging, mellowing self with the younger, intrepid me who leaped at every daring stunt. While plenty of my friends—some decades older than I—continue to leap, and while I still *want* to leap, sometimes I just really don't feel like leaping anymore. And while I wholeheartedly celebrate the fact of aging (on good days at least), I deplore the thought of slowing down. Yet I also truly enjoy the actual practice of slowing down. At the same time, the exhilaration of accomplishing something physically challenging is unbeatable.

It gets confusing.

What helps, I've found, is reading travel stories, because the more I read, the more I'm reminded that adventure is limitless, since it can mean *absolutely anything*. It's deeply personal—one woman's gutsy escapade is another's ho-hum afternoon. Adventure is also ageless, evolving as we do. I can attest to this, because in some regards I'm far braver than I was when I began traveling in my twenties. Meanwhile, certain acts I'd have classified as ordinary back then strike me as exciting now. Getting married was an adventure. Trying to start a family is an adventure. Practicing foreign languages, eating weird foods, making new friends: these all feel like adventures. Getting back on a bike was clearly a misadventure (I have the bruises to prove it), and come on: when is karaoke *not* an adventure?

Reading travel stories also strengthens my belief that adventure isn't a physical feat or even an experience, but a state of mind. I think true adventurers are those who treat every ordinary day like the mysterious gift it is; who greet strangers with an expansive mind and an eager, helpful heart; and who aren't necessarily fearless but who confront fears, little or large, and attempt to transcend them. ("I've been absolutely terrified every moment of my life," wrote the great artist Georgia O'Keeffe, "and I've never let it keep me from doing a single thing I wanted to do.")

This is precisely why many of us travel—to face fears and slake our thirst for the unknown. To force ourselves to be a little bolder, a little bigger. We seek renewal, and we've discovered it's most easily attained with passport in hand. Travel is one of the most important acts we can engage in as humans, if only because it reboots our regular lives. The more we set out to discover the universe, the more we habituate ourselves to pursuing rich opportunities and infusing wonder into every moment. Being alive—*truly alive*, not merely existing—requires a refusal to grow complacent, and a deliberate effort to routinely wake ourselves up. And in travel we have an obvious—and exquisite—wake-up call.

So answer the call to adventure. Dare to do something different. Book a ticket to a place you can't pronounce, and when you arrive, climb a volcano. Go trapezing. Or hang gliding. If you're invited to run an eel relay race, say *yes*. Or don't, but say *yes* to something. Wherever you go, find an experience you can turn into an adventure.

This year I had the great privilege of reading 450 submissions to select the 30 essays for *The Best Women's Travel Writing, Volume 10*. As always, the process was enormously fun and ridiculously challenging. The quality of writing astounded me, and I was left with heaps of stories I would have loved to include but couldn't—stories that kept me reading late into the nights, set fire to my wanderlust, gave me shivers, brought me to tears and laughter. Stories that still walk around inside my head, rearranging my notions of travel and adventure. And indeed, although the essays I selected for this year's edition are wildly diverse in geography, subject, and tone, they are all alike in that they are tales of true adventure, because each author made the same simple but critical decision: *she went*.

From Australia to Afghanistan, Thailand to Tanzania, Ireland to India, Cuba to Croatia, thirty talented writers have invited you along on their expeditions of body, mind, heart, and spirit. Some stories are of journeys requiring not only physical but also mental fortitude, such as Peggy Orenstein's deeply moving account of dog sledding in Greenland after her mastectomy. I think you'll find Jill K. Robinson's diving trip through the *cenotes* (underground caves) of Mexico moody and mesmerizing, and Serena McClain's journey of 400 miles along the Camino de Santiago in Spain—with some nasty travel companions—downright terrifying.

You'll read tales of bona fide danger, like Eva Holland's "Chasing Alexander Supertramp," a fascinating profile of the pilgrims who risk life and limb each year in Alaska to reach an abandoned bus, and Jayme Moye's "The Road Not Ridden"—about courageous young female bicyclists in Afghanistan who continue to ride, though doing so endangers their lives.

And of course, there are plenty of essays that prove adventure is beyond definition. Carly Blitz perfectly illustrates my thesis that getting married is an adventure (especially if you do it the way she did, at Burning Man). Sarah Katin finds her adventure crossing the road in Vietnam. And Judith Campbell's "Indian Ocean Commotion" illuminates, to my mind, the highest form of travel adventure: finding yourself an unexpected guest stuck in an unpopular, untouristed place—and welcoming the experience with sheer delight.

Along with chocolate, coffee, and rum, I carried something equally delicious home from Nicaragua: a clear vision of Erin and me, two little old ladies rolling our bags along cobblestoned streets someday. Misplacing our passports, riding chicken buses, hacking away at coconuts. It brings me joy to imagine. And so does the realization that Aldo was right: age doesn't matter. Nor does baggage (literal or metaphorical). What matters is continuing to sign up. Hurtling into unknown places—or merely inching out, even if all that entails is driving fast over a hill to catch some air. What matters is going.

I hope you enjoy this tenth-anniversary edition of *The Best Women's Travel Writing,* and that the thirty stories within (and Barbara's, of course) inspire you to grab your backpack—or your gigantic flowered rolling bag—*¿porque no?*—and go have your own definition of adventure.

—LAVINIA SPALDING
SAN FRANCISCO

જ્જ જ્જ જ્જ

Good Is Coming

Breakfast at epiphanies.

Every day, I walk down to the Ganges River for a swim. Along the way, I pass a small cave chiseled out of the rock. There's an old man there, a holy man. He's usually crouched low over a fire, snapping twigs. I try my best not to let him see me looking inside his home. I don't want to be disrespectful, but I'm curious. I've never seen a holy man's living quarters before. Sometimes, when I think he's bent low enough, I walk slowly to catch a better glimpse of life inside the cave. I've seen a battered pot, a wool blanket. I've spied an altar at the back: candles burning, pictures of Hindu gods and goddesses.

Today the holy man is sitting very still at the mouth of his cave, gazing at the lemon trees. It's difficult not to stare at his long, neatly combed white hair and intense brown eyes.

Every day, when I get to the river, I wait behind the rocks until the groups of white-water rafters have bobbed past, and then I come out and dive straight into water fresh from the Himalayas. The cold is shocking.

At the ashram where I'm staying, they joke that I must have Canadian blood to be so foolish as to swim up here in November. I humor them, saying I come from a people who run naked into oceans in subzero temperatures on

New Year's Day. To be honest, my blood rebels against the water temperature. It numbs my every cell. But I have no choice except to swim in it.

The river cures everything, eventually, I've been told. Rheumatism. Cancer. Snakebites. Broken hearts. Bad karma. For thousands of years people have found their way to its banks and prayed to it, adorned it with flowers, burned their dead beside it, swum in it. Millions and millions of people. I like to float along in its current, thinking of this. I like to imagine my body as a sieve and the river straining through me, the rapids crushing any molecules of disease. I like to imagine my broken heart coming dislodged and floating downstream like a dead branch, my bad karma sinking to the bottom with the silt. Like the silt, every day it seems to pile higher. Every day I remember some new misdemeanor: Lies. Jealousy. Unkindness. It's all there. Cringing in the cold water, I think back on turning thirty, and on my twenties, and all the way back to my teens, to the worst thing I've ever done—something I've never spoken of and probably never will. Do we all hold one such secret? I float there, thinking about that night I'd rather forget, and wait for the river to swallow me whole. But it doesn't.

After my swim, I walk along the beach and shiver. Sometimes I see the holy man farther downstream making elaborate gestures with a stick of incense. Other times he's just sitting and looking at the rapids. If it's a sunny day, the flattest rocks will be covered with his laundry: cantaloupe-colored sarongs, matching handkerchiefs, and towels. If he's close enough, I smile broadly, place my hands in prayer position, bow slightly, and say, "Namaste." The holy man always seems amused by this, but he never returns my greeting. I've been told by the ashram's meditation leader, Lalita, that he's taken a twelve-year vow of silence. I've also been told to avoid contact with him at all costs. But I figure even holy men like to be smiled at now and again.

I confess that, while he's busy with his incense stick at the river, I take advantage of his absence from the cave and linger for a few moments at the threshold, looking more closely at the gods and goddesses and his neatly kept fire pit, until I start to feel guilty and walk quickly back up the hill to the ashram.

I've overstayed my time here. A one-week retreat to learn the basics of Hinduism and yoga has turned into three. I've self-tailored the past two weeks to suit my own spiritual needs, which include reading novels, writing poems, and, of course, swimming in the river. Luckily the ashram is slow this time of year, and Lalita is happy as long as I keep quiet. I think she sees me as a bit of a lost soul, too fragile to return to the rigors of traveling alone in India. I think she's right.

As the river becomes colder, Lalita begins to talk of closing for the season. Though I worry the Ganges hasn't yet cured me, I decide it's best to leave. I walk five kilometers into the village and buy a bus ticket to the deserts of Rajasthan. On impulse I buy the holy man a bag of oranges and leave them by the mouth of his cave.

On my last day at the ashram I walk to the Ganges for my final swim. I see the holy man inside his cave, bent over the fire, snapping twigs. The moment my footstep falls by the cave entrance, he turns and gestures for me to enter. I look nervously back toward the ashram. He slaps the ground hard with a twig and fixes me with a scowl. I go inside.

He leads me to the altar. There, beneath the portrait of Shiva, balances a pyramid of oranges. He points to me, to the oranges, to Shiva. He places his hands between his chest in prayer position and bows his head. Then he rubs the spine of a cabbage leaf onto the dirt floor and begins to write with its juice in English: *Breakfast. Tomorrow. Seven A.M.* He looks to me for a response. I nod. He claps his hands together twice, smiling so widely I can see that he has only four teeth. Then he turns his back to me, bends over the fire, and snaps twigs.

When I arrive the next morning at seven, the holy man is stirring a pot over the fire. I offer him the only item I have left in my chocolate stash: a KitKat bar. He claps his hands and smiles, gesturing me toward a cushion atop a bamboo mat. He busies himself with the pot, and I fidget on the cushion, growing more and more nervous, but my nervousness is soon overtaken by curiosity. I'm at leisure to examine every detail of the cave: the holy man's bedroll, the symbols written in ash on the wall above it, the package of incense, the books stacked neatly in a recess. He walks to a shelf made of branches lashed together by twine and extracts an assortment of bags from a large box, then returns to the fire.

Finally the holy man presents me with a mysterious concoction in an ornately patterned copper bowl. He sits in front of me and watches as I take my first spoonful. I've prepared myself to love it no matter how horrible it tastes. But when it reaches my tongue, I raise my eyebrows in surprise, then take another bite, and another. I can't stop eating. It's as though he's captured every flavor I've ever loved. The sweet, the savory. It's all there in my copper bowl.

He laughs and gives me more. He points to Shiva, to the pot on the fire, to me. He goes outside and returns with the spine of a cabbage leaf. *Deva*, he writes, points to me and then to the center of his forehead. *I see you*, he writes. I must look confused because he squeezes his eyes shut, opens them, and then writes: *Good heart. I see you. Inside.*

I panic for a moment. Can he read my mind? I try to think pure thoughts, and he laughs again. Suddenly his expression changes to one of pain. *Suffer*, he writes quickly, the cabbage stem beginning to turn to mush. *Too much.*

"I've suffered too much?" I ask, and he nods his head. "Yes," I say. "Yes, I know."

The holy man claps his hands and smiles. He throws the cabbage stem aside and picks up a twig. *Good is coming,* he scratches into the dirt. He points to every word. "Good is coming," I say, and he claps again. "Good is coming," I say, liking the feel of the words in my mouth.

At the age of eighteen, Angela Long flew from Toronto to Frankfurt to begin a long-term love affair with faraway lands. She's hitchhiked, cycled, bussed, walked, driven, sailed, and ridden trains throughout Europe, Mexico, Central America, Northern Africa, India, America, and Canada. She's volunteered in soup kitchens, orphanages, literacy centers, and farmers' fields. She's worked in restaurants, tree-planting camps, hotels, hostels, English-language schools, tutoring centers, gardens, pottery studios, and transition houses. Her writing is a distillation of these experiences and has appeared in numerous publications including The Sun, Utne Reader, *and* The Globe and Mail. *She's also the author of* Observations from Off the Grid, *a collection of poems about the nomadic life.*

FAITH ADIELE

ॐ ॐ ॐ

Snails

Witchcraft was the least of their troubles.

> In pre-colonial Nigeria, witchcraft was
> regarded as the most heinous crime anyone
> could commit. . . . Witches could enter the
> womb and devour the unborn child. . . . A
> witch with a humorous disposition might
> cause monstrous births. . . . In 1976 there was
> a stampede at the Port Harcourt General
> Hospital as the rumor that a woman had . . .
> delivered . . . a snail spread rapidly. A witch
> was said to have been responsible.
> —Elechi Amadi, *Ethics in Nigerian Culture*

*O*n this, my third visit to my father's homeland, I kidnap
my Nigerian-born sister and drag her out of our ancestral compound, away from her endless chores, away from the
roar of the Chinese generator, the indignant bleating of her
pygmy goats, my stepmother's constant, teary-voiced calls.

"I have to see the tree!" I beg. My favorite spot in the whole
country.

"It's much smaller now," she warns as we stroll the quiet, dusty
path toward the village crossroads. "They've been chopping it

back." Her smooth, perfect brow crumples and her flower-petal lips turn downward, anticipating my response.

I double over like I've been stabbed. "The tree that saved us?"

That first visit, sixteen years ago, my new-father and stranger-siblings stopped en route to our ancestral village to show me the tree. The dirt road, so feverishly red and potted it resembled a victim of war, suddenly grew cool and dark. Ahead, several paths and roads met, rising up into the largest tree I'd ever seen. The ancient Peugeot, piloted by my teen-aged brother, cautiously approached.

It was just an *achee* tree, the leaves good for soup, but huge, gnarled roots taller than a man erupted from the vivid soil, arced and undulated along the forest floor, forming a series of natural seats nearly a block long. Branches stretched from one side of the road to the other, forming a canopy over our heads, over half of the entire village.

The car fell silent, and my sister explained how the tree had saved the village during the civil war. "When the Nigerian Federalist troops finally made it this far south into Biafra," she began in that lilting voice, as if speaking from far away, "they marched into the village and began looting houses and setting farms on fire. Ours was one of the first to go."

Her dark eyes stared dreamily out the cracked window. "When they saw the prize *achee*, they rushed to chop it down." She shivered, chilled by the shade or the history. "They say that wherever Nigerian axes struck the tree, blood ran like sap. The soldiers fled the village in terror."

And though our father generally discouraged such super-natural talk, this time he sat silent in the front seat, his narrow, weathered face set in its any-talk-about-the-war mask.

Now, sixteen years later, suddenly we're in deep shade, the air cool around us. "This-o?" I demand, looking up. "The villagers are chopping this tree that bled for us?"

She fumbles for my hand and pulls me close. "They think witches gather here," she whispers.

Back at the compound, my brother's fiancée—noticeably pregnant, with four-inch heels and a shiny black weave—lounges on the porch of our father's newly painted, dollhouse-like bungalow.

"Ah, Faith, I hope you brought me something very good from America," she says with a smile that feels like a threat. "I told all my friends I now have an American sister-in-law!"

My stepmother starts up again, and this time my sister departs eagerly, a warning glance over her shoulder. My brother's fiancée leans back against the shutters in her filmy, purchased-in-Dubai blouse, looks me up and down, pats her swelling belly, and waits.

Over the coming days I will drag the countless extended family members who pass in and out of the house to the porch and demand, "This fiancée. Who is *she*?"

No one knows, they will reply. My aunties dig their fingers into the sensitive crook of my elbow and pull in opposite directions. *Eh heh! Now that you are finally here, let us Whisper in Your Ear.*

She comes from—they whisper—*a family of uneducated traders! Her parents attend one of those churches where everyone dresses in white.* The aunties arch their shaved-off-then-painted-on eyebrows. *Clearly she used traditional witchcraft to ensnare him, the first son of the great Commissioner! He hasn't been the same since the day he laid eyes on her.*

He left his long-term girlfriend, sweet girl. They drag the backs of their left hands across the palms of their right, flinging manicured fingers up dismissively. *You can't talk to him. Try, now!* They gesture at me, palms up.

He just wants to do what he wants to do. The aunties' voices dip as they lob their basest accusation: *Like an American!*

After they depart, their British perfumes and face powders leaving me weak and asthmatic, I turn to re-enter our

ancestral home, newly renovated with my brother's mysteriously sourced but seemingly unending stream of wealth.
Below the tin roof awaits a father battling dementia; a stepmother paralyzed on one side from a stroke; one thoroughly
depressed (or perhaps exhausted) sister; and a second brother
with autism/retardation/social anxiety/whatever-the-hell-
we're-not-naming/not-noticing. Witchcraft is the least of our
troubles.

In the morning, my brother roars with frustration. First he
shouts directions to the armed guards he has hired to protect us from robbers and kidnappers. Next at the family:
"Mommy," he bellows, "stop that your Fussing! Sister, stop
that your Dawdling! You People get into the car! Our Bride's
People await!"

It seems the smaller our father shrinks, the larger my
brother grows. This morning he is huge and handsome, skin
glossy-dark in a new up-and-down of mint-and-buttermilk
lace with matching cap.

We prepare to pile into the car, and Daddy shuffles out in
moth-eaten sweater and bedroom slippers. He pounds me
on the arm: "Enjoy the church services, My Daughter!" My
sister, elegant in chignon and Swiss lace, smiles sadly. Upon
the first car's return at dusk, he has no idea that his heir has
married.

No idea that when the drummers entered the *fútbol* field,
Our Bride in matching mint-and-buttermilk lace dancing
behind, flanked by bridesmaids in head-ties as colorful as
birds, The Groom ducked behind his boys. No idea that the
women danced up to the laughing men and made a show of
looking up, down and around for The Groom, who for his
part was making a show of not wanting to be found, crouched
down behind the men, who were crowding together and swaying like a rugby scrum. No idea that when she spotted Her

Groom, Our Bride held out the calabash of palm wine she was carrying, and he jumped to his feet, took the gourd from her hands, and married her with a sip. No idea that with this, my brother's leap into manhood, the balance of power has shifted.

Upon our return, my stepmother immediately starts calling for my sister to fetch water from the cistern, fetch food, start cooking, start Daddy's bath, find her purse, find that letter from Mr. So-and-So.

"What are the housegirls and houseboys for?" I complain as my sister hurries by, cranky and sad.

Through the wall I hear our father working on his sound effects. In his stories there are always soldiers and policemen *bum-bum-bumping* with loud guns and *whap-whap* beating sticks. He puffs his cheeks and marches in place: baggy shorts, striped socks, house slippers. *Bum-bum-bum!* "My father Samson was more than seven foot tall!" he often declares.

Through the other wall I hear ghosts and threats of juju and death curses as our silent second brother and the houseboys and girls watch lurid Nollywood movies all night.

Finally, when the sky over the courtyard is forest-black and Daddy long since tucked into bed, reliving the war, and the villagers who have come to welcome Our Bride have subsided into low mutters and sleepy demands for *More Drink!,* my brother returns with Our Bride.

The village women rush the car, ululating and singing songs of welcome barely audible over the incessant generator. The newlyweds emerge in their mint-and-buttermilk finery, shaking from witnessing the bloody car crash that delayed them, and the villagers cluck their tongues at their near escape, cry *Aeh-yah* and *Heyyyyyyyy*, slap their palms, and raise their faces to the sky to declare, *God is Great* and *Thanks Be that you were covered with The Blood of Jesus!*

Toting shiny boxes and plastic buckets of cash, the new-lyweds move into the master bedroom, the only room in the house with air conditioning: our father's room.

Four days after the wedding, the day of the Great Bride Soup, Daddy shuffles out into the courtyard, and my brother, who is perched on a stool in his pajamas drinking schnapps for breakfast, tries to lure him into a game of cards.

Nearby Our Bride cooks us her first soup. Several house-girls and cousins have been rounded up to aid in the endeavor, which by all the moaning and sighing and declarations of great suffering and exhaustion being performed by Our Bride, appears to be an undertaking epic in proportion.

Neon-orange palm oil is being drizzled into pots. Onions and peppers and dried crayfish are being ground in blend-ers. Small green boughs of *oha* are being stripped of leaves. Bright-white buds of *cocoyam* are being pounded to paste in mortars. Dried Norwegian stockfish is coming to life in pans of boiling water. Tiny knots of fluorescent-blue snails are being flushed of grit.

"We prepare it differently on my side!" Our Bride shrieks between feigned bouts of fainting, hand to hairnet. "I'm tell-ing you, you will love it!"

When she sees me roll my eyes, my stepmother steps in. "Daddy," she cajoles, "Our Bride is making a very good soup that you should be prepared to take."

"Take it where?" he quips, slaying the crowd. "Where does this soup want to go?"

"Daddyyyyy," Our Bride purrs, teeth hidden. "I hope you can eat my very good soup, that nothing in it disagrees with you."

Daddy ignores her. Instead, he turns to me and switches to The Queen's English, an intimidation tactic from his years as Commissioner of Education. "So, young lady, who is your father?" He peers closely at me, and I hold my breath, willing him back to us. "I know him, don't I?"

I bite my lip and nod, praying for the spell to break.

After dinner he refuses to take his medicine, knocking the glass out of my sister's hand and shouting that the Nigerian Federalists are trying to poison him. Our Bride intercedes, playing the devoted daughter-in-law, her performance high-pitched and cloying.

"Daddyyyyy!" she screeches, "I brought you banana, so you should take this small-small pill and then you can have it."

"Aha, that's the very reason I should not!" he lobs back, withered arms crossed.

"I'm preparing *pawpaw* for you," she chirps at a frequency that drives dogs and sisters-in-law mad, waving a dull knife and platter of papaya. "Daddy, I'm sure you will like."

"Ah, that is my worst enemy!"

I smile. Even half out of his mind, he can smell rotten stockfish.

That night the Great Bride Soup exits my body out of every available orifice. I crouch in the bathroom for what feels like hours, plastic buckets positioned strategically. The Great Bride Soup reappears, virtually intact: Orange palm oil slimes down my legs. Green *oha* leaves flake to the floor. Lumps of off-white *cocoyam* plop out like beaten slugs, followed by blips of blue snail, looking like eyes.

Despite my loud retches and explosions, my moans for help, no one appears. In the morning Our Bride refuses to speak to me, huffing icily.

"Uh oh," my sister whispers with a grin, "she must be convinced you got sick on purpose."

"Or that I thwarted her evil plan to kill me," I quip to make my sister gasp and scurry away giggling, as my stepmother calls for her.

*   *   *

The villagers claim that witches have been living in the *achee* tree.

The tree's history doesn't sway them, my sister reports. They hack at its taller-than-a-man-sized roots and its blocking-the-sun foliage, bludgeon its reaching-from-one-sid e-of-the-road-to-the-other branches, though I don't know how anyone could forge instruments that powerful or reach that high.

With each visit the tree is shrinking.

Finally, though their efforts have not lifted the epidemic of armed robberies and kidnappings, of plane and car crashes, of corrupt politicians using public funds to take their mistresses abroad, of deaths to sickle cell and malaria and childbirth, of no light nor running water, or whatever-it-is that the villagers attribute to these witches, they fell the thing completely, leaving just a scarred stump at the village crossroads that refuses to bleed.

     ✍   ✍   ✍

Faith Adiele has been a Buddhist nun, community activist, diversity trainer, and petty bureaucrat, and appeared in a national television ad, in the pilot for a new reality show, and in "A Day in the Life of Faith Adiele" *for* Pink *magazine. She is the recipient of sixteen artists' residencies in five countries; author of the award-winning travel memoir* Meeting Faith; *writer/narrator/subject of the PBS documentary* My Journey Home; *and co-editor of* Coming of Age Around the World: A Multicultural Anthology. *Named by* Marie Claire *as 1 of 5 Women to Learn From, Faith has taught travel writing in Bali, Chautauqua, Ghana, Iowa, Nigeria, the San Francisco Bay Area, South Africa, and Switzerland. Visit her at www.adiele.com.*

ℬ ℬ ℬ

Bad Pilgrim

She finds some unusual travel
companions on the Camino de Santiago.

The room slowly stirred to life. Martin, a recent graduate from California, wrestled with his sleeping bag on
the bunk above me. In the corner, Jack from Canada held his
sleep apnea machine in one hand and his ukulele in the other,
and I suspected it would not be long before he decided to sere-
nade the room with a morning greeting. The Germans across
from us were already dressed, packing up their belongings so
fast they looked robotic. An Italian girl made her way to the
bathroom, clad only in a towel, while an older French man
wearing just tiny white undies walked by me and groaned. I
struggled out of my lower bunk and looked out the window.
More rain.

Months ago, when walking the Camino de Santiago was
nothing more than an idea, I couldn't have fathomed how
normal this scene would become. How common it would be
to stay in a room full of strangers. To fall asleep listening to
a cacophony of snores and wake to hairy legs dangling over
you. To no longer blush when a wrinkly old man walked by
you in his birthday suit. To spend five minutes every morning

covering your feet in Vaseline. To have no idea where you'd be sleeping that night.

We'd planned the trip for more than a year. Walking the Camino de Santiago, a five-hundred-mile pilgrimage across Northern Spain, had been my husband's dream for well over a decade. He'd first learned about it in high school, and the idea of traveling across a country by foot had stayed with him since. We'd been married just shy of two years, and this was to be our last hurrah before settling down and starting a family. But we were looking for more than a vacation; we wanted— maybe even needed—a shared adventure, an *experience*.

Almost three weeks in, we were getting an experience.

Nestled in the sleepy mountain village of El Acebo, Apóstol Santiago was quickly turning out to be the weirdest *albergue* we had come across so far. A *donativo* refuge, it was associated with the tiny cobblestone church next to it. Rosaries hung from the ceiling and crosses adorned its wooden walls. When we'd arrived, the *hospitalero*, an eccentric little man named Javier, handed me a postcard with a photo of himself dressed as St. James.

I sat down on Kevin's bunk, leaning forward to avoid hitting the low wires of the bed above. "How did you sleep?" I asked. He looked at me, a deadpan expression on his face, and said nothing.

"Yeah, me too." I said. "But I don't think I got bit, so that's good, right?"

The rumors had started shortly after we'd checked into the *albergue* and unpacked our bags. "I think I saw a bedbug," I heard someone whisper from across the room. Kevin and I had looked each other in horror. It was already dark out, and the next village was more than three miles away. Our hardest day yet, we'd just hiked fifteen miles through freezing rain and howling wind. The terrain was treacherous, covered in tiny sharp rocks that caused my already blister-laden feet to

sear in pain. More than once I'd stopped walking and simply sat in the middle of the stony, muddy path trying not to
cry, while Kevin trudged ahead looking for a magical short-
cut that didn't exist. We assessed our options and came to the
dreadful conclusion that we didn't really have any.

Over dinner that night at Apóstol Santiago, Javier announced
that he wanted everyone to go around the room and share
their personal stories with the group.

Why are you walking the Camino?

I had come to loathe this question. The Camino equiva-
lent of "What do you do?" it was one of the very first things
people asked, coming shortly after "What's your name?" and
"Where are you from?" It hadn't bothered me at first, but
lately it seemed like a competition for whose story was the
most transcendent.

In the middle ages, the Camino de Santiago was revered as
one of the most important Christian pilgrimages in the world.
According to Catholic legend, the remains of the Apostle
St. James were buried in the cathedral in Santiago de Compostela. Once there, medieval pilgrims would receive a ple-
nary indulgence, lessening their time in purgatory by half.

Though yellow painted arrows and scallop shells now
adorn the path, and a highway often runs parallel to the trail,
the route itself remains largely unchanged. Every year hundreds of thousands of modern pilgrims continue to make their
way to Santiago, each drawn to it for different reasons.

There were the lost souls searching for the meaning of life.
The Catholics walking in the name of Christ. The hardcore
fitness buffs testing their physical limits. There were those on
pilgrimage seeking spiritual transformation, and others walking in order to cope with tragedies so heartbreaking they were
beyond comprehension.

And then there was me.

I wasn't religious. I wasn't on a personal quest for enlightenment. I wasn't overcoming a terrible obstacle, mourning a death, or escaping a bad marriage. I wasn't looking to find myself. I wasn't even fond of hiking.

My story seemed shallow and insignificant in comparison to others. I was doing it for fun.

Which was ironic, considering my feet were blistered and bleeding, there was a constant ache in my Achilles tendon, and I'd begun to fear I was suffering from a collapsed arch. Taking into account the latest bedbug rumor, this wasn't my idea of fun. Why was I walking the Camino? I'd been asking myself that question for days.

Javier went first. The star on a stage of his own making, this was clearly his favorite part of the night. For ten minutes he talked about his life in Spain and the bad decisions that had led him to walk the Camino. Once he arrived in Santiago de Compostela, he said, God had told him that he needed to be of service to other *peregrinos*, so he'd left his wife and kids and gone to work at this *albergue*. St. James spoke to him often.

Before long only one person was left until it was my turn to share. I had already learned that the woman sitting beside me was a devout Catholic from Ireland, and I wondered what motivational tale she had in store for us. I braced myself for yet another moving account that would bring the group to tears, but she surprised me.

She snuck a glance at me, rolled her eyes, and then stood up. "Only God knows," she said. Then she sat down and resumed eating her dinner.

Javier looked perturbed, and I tried not to laugh. I found solace in her simple answer.

Why was I walking the Camino?

Only God knows.

* * *

"My paranoia is starting to get the best of me," I told my friend Carmel, a vivacious Australian mother of three, as we maneuvered up a soft path covered in mud. "Last night I dreamt they were crawling around in my hair and laying eggs *in my ears!*" I was trying to restrain myself from scratching the new spots that had sprouted on my face.

A few days after leaving Apostol Santiago, I'd discovered a small cluster of tiny red bumps on my arm. The next day, a new swarm appeared on my knee. Now, worst of all, they'd found their way to my forehead.

"At least you're not walking in shit," Carmel responded, realizing she'd stepped into another pile of squelchy manure. We had just entered Galicia, a stunning region characterized by lush green farmland, rolling hills, pastures full of cattle, and a lot of dung. "It's probably my penance for being a bad pilgrim and taking the bus."

We met Carmel and her husband Ken the day we left Apóstol Santiago and became instant friends with them over multiple bottles of local Ribeiro white wine, *caldo* soup, and each evening's mystery meat of choice, which ranged from mind-blowing to utterly inedible. Like us, they walked slowly, stayed at the occasional hotel, drank wine with lunch, and enjoyed a good meal. Unlike us, they were over sixty and retired.

As a childfree couple in our thirties, Kevin and I were a minority among *peregrinos*. We'd come to understand that most pilgrims fell into one of three camps: Early twenties, full of wanderlust and low on cash; mid-life soul searchers walking alone; and older retirees, embarking on the Camino as a walking vacation. Most of our friends fell into the third category. On the Camino, age is irrelevant, but the retirees and us, we understood each other.

When we stopped for lunch later that afternoon, we opened a bottle of wine.

"Drinking again? It's like you're on holiday or something!" said Daniel, a young Canadian we'd met earlier in the week.

We had picked up the bottle during a spontaneous winery detour the day before. We'd wandered in tired and sweaty and wandered out with a bottle of rioja and a jar of foie gras.

"We *are*," Kevin responded.

A few days before leaving for Spain, Kevin had arrived home to find our living room in chaos. Sleeping bags covered the floor of our tiny San Francisco apartment. Clothing was haphazardly strewn over furniture. Ace bandages. Compression sleeves. Socks. Gloves. Everything we could possibly need for the following six weeks was spread around the room like hand-me-downs at a garage sale. And I was standing on the couch, dousing it all with a non-toxic insect repellent.

"Don't you think you're going a bit overboard?" Kevin asked as he tiptoed around the mess.

"Better safe than sorry," I said. "You'll thank me later."

Horrified by the thought of bedbugs, I wasn't taking any chances. Even our toiletries got a slight mist of protection.

I was thinking back on this conversation as Kevin and I sat on the floor of our private room at Albergue Paloma y Leña and sorted through our backpacks item by item. We turned pockets and socks inside out, combed through our guidebook page by page, even dismantled our camera in case something had crawled deep inside. And after two hours of searching, we breathed easy again, convinced we were in the clear.

As we prepared to leave for dinner, I noticed my red backpack cover leaning conspicuously against the room's bright yellow walls. It was the only item I hadn't checked. I walked over and spread it on the floor in front me. Huddled in the crevice of the nylon rain cover was one tiny *chinche*, the infamous and hysteria-inducing gremlin whose English name was bedbug.

It was past midnight. Standing outside in our underwear, Kevin and I finally started to laugh. After it was confirmed that the creepy crawler living in my backpack was indeed a bedbug, the *albergue* inhabitants had sprung into action. Thomas, a recent bedbug victim himself, gave us his toxic bug spray. Paloma, the *hospitalero*, washed our clothes at a temperature hot enough to ensure insect mortality. Carmel taught us to use vinegar to wipe down everything we couldn't wash. Ken found some trash bags so we could throw out what couldn't be sanitized. And Cory, who spoke not one word of English, shouted "*¡Muere! ¡Muere!*" as I attempted chemical warfare on our backpacks.

There had been no spiritual transformation or eureka moment of enlightenment, but over the course of the past few weeks, I'd become stronger. *We'd* become stronger, together. My worst Camino fear had come true, and it wasn't that bad. So we'd had bedbugs. Even carried them with us for days. But we vanquished them. We prevailed.

The next morning, we would wake up late and be the last to leave. Our backpacks would smell of chemicals and vinegar, a scent that would linger long after returning to California. We'd eventually make it to Santiago, arriving in the midst of a torrential downpour, sopping wet and full of gratitude. People would ask us if we'd do it again, and we'd surprise ourselves by saying, yes, yes we *absolutely* would. Because despite all the misery, pain, and gloom, we had a blast.

Especially the night we stood in a small garden in Northern Spain, outside an *albergue* whose slogan was "An Oasis of Peace and Tranquility," stripped down to our skivvies, chanting, "Die, motherfuckers, die" as our new friends from around the world cheered us on.

❧ ❧ ❧

Serena McClain is a terrible hiker, but she tries her best. She has crossed the Atlantic Ocean by ship, worked as a barmaid in Edinburgh, changed diapers in Phnom Penh, and is always on the lookout for her next big adventure. A citizen of the world at heart, she currently lives in San Francisco with her husband. This is her first published story.

ॐ ॐ ॐ

Day Dreamer

Those who dream by night in the dusty recesses of their minds wake in the day to find that it was vanity: but the dreamers of the day are dangerous men, for they may act their dream with open eyes, to make it possible.

— T.E. Lawrence, Seven Pillars of Wisdom

*C*orbin looked as though he had left his head in the clouds as he stumped down the stairs of the Eiffel Tower. From the Champs des Mars below, I kept my eye on his blond head, bobbing above the others in his fast-growing teenaged body.

"You should never have left him up there, Brendan, how will we find him in this mob?" I hissed. "I don't care if you got vertigo. Get up there and grab him before he's completely lost!"

We were already an hour late to meet my friend at Musée d'Orsay, where she and I would visit Georges Seurat's pointillist paintings—in peace, I hoped. By the time we traveled on foot and by metro, waited in line, and arrived inside the museum, my lofty aim to turn my son Brendan and his friend Corbin into art aficionados had shrunk to a disappearing dot.

"Here." I scribbled a list, remembering how they'd always loved treasure hunts. "Find these in the museum. I'll meet you here in one hour." They were getting hungry; that was all the time I'd have.

The List:
1. Statue of woman's head, cut off at the neck.
2. Painting of guys playing cards.
3. Statue of girl in tutu with real tulle, hair, ballet slippers.
4. Painting of empty church, blue inside.
5. Find the Louvre across the river [*surely they could?*].
6. Painting of people dancing outside.
7. Black and white photograph by Degas.
8. Painting of snow.
9. Opéra Garnier model.
10. Big clock.

"What if we can't find all this stuff?"
"One hour."
"What's a tutu?"

The artist was obsessed with the weather. In 1885, he was chasing clouds in Étretat, France, engulfed by a surging desire to capture the sea on canvas. One day, he was on the beach at his easel, and as mist rose off cresting waves in droplets of white foam and caught the sunlight, he painted in a fevered froth. When the moment passed, he saw that he had done it: He had caught the sea. But, he noted with despair, he now needed the matching sky, and dusk was falling. He returned the next day and, absorbed, did not hear the increasing thunder of the waves.

I didn't see a huge wave coming, it threw me against the cliff and I was tossed about in its wake along with all my materials! My immediate thought was that I was done for, as the water dragged me down, but in the end I managed to clamber out on all fours, but Lord, what a state I was in!

Oscar was soaked. His palette had splattered his beard with blue, yellow, and green. His painting was *torn to shreds by the sea, that "old hag."*

He needed identical conditions to appear and remain long enough to complete the painting. If only he could suspend time so that a shadow lingered before skittering off, the light brightened a fraction and held, and the clouds stopped.

Oscar cursed, slashed his paintings, and became *terrified of light.*

I'm very unhappy, really miserable and I haven't the heart to do anything, the painter in me is dead, a sick mind is all that remains of me . . .

Before our trip to Paris, in my quest to interest these two teens in art, I'd left heavy tomes, *Art Through the Ages, Treasures of the Louvre, Musée d'Orsay* lying on top of *Sports Illustrateds* around the house, but they served as mere paperweights. I wished just once someone would pick one up and thumb through it.

During our week in Paris, I'd dropped tidbits about the Impressionists.

"Cézanne was the grouchiest, kind of like you, Brendan, last night when you were trying to pronounce *boeuf bourgui-gnon*. He was from a place called Aix."

"Van Gogh slashed his own ear. Could have been too much absinthe, or epilepsy. No one knows for sure."

"This statue by Rodin is of a famous writer—Balzac."

They both emitted choking hacks.

"What's so funny?"

"Balls-sack?"

I shared my wisdom: This artist was wealthy, that one went by his middle name for years, another strapped paintbrushes to his arthritic hands. Brendan and Corbin's eyes became hooded; they puffed out their cheeks, stifling yawns.

Still, I stopped them at Rodin's statues, smiling at their snickers, pointed out artists' studios, and planned a trip to Giverny. I knew they'd like that pond.

After our trip to Musée d'Orsay, we had lunch in a café.

"What did you like?" I asked, flushed with hope. Perhaps they'd spotted *Impression, Sunrise*, the painting that had defined the movement.

"Nothin'."

"Back in the day, the critics didn't like those works either; they rejected them for the big Paris art salon, so the artists got together and had their own and called it '*Salon des Refusés.*'"

"There *was* this one painting," said Corbin. "It was of a fence in the snow, and there was something really cool about the air."

"Yeah," said Brendan, and I could tell this was the first time they'd discussed this. "That was wild, like I felt the air."

In the early years, the artist's obsession had been survival. He and his wife and son had moved from place to place, creditors in pursuit, and often went hungry. He penned a constant stream of letters:

> *Please, I beg of you, send me a bigger sum tomorrow without*
> *   fail.*
> *I am utterly without hope, and see everything at its blackest*
> *   and worst.*
> *For a month now I have been unable to paint because I lack*
> *   colors, but that is not important. Right now it is the sight of*
> *   my wife's life in jeopardy that terrifies me . . .*

His wife had another baby, their desperation continued, and she died.

We lingered over dessert.

"What else did you see?"

Brendan and Corbin smiled at each other and nodded.

"I was gonna talk to her, but she looked Czechoslovakian."

"Like Maria Sharapova with green eyes."

Their goal was to exchange sightings and *bonjours* with girls from as many countries as possible, a bevy of gesturing Italians, willowy French girls, tall Swedish beauties.

Perhaps it had been vanity for me to think I could lure them into appreciating art.

The artist's lasting obsession seemed impossible. His work began to sell, and he married a woman with six children. They lived in the country, where he could finally paint in peace, *en plein air*, out of doors, with a lasting paint supply.

He squinted at red poppies and let their round edges ravish his canvas as they had his eye. In quest of *the luminous envelope surrounding the model,* he placed one of his stepdaughters at the top of a hill holding a parasol. Every whoosh and wafting breeze appeared in her white dress as clouds spun past. He caught the golden Thames flashing at sunset, gondolas shimmering in Venice, a small red house in Norway.

It's only now I see what needs to be done and how.

His dream was far-reaching. He'd articulated it once and knew people thought him a bit mad.

He was driven, regardless.

Then his eyesight began to go.

Six months later, I remembered the single painting that had attracted Corbin and Brendan.

"Yeah, I remember, the painting of the snow, that one that showed the air."

Corbin drew a picture: a fence with a ladder on the left and a bird on top, a house on the right with trees in front.

Brendan's drawing was identical.

"Yep, the painting of the air." He caught Corbin's eye. "But it wasn't the most beautiful thing we saw that day, was it? Green eyes."

I blew the dust off my *Musée d'Orsay* book, finding Sisley and Pissarro, Impressionists who had often painted snowy scenes. I interrupted the boys' viewing of a college basketball game on TV.

"Is it this one?"

"No."

The halftime buzzer rang.

"This?"

"No."

"Let's find it," said Corbin. He grabbed the book and Brendan hauled himself out of the recliner to flop onto the couch. Heads together, they lingered on images of ships sailing on green-blue squiggly seas, apples leaning against blue china pitchers, pillowy nudes in patches of sun.

"Here it is!"

The Magpie. A rare painting of snow, completed the year his rejection at the Salon had caused him to conclude, *I can no longer claim to cope.*

I knew that the artist had achieved his goal.

I am chasing a dream, I want the unattainable. Other artists paint a bridge, a house, a boat, and that's the end. They've finished. I want to paint the air which surrounds the bridge, the house, the boat: the beauty of the air in which these objects are located, and that is nothing short of impossible.
                                        —Claude Oscar Monet

✿   ✿   ✿

Erin Byrne writes travel essays, short stories, poems, and screen-plays. Her work has won numerous awards, including three 2014 Travelers' Tales Solas Awards, and 2013 and 2012 Grand Prize silver and bronze for Travel Story of the Year. Her work appears in a wide variety of publications, including Points North Atlanta, World Hum, *Travelers' Tales* The Best Travel Writing *and* Burning the Midnight Oil *anthologies, and* Vestoj, The Journal of Sartorial Matters. *She is the writer of* The Storykeeper, *an award-winning film about occupied Paris and* Siesta, *to be filmed in Spain in 2015. She is occasional guest instructor at Shakespeare and Company Bookstore in Paris, and is co-editor of an anthology of writings from the bookstore,* Vignettes & Postcards From Paris, *winner of ten international awards. www.e-byrne.com.*

✿ ✿ ✿

Fly Girl

Even as a visitor, one traveler made the perfect host.

*T*ravelers have long observed that wherever you go, you leave a piece of yourself behind. But in Uganda, I went for a singular variation on the theme.

The decision wasn't actually mine, but that of the good Dr. Ndagijimana, head of general services, obstetric and gynecological services, laboratory services and—for good measure—dental services at the roadside Sts Cosmas and Damianus Clinic in Kisoro, a dusty western border town where I turned up in desperation, mid-gorilla-trek.

In a tiny yellow room outfitted with only a peeling vinyl exam table, a cracked bathroom scale, a bare, hanging bulb and what appeared to be Doc Baker's stethoscope on loan from the Paramount prop closet, Ndagijimana solved the mystery that had been plaguing me—in the biblical sense, as I'd soon learn—for days.

"Ripe, painful gluteal abscess," he began writing in billboard-sized cursive that didn't want to be contained by his official Clinical Notes pad. "*Very* painful," he continued aloud as he studied the angry-looking, crack-adjacent tumor. Then, without further ado, he delivered the verdict: "Mango fly!"

Turned out this degenerate insect—also known as the tumbu fly or putzi—had hidden in some air-dried linens, as it was apparently wont to do, then shamelessly violated my left butt cheek at a jungle lodge while I slept off the two-day trip from New York. "The larvae penetrate the skin and lie in the subcutaneous tissue," reported a couple of Belgian doctors in the 1911 edition of *Entomological News* that came up in my requisite, instantaneous Google search. "On reaching full growth, the larvae leave the host, fall to the ground, bury themselves and there pupate."

God help me.

I didn't have an infection. I had my own budding fly colony. But before I could even begin to process my horror, Dr. Ndagijimana called a colleague at a nearby hospital to get me on the day's surgery docket. So I paid a whopping $20 for the consultation and my first ever prescription of Olfen-100 ™ Retard pills, then proceeded to the theater of operations.

Of course, I had been hoping to avoid precisely this scenario. And during the days leading up to it, I sent a whole desperate series of ass selfies to a dermatologist friend back home so he could tell me that with time—and maybe a couple of hot compresses—I'd be totally fine.

Resorting to the subject line "I'm so sorry!"—because really, I was—I continued with this: "As you can see, I've been bitten in a most unpleasant place, and the resulting inflammation is painful and hardened, with a delightful, pus-filled dome. I think the culprit was probably a spider . . . and I'm just hoping to make sure that I need not visit a local hospital. A thousand apologies again!"

But after monitoring the worsening atrocity via Gmail for about forty-eight hours, he insisted I see a doctor in person. And by then, I was in too much pain to object.

I could focus on little else on the ride from Dr. Ndagijimana's to the hospital and had to lie face-down in my guide's jeep as we four-wheeled through stretches that were more rut than road. I tried to distract myself with the occasional glimpse of bright blue, wide-open Ugandan sky, but my embedded guests demanded my full attention.

Mercifully, we soon arrived at St. Francis Hospital Mutolere, and though my turn on the table wouldn't come for hours, the wait proved shockingly comforting. Just outside the window opposite my seat, sequin-turbaned maternity ward patients sat in a circle on the grass—most of them chatting, many nursing, and a few occasionally singing. While the melodies were clearly meant for the babies, I couldn't help but feel I was getting a little music therapy myself.

Meanwhile, the surgery waiting area—a hallway lined with benches and the odd stretcher—also served as a lizard and bird superhighway. Plus a bazaar: Street vendors bearing buckets of freshly caught fish considered everyone a potential customer, and the patients, orderlies and doctors were no exception. So I never went long without a reminder of life beyond these walls.

Sometimes, of course, those reminders were grim. But for every anti-sexual violence poster or HIV-exposed infant care schedule that hung on the walls, there was a framed sentiment so sweet ("My auntie gets me my medicine and makes sure I take it!") that I was comparatively relaxed by the time I entered the operating theater.

The surgeon—a wise-cracking Dutch guy in a Winnie the Pooh scrub cap—put me even more at ease. Good thing, too, as I would soon have to drop trou and hop on the table in front of a group of med students there to observe. (Gowns? Changing rooms? Don't be absurd.) Of course, I could have done without the audience excitement: As soon as the doctor numbed the site and began digging, there were whispers of "I think I see something!" and the ever-assuring "Wow! Wow! Wow!"

Still, I was so elated once the deed was done, I practically kissed everyone on my way out.

And however vile the excised larvae, I felt strangely grateful to them for bringing me here. With all due respect to the apes I failed to ogle that day, I would never trade the display of humanity I dumb-lucked into instead. Nor would I doubt that wherever you go, you *do* leave a piece of yourself behind. In fact, somewhere between the singing mommies and the caretaking aunties, I left not only a piece of my ass in Uganda, but a little piece of my heart, too.

Abbie Kozolchyk is the Beauty and Travel Editor at Every Day with Rachael Ray *and a longtime Travelers' Tales loyalist.*

KATHERINE JAMIESON

ॐ ॐ ॐ

Miss Associated Supermarket

Winning isn't easy in Guyana.

The summer I moved into the Kings' house, Nikki was practicing for the Miss Georgetown Pageant. "Come Katrin!" came the call upstairs every afternoon. I would drop my book and creak down the wooden steps, past the cracked figurines of little Dutch girls nestled between the concrete blocks. Regina would already be slouched on the sofa, and as the afternoon sun burnt through the curtains, we'd drink glasses of Shirley's passion fruit juice, sweet and tangy. Shirley herself would stand in the kitchen doorway, one eye on dinner simmering over the gas flame, while Reggie in his recliner would glance up occasionally from the *Stabroek News,* lowering his glasses as if he couldn't quite believe what he was seeing in his own living room. "Y'all must tell me the truth," Nikki commanded, bending over the tape deck to cue up her song. "Ya must tell me how I *sound.*"

Nikki was nineteen years old. There were shades of the gawky adolescent in her loose-limbed flop on my bed, but grace was overtaking gangliness by the day. Unusually tall for a Guyanese, she had deep brown skin and a face made up of circles: high curving cheekbones; plump lips that broke over large teeth; hair set in wide coils. The repeated roundness made her seem young, but her hips pushed out to reveal a tiny waist, and small breasts rose from an otherwise narrow chest. She seemed to still be trying beauty on, as if it were a fancy dress that had just arrived in the mail one day. I did not yet know that she had nothing else to wear.

She took her place in front of the muted TV, lifting her chest and striking a pose while the tape buzzed and clicked. Then one of the latest R&B hits would start up: "I Believe I Can Fly" or "I'm Everything I Am Because You Love Me." Depending on the mood of the song, she would draw her arms overhead as if in prayer, she would tighten her face in grief. Her long fingers stretched to soothe a broken heart, to catch a fleeting dream. She pranced across the floor, making eye contact with each of us in an unwitting parody of seduction.

As soon as the artist began his crooning, Nikki subsumed it, pushing the vocals far beyond their intended range. She matched him word for word, until the real singer was reduced to a harmonizing hum. And what can I say of her voice? All bad singing is at heart the same. Nikki's was distinguished only by volume. She managed to silence Guyana, drowning out the barking dogs and crowing roosters, the rush of rusty water from the pipes. I cringed for her, embarrassed that she could not hear herself, and that she didn't know to stop. I was three years older, and I didn't realize that she was teaching me something in those performances; I could not admit I might have anything to learn from her at all. Nikki's terrible voice sang of love and loss and desire and hope, and we listened. Our applause sent the lizards scurrying up the walls.

Nikki and I lived together in Aunt Shirley's house on Hadfield Street in a rundown neighborhood of Georgetown. Shirley King and her husband Reggie had been police officers for years, and they supplemented two meager government pensions by renting out a room. In early July, I had dragged my enormous duffel bags to an upstairs bedroom with a square hole cut out for a window. My "host family," who I was assigned to live with for my first few months in Guyana, included two sisters: Nicola—Nikki—and Regina, Reggie's sixteen year-old daughter. In the mornings, I passed Nikki sleeping in the upstairs bay window, wrapped head to toe in a thin blanket like a mummy. It took me weeks to realize that I'd been given her bedroom.

Shirley and Reggie had been in the house forty years, building it from a wooden frame, adding concrete floors and walls, and then accumulating, with painstaking frugality, the accoutrements of a middle-class life. The house was a repository of these efforts, with every successive material acquisition still in residence, whether it worked or not. There were old refrigerators, washing machines and typewriters, clocks long since frozen to a false time. The house had the feel of a yard sale come inside, an attic shifted haphazardly south. Decoration seemed to have been a similarly accumulative process, with acrylic paintings of waterfalls, family photos, and contoured woodcuts the shape of the nation of Guyana lining the walls. Clothes from several decades hung in stacks on the walls or peeked from bursting suitcases. To enter the house was to navigate a maze of papers, magazines, and moldering phone books.

I struggled to fit all my stuff into the King's already packed house. I was ashamed to have so many bright, new possessions. The girls, however, had no qualms about my mass of material wealth, especially my clothes. Regina and Nikki stroked the unfamiliar synthetic blends and pulled at the cotton-lycra pants, slowly releasing them back to shape. These clothes were almost as foreign to me; during college, I had affected a worn and gender-neutral style, my wardrobe comprising a selection of ratty flannel and denim, much of it secondhand. The Peace Corps recommended more traditional attire, so I bought skirts, blouses, and dresses I imagined could survive tropical weather. I replaced pilled sweaters and baggy pants with light fabrics the saleswomen assured me could "breathe." To begin the first adult job of my life, I returned to the styles of my early childhood, practical and girly.

Regina had a thick frame, and only my shorts fit her well. But on Nikki's svelte figure, every garment seemed to cling and drop in the right places. "Look, ya shart dress!" she said, holding the piece up to her body and twirling back and forth in the narrow mirror.

"Like ya posin' fuh George already," Regina teased her. George was Nikki's forty-year-old boyfriend. When I'd first asked her about his age, she'd sung me a song by Sparrow, the Calypso King: *Age ehn't nuting but a numbah!* She smirked at Regina.

"Don't be lickerish now, gal," she said. Turning back to me, "Ya must let me borrow it when we go an' party, Katrin." As she slipped off her shirt and pulled the dress over her head, I watched her face and arms and legs appear where mine usually did. While the color made me look twice as white, Nikki's rich skin tone drew a depth from the simple black garment never imagined by its pale designers. She flashed a smile, and I was reminded of the Guyanese children's song: "I black and I shine, multiply by nine!" It was Nikki who would make my wardrobe enchanting, who seemed to fit my new clothes better than I ever could.

Every day I went to the training center wearing my flowery skirts and knit tops to learn the buzzwords of my new job: *sustainability, counterpart, appropriate technology.* We were visited by local leaders and Ministry officials, activists and theorists. We were taught to "map" communities and "facilitate" conversations. I felt the possibility of my new volunteer job, the weight and excitement of it, though I still had very little idea *how* I would actually do it.

I'd always been a good student, and I set myself to studying my new endeavor: helping the people of Guyana. Especially women and "at-risk" girls. Helping them do what was not entirely clear. Teaching them something, perhaps. In training, we threw around the word "development," a term that spoke of maturation and change, though it was vague to me. I still had no specific work to do, so I thought I might develop Nikki.

She seemed a good candidate, as she was on her own, having no parents or family. Nikki was not related to the Kings. She was the granddaughter of a family friend and had come to live with them as a child from a small village in a rural area. One night, as she painted my nails in orange glitter, Nikki and I talked about her plans for the future. She told me she wanted to be a doctor, or a fashion model if that didn't work out. I reported her medical aspirations back to Valerie, one of our Guyanese trainers. She narrowed her eyes. "These girls talk big," she said, "but what is she really doing to become a doctor?" I pictured Nikki practicing her dance routine for the pageant and rifling through my closet for outfits.

"I think she might take some computer classes next month?" I said.

She shook her head. "What kind of work does she do?" she asked.

I told her about Associated Supermarket, a one-room grocery store where Nikki rang up overpriced imports. She liked it because they let her come to work in her regular clothes: bati-riders—shorts that rode high up her thighs—and baby t-shirts.

"They're sponsoring her to be in the Miss Georgetown Pageant," I said. Valerie raised her eyebrows.

"She has no idea what it takes to be a doctor, and no plan to make it happen," she said.

I had to agree this was true, though it didn't seem to bother Nikki as much as it did Valerie and me. Every week she came home excited about something else her job had agreed to pay for—false eyelashes, hair extensions—and a new song to practice on the living room stage. Nikki seemed as oblivious to her "at-risk-ness" as she was to the true pitch of her voice.

In truth, I was the one at risk. Walking home, I wandered into the Tiger Bay ghetto, which was notorious for street violence. I accidentally jogged through a jungly area in the National Garden, a favorite spot for drug dealers and prostitutes. Wherever I went, catcalls and leering followed, and the madmen harassed me in the market. Right in front of Shirley's house, I panicked when a herd of bony cows surrounded me on the road.

After witnessing a few of my mishaps, Nikki stepped in. As it turned out, she would develop me. I'm still not sure why she did it. One of few foreigners in the country, I was a novelty, and she may have liked the attention I brought her. Perhaps she thought a friendship with an American might gain her favors in the future. Whatever her motivation, I was tired of sitting around the training center listening to theoretical lectures about theoretical Guyanese. I knew this girl could show me parts of the country I would never see on my own. I put myself in Nikki's hands.

"Come, Katrin!" began her high-pitched recruitments each weekend. Saturdays Nikki cleaned the house, but her hair was up in curlers by eleven o'clock. By noon she was selecting my clothes, reminding me to wear makeup and paint my toenails. And before she had scrubbed the last pot, she would sing again from downstairs, "Come, Katrin! Bathe your skin, we goin'!"

After promising Aunt Shirley in vain that we'd return before midnight, Nikki and I ambled on the periphery of D'Urban Park, a large oval field where animals grazed amidst rusting machinery. We walked slowly as she negotiated the unpaved roads in her high sandals, her powder-hairspray blend masking the smell of the smoldering trash. Our street was once part of a colonial horseracing track, but now an irrigation trench and houses lined the long dirt road. Across the field, the straightaway had been paved, and minibuses used it as a staging ground for highway speeds.

Nikki let the older "corkballs" pass, and made us wait for a "boom boom" bus vibrating with deep bass lines, chrome bumpers and hubcaps glinting hard in the sun. When a "shiny" bus finally squealed to a stop in front of us, the tout slid back the door for me while offering the seat next to the driver to Nikki. She had what the Guyanese call a "front-seat face," her smooth skin and thin neck as prized a detail as the fuzzy dice swinging from the rearview mirror. As I crammed myself in between knees and parcels to find a small patch of sticky vinyl, I heard Nikki's familiar shriek: *How ya do, man?* In the mirror, I could see the driver's wide grin. Lurching to our final destination, the touts waved off her money, while I emerged from the dim interior to pay my fare like all the rest.

Nikki's transformation fascinated me. I knew she had almost nothing: few possessions, little education, not even a guaranteed bed to sleep on. But as soon as we walked off the cracked concrete path away from Shirley's home, these facts faded away. On the road, Nikki was a connoisseur of minibuses, a street celebrity, a pageant queen. Even when men catcalled her, she acknowledged them with a dismissive wave that garnered her only more power. While my own looks had always made me feel vulnerable, she used hers to convince the world that she deserved more. I envied her confidence even as I resented it.

Nikki was a ruthless tour guide. She kept us out for ten or twelve hours, rarely asking what I wanted to do. She explained where we were going only in the sketchiest terms, ignoring me when I pressed for more detail. *Katrin, like ya worry too much!* She did not guarantee safety. One night at the

Sea Wall, two young men yelled at each other and one pulled out a gun. I looked at Nikki to see if we should run, but she waved me down. The boy screamed a few more threats, but sped off without firing a shot. "See, Katrin, nothing is happen!" she said later, clapping my arm.

Sometimes I hated Nikki after a night out together. I rubbed the nail polish off in a huff, washed the tangled curls from my hair. Time after time I swore I would never again submit myself to her haphazard plans. But I always did. As aggravating as she was, Nikki was my first entrée to Guyana. I could stay at home, or I could follow her into the long nights. Nights that pulsed with desire and danger, set to a constant, deafening beat. Nights when I never knew where I was, or the name of anyone around me. In spite of myself, I came to crave these times when I too could become something I'd never been before.

Months later, after I'd started teaching at a school for teenage girls, a few of my students said they'd seen me on television. I denied it. "Miss, you were dancin' up!" they insisted. Apparently, one of the country's two television stations had a popular music program that videotaped live parties. In a recent show, the patio had been full of Guyanese, but there was one white woman right in the middle. And then I remembered: the hour-long minibus ride and the boys toting five-foot speakers. The hard wooden benches where we waited hours until other guests arrived. The dub music blaring so loud we had to scream to be heard, and the bright lights on the dance floor flashing in my face. Only Nikki could make me famous.

"Nobody can't beat Nikki in Monopolee!" Aunt Shirley had warned me, and so I avoided the showdown, begging off for exhaustion, heat, and mosquitoes, until my excuses ran out. Dinner was finished and Nikki knew my training was cancelled the next day. "Come Katrin. We must play tonight.

Regina gon' play too." She unfolded the faded board and counted the money like a banker, licking her fingertips to get better traction on the little stacks of worn paper.

The metal playing pieces were preordained: Nikki the hat, Regina the dog, and I was the shoe. She lifted her arms high, shook the die, and let them drop hard on the board. Regina and I rolled, both of us coming up short of Nikki's snake eyes. She grabbed the die again, and we were off. I remembered the game from childhood as a languorous, complicated affair, lasting hours, if not days. In contrast, Nikki's Monopoly was a cutthroat whirlwind. "Mahvin Gardens!" she yelled, sliding the hat up eight spaces, and counting out the $340 to buy it. Her strategy was to constantly buy: properties, houses, favors. When she didn't have the cash, she wheedled. "Look, lend me hundred dollars, nah, and if ya land on any of my hotels ya don' have to pay."

As the match wore on, I wondered when Aunt Shirley had gotten this game, and when Nikki had mastered it. Guyana was a socialist country until 1985, and some of its public buildings still bore slogans about "production" and "a new tomorrow." Shirley and Reggie had been police during this era, and there were pictures of them marching in Soviet-style regimentation. But they seemed to hold no nostalgia for the bans on flour and rice, rigged elections and graft that characterized those decades. Nikki and Regina had been born at the tail end of it, when everyone who could afford to was leaving for the U.S. and Canada.

My head was spinning with Regina and Nikki's clipped Monopoly Creolese as my little shoe moved faster and faster around the board. First I was in jail and then, before I knew it, going bankrupt. When I finally had a stroke of luck and landed on Park Place with just enough cash to buy it, Nikki set in on me. "Waterworks and all the Reds," she offered, pressing the cards into my hand as she reached for the matching blue she needed to wipe Regina and me off the map. She had Boardwalk already, of course, and her houses and hotels dotted the luxury properties leading up to her final conquest. But before she could complete the deal, I snatched up Park Place and held it to my chest. Nikki glowered at me, then grinned. "Come Katrin," she said, reaching her hand out for the card, "ya know ya can't win."

I know, I thought. A month before, she had asked to borrow money for some classes, assuring me that George would reimburse me in a few days. I gave her fifty dollars and waited weeks before asking about it. "Just now, Katrin," she told me, employing the universal Guyanese stalling expression which could mean anywhere from a few hours to a few years. I stewed about this, but I was hamstrung. Nikki knew I was too proud to go to Aunt Shirley, the only one who could make her return the cash. The money was between us now: my ease in giving it to her, and her ease in taking it from me and never paying it back.

The room was still, the ice in all of our drinks long since melted. My body was cramped from sitting on the floor so long. Shirley and Reggie had been laughing and calling out as the game sped up, but now everyone quieted, watching what the American would do. Regina, accustomed to losing, looked sullen. Nikki stared at me, alert and energized, poised for her victory.

I realized that we were playing at different games. I had grown up well off and spent years trying to conceal it. Nikki was poor, but worked hard to create a pretense of riches. Shirley told me that when she first came to stay with them, she had found stashes of missing buttons, shiny coins, and pieces of cloth in Nikki's room. I was struck by the poignancy of this little girl scavenging the house for something to call her own. But now I felt that she was scavenging me. In truth, Nikki was just teaching me the rules. Guyana is a nation of scarcity, not excess, and if you weren't smart enough to protect what you owned, it was taken from you. This wasn't malicious. It was just the way things worked.

I turned to Regina. "Do you want my properties?"

"Ya wan' give me everyting?" she asked with a glint in her eye.

"No, no Katrin, ya can't do it!" Nikki protested, but I was already handing Regina all my cards and cash. Reggie and Shirley hooted and clapped their hands at the sudden reversal of fortune.

"Sorry Nikki, I'm just too tired," I said. She'd already turned back to the board to count out her remaining properties. As I passed up the wooden stairs, I felt a slight pang of guilt, but by the time I reached the top floor the thought had evaporated into the thick heat.

The night of the beauty pageant finally arrived, and Regina and I took a minibus to the gymnasium of a local high school. The ticket said that the pageant was supposed to start at eight, but when we arrived the organizers were just beginning to put out the potted plants and hang streamers. We were alone in the wooden bleachers until ten, when everyone else started showing up.

We saw Nikki down below, wearing white shorts so tight they seemed to disappear into the crease of her thigh. She waved with her whole arm and came up to see us. Under the lights I could tell she had used skin bleach, but her complexion was so dark that the cream just gave her a ghostlike pallor.

"How y'all doin?" Nikki said, bending over to kiss Regina and me on the cheek. Her voice sounded higher than usual. Glistening under the fluorescent light, her lips were garish with red gloss. Bright pink rouge stained her cheeks, and her eyes shone dark with liquid black liner and sky-blue eye shadow. The makeup was startling, and it made her look like a grown woman. She flashed me her bright white teeth, and I had a memory of a time we'd eaten crabs together, a giant claw sticking out of her mouth.

"Y'all ehn't seen George?" she said, swiveling her head back and forth around the room, her "Miss Associated Supermarket" banner riffling out with each movement. We shook our heads. "Ya must call to me if he comes," she commanded.

"Good luck, Nikki," I said. She clomped unsteadily back down the steep stairs, her plastic high heels unsuited for the climb.

The day before, I had asked her about the money again, and she told me that George would bring it with him to the concert. But George never did come that night. A few months later, when I moved into my own place, Nikki showed up on my doorstep with a ring made of some of Guyana's cheap yellow gold, my unspoken reimbursement. The band had a little dented heart soldered onto it. She tried it on my ring finger, but it didn't fit, so I let her push it over my pinkie knuckle. It pinched my skin. "Look Katrin," she said, holding my hand up, "it look nice." When I didn't respond she said, "You could always melt it down and sell it too, ya know."

As I watched her on stage, giggling with "Miss Kwality" and straightening "Miss Guyana Stores'" banner, I thought back to Nikki rehearsing in the living room. Her long limbs gliding across the concrete floor; her mouth wide and dramatic unleashing its incredible sounds on us. She was unafraid to demand what she wanted. Her desire scared and fascinated me. I wanted to want that way.

By midnight, the talent section was just beginning, and it looked like the pageant might go on until two or three A.M. Shirley had asked that I bring Regina home before one A.M.; after that we couldn't guarantee transportation. So after watching all of her rehearsals, I never got to see Nikki perform, or witness her loss to another girl whose shorts were just that much shorter. But I have no trouble conjuring her in front of the audience, under the bright lights. In my memory, Nikki is always on the stage, ready to sing what she can sing to anyone who will listen.

Katherine Jamieson is a graduate of the Iowa Nonfiction Writer's Program, where she was an Iowa Arts Fellow. Her essays and articles have been published in The New York Times, Narrative, Meridian, The Common, Alimentum, Brevity, The Best Travel Writing 2011 *and* The Best Women's Travel Writing 2011 *and* Volume 9. *Based in the woods of Western Massachusetts, Katherine leads a dual life as a reclusive writer and road manager of an internationally touring musician (her husband). You can read more of her writing at: katherinejamieson.com*

EVA HOLLAND

ɛ̃ɔ ɛ̃ɔ ɛ̃ɔ

Chasing Alexander Supertramp

The dangerous journey to Alaska's "magic bus."

Alaska's Teklanika River runs fast and cold. One chilly, drizzly day in early September, I stood on its eastern bank and watched two young hikers strip down to boxer shorts and sneakers, stuff their clothes into drybags and then into backpacks, and attempt to cross. Three more hikers stoked a small fire a few feet away, in case their friends fell in and needed to warm up fast; the plan was for two members of the group to tackle the river first, with the other three following if the first pair succeeded.

Scott Wilkerson settled his pack on his back. Minutes earlier, when the twenty-two-year-old had agreed to go first, he'd joked, "I volunteer as tribute!" Now he turned to me and deadpanned, "I have a good feeling about this."

I'd traveled to Alaska because I was interested in the so-called "McCandless pilgrims"—people, mostly in their teens and twenties, who came from around the world to hike to the abandoned bus where Christopher McCandless died.

McCandless's story had first been told in a January 1993 *Outside* magazine article by Jon Krakauer, "Death of an

Innocent." Three years later, Krakauer's book-length account, *Into the Wild*, was published and became a bestseller. The 2007 movie version, directed by Sean Penn and starring Emile Hirsch, brought the story mainstream movie-house fame. In the years since, a growing number of hikers inspired by McCandless's free-spirited idealism have made the journey to Alaska in search of the famous bus. Fairbanks City Transit System Bus #142 has become a shrine, its rusting shell etched with motivational phrases left by visitors. But the pilgrimage is risky. One hiker died while crossing the Teklanika in 2010, and dozens more—twelve in the summer of 2013 alone— have become lost, hurt or stranded by the rising river and have needed to be rescued by local authorities.

I wanted to find out what kept the pilgrims coming—more than one hundred every year, by one local's estimation— despite the risks. I wanted to see the terrain for myself. And I wanted to hear what the locals thought of the phenomenon. But what I hadn't bargained for was learning firsthand just how treacherous the pilgrimage could be.

Raised in Virginia, Christopher Johnson McCandless began his long journey to Alaska in the summer of 1990, shortly after his graduation from Emory University. He donated the remaining contents of his college fund to Oxfam, packed his Datsun and headed west—without telling anyone his plans. After abandoning his car near Lake Mead, McCandless adopted a new name—"Alexander Supertramp"—and hitched and hoofed his way around the western United States for nearly two years. Then, in April 1992, he headed north. He planned to spend the summer living off the land south of Fairbanks, sustaining himself on wild plants and any game he could bring down with a .22-caliber rifle he'd picked up.

In his journal entries and letters to friends, first published in *Into the Wild*, McCandless spelled out the philosophy that motivated his travels. He was seeking freedom and adventure, an escape from consumer culture and the 9-to-5 lifestyle. Not long before he left for Alaska, McCandless wrote to a friend: "So many people live within unhappy circumstances and yet will not take the initiative to change their situation because they are conditioned to a life of security, conformity, and conservatism, all of which may appear to give one peace of mind, but in reality nothing is more damaging to the adventurous spirit within a man than a secure future . . . If you want to get more out of life, Ron, you must lose your inclination for monotonous security and adopt a helter-skelter style of life that will at first appear to you to be crazy."

On April 27, McCandless sent a postcard from Fairbanks to a friend in South Dakota. "It might be a very long time before I return South," he wrote. "If this adventure proves fatal and you don't ever hear from me again I want you to know you're a great man. I now walk into the wild."

The next day, he thumbed a ride south from Fairbanks to the Stampede Road, near the town of Healy and the main entrance to Denali National Park and began his trek into the backcountry. He followed the Stampede Trail through the late spring snow and across a still-frozen Teklanika River until he stumbled upon a derelict bus and made the 1946 International Harvester K-5 his home. He hunted squirrels and porcupines and birds and eventually shot a moose. He read Jack London, Leo Tolstoy, and Henry David Thoreau.

But by midsummer, McCandless was ill and starving. He deteriorated rapidly and died in mid-August. His body was found by a group of moose hunters in early September. Krakauer's story was published the following January, and a legend was born.

On my first night in Healy, I told a bartender that I was there to write about the bus's ongoing hold on people. He shook his head.

"It'll be gone soon," he said. "Too many people are getting stuck out there."

"You think they'll take it out?" I asked. Over the years, local authorities had talked about removing the hulk by helicopter to eliminate the temptation.

"Nope. I know some local boys that are gonna blow it up."

Whether the claim was simple bravado or not, the sentiment was real. Alaskan reactions to the *Into the Wild* saga vary, but almost always fall somewhere between a resigned eye-roll and full-blown hostility. A few young Alaskans I met told hand-me-down stories they'd heard from Healy locals about McCandless's behavior in the Totem Bar. "He wasn't charismatic," one of them said. "He just sat in the corner, drinking and talking to himself."

Never mind that in three years of research for his book, Krakauer didn't find any evidence to suggest that McCandless ever went near the bar or even the town of Healy proper. For some Alaskans, the mythic aspects of *Into the Wild* form a balloon they feel compelled to puncture. Instead of Sean Penn's healing, quasi-mystical vagabond, who changed every life he touched for the better, some locals see an antihero—one whose sad, predictable end has been hyped into fraudulent legend.

Rusty Lasell, the chief of the Tri-Valley Volunteer Fire Department in Healy, coordinates rescues of lost, stranded and injured bus-seekers. He's more sympathetic to McCandless than most Alaskans. "The kid was a decent kid," he told me as we sat in the fire hall on my second day in Healy. "He just bit off more than he could chew." But Lasell also sees the local perspective. Alaskans grow up understanding the dangers of the north country, he said. They know it isn't a place to be flirted with or taken lightly, nor a place to fulfill dreams hatched in a southern suburb. "You come to this state, you've got to bring your A game," he said. "And so when you see people that come up here and want to try it out, it aggravates you."

Lasell has been on the job for twenty-five years, since before McCandless set out from Atlanta. By the time I met him in early September, he'd already rescued twelve Stampede hikers that summer—most of them stranded on the far side of the Teklanika by fast-rising waters. Every time he gets a call from a worried parent about a kid who's failed to check in, he has to commandeer a helicopter from a local sightseeing outfit and go on the hunt—with the state of Alaska footing the bill.

"We've had people die out there," he said. "We've flown I don't know how many people out of there who've gotten sick, we've had people in winter that overshot it." He has no idea how many hikers have attempted the trip over the years and either reached the bus successfully or turned back without incident. "They don't check in with us, they don't check in with anybody." But he knows that the problem has been growing over the last six years. "We didn't really feel an impact from the bus until the movie came out."

Healy local Steve Tolley figures it was 1975 or so when he and a friend decided to make the old bus their home base for the winter trapping season. The vehicle had been abandoned in 1963, back when the Stampede Trail led out to the now-defunct Clearwater mine. Wilderness had since grown over the one-time mining road, but the bus labeled Fairbanks City Transit System #142 was still there. "The bus had all the windows in it," Tolley recalled, "so we took some mattresses, stuff to make it comfortable." The place became a popular shelter for hunters and trappers each fall and winter. But in summer, when the Teklanika River ran ice-free, the bus stood empty—until McCandless arrived in 1992.

Like Rusty Lasell, Tolley is sympathetic to McCandless. "I think he just wanted to go out there and prove that he could live on his own," he told me over beers in his homemade cabin, up on a ridge outside Healy. "But that's a rough spot to try and do that. I think everybody has a stage in their life where they want to test themselves. But I tell you what: it's a challenge, even living here a mile away from the grocery store."

Tolley and another local friend, Roger Phoenix, don't stay in the bus anymore. Two different groups head out to the bus these days, they told me: the pilgrims themselves, and a handful of young locals hostile to the McCandless mythology. "The young punks from around here shot the thing full of holes," Phoenix told me. "The windows are broke out. You can't even stay out there no more." The bus has long since been covered with graffiti from McCandless's fans—the ancient paint etched with "Please respect Mother Nature," "The best things in life are free" and other McCandless-esque mantras. But over the years, Phoenix has seen another kind of graffiti appear. One such inscription reads, "Stupid people die fast!"

On the day I headed down the Stampede Trail, I was up and out of my tent before sunrise. I had hoped, when I first set out for Healy from my home in the neighboring Yukon Territory, that I might be able to get to the bus on my own. The worst of the summer floods had passed, but I'd asked around when I arrived in the area and was quickly discouraged from even thinking about crossing the Teklanika solo. It had been a rainy week, and the river was running high. "ATVs are being washed downstream," one local told me. Only Argos—amphibious all-terrain vehicles—were able to make the crossing. So I planned instead on a daylong hike, down the Stampede Trail to the Teklanika and back again, twenty miles round trip. I figured I would at least get a sense of the terrain McCandless and his followers were contending with, a firsthand taste of the trail and a good look at the river, the pilgrims' biggest obstacle.

I hoped, too, that I might encounter some pilgrims on the trail. A musher who lived on the Stampede Road had told me he saw them daily in the summer.

The sun rose as I drove along the four paved miles of Stampede Road. I bounced along rutted gravel for another four miles, passing moose hunters who were unloading ATVs from pickups and trailers. At Eight Mile Lake, the gravel road narrowed abruptly into a trail and descended into dense bush. I loaded my pack with a full change of warm, dry clothing, plenty of water and food, a headlamp, and a cold-weather sleeping bag—just in case I got stuck out overnight—then I headed down the trail.

I'd always had mixed feelings about McCandless and his story, despite moving to the Yukon Territory in my twenties and enjoying a relatively unconventional life myself. I shared some of his beliefs and passions, but for me the sticking point had always been his refusal to contact his family during his journey. I could imagine the resulting pain and anxiety, and that, as much as anything, kept me from considering McCandless someone to emulate. But at the same time I understood the pull that his story exerted on people: Plenty of us dream, but few make those dreams a reality. What's more, the young men and women inspired by McCandless today live in a world more wired and connected than anything he could have imagined. Small wonder that some of them are seduced by the idea of chucking their iPhones and disappearing into the wilderness.

I hiked alone for two hours, yelling occasionally to let any nearby bears know I was coming. The trail was coated with fallen yellow leaves, wet with the previous night's rain. Fall's bloom was fading, and winter's arrival was imminent. I was taking a break, snacking and working on my notes, when a group of hikers came around a bend, laughing and chatting. "Are you guys headed to the bus?" I called. They were, and after I'd introduced myself and explained my mission, they agreed that I could hike with them as far as the river and watch them cross.

They were a group of five friends—Scott, Matt, Jake, Liz, and Rick—who worked at a hotel near the park entrance. Four were in their early-to-mid twenties, and the fifth, Rick, was in his forties. With one exception, they told me, they weren't diehard McCandless fans. They had spent the summer working and playing together, and they thought the hike to the bus would be a fun way to end the season before they went their separate ways.

All five had seen the movie, but Jake was the only one who seemed particularly taken with the story. The book and the movie were the reason he had gone to Alaska. He didn't see how he could spend the summer there without visiting the bus. He'd already been to the replica, a leftover from the movie set, now parked outside the brewery in Healy. In fact, his Facebook profile photo showed him in a plaid shirt, leaning against it. The shot is a near-perfect imitation of the iconic McCandless self-portrait.

We reached the banks of the Teklanika just after noon, and the moment I saw the river, I was relieved I hadn't planned to cross. A sunny early morning had slumped into a grey, cold afternoon, and the river raced by us, its silt-choked waters moving unexpectedly fast. As we scouted upriver and down, checking to see if there were any better crossing options, an icy rain began to fall. The group made plans for the crossing, and I wondered briefly if I should say something to discourage them. I wondered if they would be second-guessing themselves if there weren't a reporter standing over them with a camera. But grim jokes aside, no one seemed too worried.

Scott and Matt made a fast crossing, facing upstream and sidestepping quickly as the water rose and foamed around their knees, then thighs, then hips. One unfurled a red climbing rope behind them, its near end secured to a young spruce tree on our side. They were a few feet from the far bank when Scott lost his footing and the pair went down briefly, then thrashed their way to shore. Now it was time for Jake, Liz, and Rick to take their shot.

Facing upstream and clutching the rope that Scott and Matt had secured on the far side, the hikers shuffled into the fast-moving water. They were in the middle of the river when Rick went down, splashing face-first into the water but keeping his grip on the rope, now bowed under his weight. Jake and Liz staggered, trying to stay on their feet as they were pulled downstream by the stretching rope. Jake fell, and then Liz splashed down next to him. She scrambled up, pulling herself hand over hand a few steps closer to the far bank, and I thought that, like Scott and Matt, the three might yet make the crossing after stumbling. When she fell again, all of them hung prone for a moment, gripping the rope, their faces in the water. I couldn't imagine any of them being able to breathe. "Let go! You have to let go!" Matt yelled from the opposite bank. Rick released the rope first, then Jake, and then Liz, and it snapped back with a wet twang, loud enough to carry clearly over the sound of the river. I stood frozen, disbelieving, still holding my iPhone to record the crossing as all three hikers were swept out of sight downstream.

We had joked around, before their attempt, about which of them might not survive the crossing. The grim banter papered over an uncomfortable truth: Someone a lot like them *had* died en route to the bus, in the cold, dark waters of the Teklanika, on a summer day just three years earlier.

Claire Ackermann and Etienne Gros, young European travelers who'd first connected in an online forum, arrived in Denali National Park in August 2010. They spent a few days hiking in the park itself, and then, on a whim before heading out of the area, decided to hike to the McCandless bus. Though both had seen the movie, neither was a serious devotee. But when another traveler they'd met suggested the trip, they figured they were already in Healy; why not go see what all the fuss was about?

They started down the trail early on the morning of August 14, and by noon had reached the banks of the Teklanika, where they found a rope already strung across the water. After scouting and debating their options, Gros and Ackermann decided to use the rope to make the crossing. Stripped down to their underwear, clothes packed into drybags, each looped a length of rope around the waist and then around the main line. Their individual loops would slide along as the pair crossed, allowing some freedom of motion plus a link to the main rope.

Ackermann and Gros were three-quarters of the way across the icy river, water up to their waistbands, when she went down. Her weight pulled the main rope downstream and underwater, and soon Gros lost his footing, too. The rope bent into a taut V, and the force of the river pinned them into the point. Struggling to hold their heads above water, neither could reach the main rope. They were trapped.

Gros reached back over his shoulder and pulled his knife from the top of his backpack. He had only seconds to make a decision: cut himself free first and try to make his way to shore and back upstream to free Claire, or cut her free and hope she wasn't lost downstream. He paused, then cut his own rope. As the river seized him and carried him downstream, he was able to see that her head was still above the water.

He kicked and fought his way to the bank and hauled himself out of the water 300 yards downstream. Then he dumped his pack and ran back up, knife in hand. When he got to the rope and waded back out into the river to reach Claire, she was underwater. He cut her free and swam after her downstream for more than half a mile before he was able to get them both onto dry land. There, on the riverbank, he attempted CPR, but he already knew he was too late. Eighteen years after McCandless expired in the bus just a few miles away, Ackermann became the second young adventurer to die on the Stampede Trail.

Gros, now thirty-three, still finds himself questioning the decisions he made that day. "It could have been the opposite," he told me. "I could have cut her rope and she could have been unable to make it to shore. I mean, if I would have done the opposite, maybe . . . hard to say. Hard to say." These days, he's on the periphery of a discussion about the possibility of getting a bridge built across the Teklanika, to allow the pilgrims to visit the bus more safely. Ackermann's family is involved in the talks; apparently, so is Carine McCandless, Chris's sister. Given the annual cost of the rescues, Gros thinks a bridge should be taken seriously. "It could be a small rope bridge, it could even be something that you could remove in wintertime," he said. "I guess the biggest problem is, are the locals for it?" He's dismissive of the idea of moving the bus to the near side of the river—another proposal. "It would change nothing," he told me, adding that hikers would still head for the area where McCandless actually died.

Of course, the river is only one way for pilgrims to get themselves into trouble. They also face grizzly bears, injuries, and exposure. And the debate over how exactly McCandless himself died has been ongoing for two decades: In mid-September 2013, Krakauer published a new theory about an amino acid that's found in the wild potato plants McCandless consumed and that can induce fatal paralysis in undernourished people. Still, the Teklanika River is the main source of the hikers' troubles. Indeed, McCandless tried to hike back out to civilization several weeks before his death and was stymied by the swollen river, so you could argue that he, too, was a casualty of the Teklanika.

*　*　*

From my side of the river, I watched in horror as Rick, Liz, and Jake vanished around a bend. After a moment, I stopped the video recording on my phone; I wasn't sure I wanted to document what might happen next. I could see Matt and Scott running down the far bank, trying to keep their friends in sight. I stuffed my camera in a pocket and did the same, my adrenaline surging as I sprinted down the sandy, rocky shore. Liz reached the other side first, maybe one hundred yards downstream on the far bank, and as I came around a bend I could see Jake clinging to the bank a bit farther down. Scott shouted, "I've got Liz!" as he pulled her out of the water, and when she was on dry land, he hurried to pull Jake clear, too. Matt and I kept running, dodging trees and brush, hurdling over downed logs, watching Rick bob in the water as he floated downstream. We must have run for half a mile. I was pretty sure I'd never run faster in my life, but I could barely keep Rick in sight. Every time his face reappeared above the churn, I squinted to see if he was still conscious and breathing. But drowning was only one concern; the river hovered just above freezing, and hypothermia loomed, too. I knew that in minutes, he could be past saving.

I cut inland to dodge a thick stand of brush and trees, and when I'd gone around the tangle and come back in sight of the water, I saw that Rick was clinging to a steep gravel slope on the far side, his feet just inches from the rushing water. Matt caught up and scrambled down to him and the pair climbed carefully back up to solid ground.

Rick was forty-seven, the oldest of the group by a couple of decades. He'd spent three seasons working in the Denali area and plenty of time backpacking alone in the park. He told me later that he kept pretty calm as he plummeted downstream. He tried flipping to paddle toward shore, but on every attempt his heavy pack drove him underwater. Soon, he realized he could no longer feel his arms or legs. He wasn't cold anymore, just numb. Rick looked over his shoulder and saw that the river had swung him close to the gravel bank. He gathered himself for one last effort and thought, "I've gotta get over there somehow." Though he couldn't feel his limbs responding, he was soon free, splayed against the rocks.

After Matt reached him, he retrieved his dry clothes from the pack. Matt tied a bandana around a big, bloody gash in Rick's leg, and then they started a slow walk upstream to find the others. Halfway there, Rick started shivering—a good sign, he figured, that his body was coming back to life.

By this time, Jake and Liz were bundled into dry clothing, too, and they had a tarp up and the fire going. All three were scraped and bruised; Jake would later learn that he had torn his right rotator cuff trying to grab the bank, and Scott had cracked his kneecap during the crossing. When Matt and Rick reached them, Matt took a good look at the cut in Rick's leg and pulled out his multi-tool to remove the worst of the embedded rock and gravel. He took out a flask of whisky and told Rick to brace himself. The alcohol on the open wound would burn. Rick shrugged, still unable to feel his legs anyway.

I stayed on the riverbank, anxious and watching from afar, until everyone was warm and dry on the far side. Then, my stomach still churning from witnessing the ordeal, I retraced my steps to town. The trail is nobody's idea of a lovely hike—one of many things that mystify the Alaskans who watch the McCandless pilgrims set off each year. ("Of all the places you could hike in Alaska . . ." one local had said to me two nights earlier, shaking her head in disbelief.) The Stampede Trail is a boggy thoroughfare for motorized off-roaders. During the day that I spent on it, I counted seven bus-bound hikers, twenty-two four-wheeling moose hunters, two guided Jeep tours, and one guided ATV tour.

Hiking there today is no way to capture the solitude and engagement with nature that McCandless was seeking. As I slogged back to my waiting car, I could not see the point of the pilgrimages. Nor could I fathom how the loss of more young lives honored his memory.

The pilgrims, of course, see the journey differently. A spiral notebook left in the bus by the McCandless family when they visited by helicopter in 1993 has since been filled with handwritten entries, each praising McCandless and the impact his story has had on the writer's life. One 2002 visitor left a poem: "I came up here to get away / It's the last frontier they say / I came across this bus today / It's gorgeous here I think I'll stay." Another entry, left by a man in 1999, reads: "I started my journey here hoping for two things, one that somewhere out here I would find myself, and two that I would find some hope for the future. Now I am here at the bus, and I am happy because the future looks up and I know who I am."

One undated entry, written in pencil, is addressed directly to McCandless: "Christopher J McCandless, AKA Supertramp, I envy the ability you had to put this world aside and live out your dream, something so many of us lack. If your spirit still looms here, if this is your eternal paradise and you watch us come and go year by year season by season, I hope you help instill some of your awesome qualities in each of us that make the grueling trip to your resting place."

Dan Grec, an Australian who now lives in Canada, visited the shrine in 2009, at the start of an epic road trip from Alaska to the southern tip of Argentina. When I spoke with him, he explained why he kicked off his journey at the bus. "I really associate with Chris not liking the world, not liking society, and not turning his back on it, exactly, but wanting to pick and choose the parts he wanted to be involved in." In Grec's estimation, McCandless was a social guy who just didn't want to be stuffed into a cubicle for eight hours every day.

Grec has powerful memories of his visit to the bus. "The most vivid thing that I remember," Grec said, "[is that] you get inside, and Chris died there, you think it's going to be like a funeral. But there's something going on there that I don't understand—some kind of happiness or energy. That's why I want to go back—I'd like to spend a week there and just soak it in."

Grec is what you might call a true believer—someone who sought out the bus because he felt a connection to McCandless after reading the book and seeing the movie. Within the core group of like-minded pilgrims, some go back again and again. But many others are more like Claire Ackermann and Etienne Gros, or Scott Wilkerson and his friends —young people who find themselves in the Healy area and are drawn to the bus out of sheer curiosity and a sense of adventure.

Back in the fire hall in Healy, Chief Lasell doesn't see anything changing on the trail anytime soon. Until more people get hurt or die, there will be little motivation to remove the bus, he said. As for a possible bridge over the Teklanika, he added, "I don't see that happening." The environmental permits and other paperwork involved would be intimidating, he figures, and without local support—with active local hostility, in fact—there is little incentive.

He seems resigned to more rescues. The flow of pilgrims shows no sign of tapering—"It might actually be growing," he said—and because the Stampede Trail is public land, there's no way to ban the hikers from making the attempt.

More than a month after my visit to the Stampede Trail, I was still trying to wrap my head around the whole phenomenon. Just days after I'd gotten home, Krakauer's new theory about McCandless's death was published, and I watched it light up the internet for the better part of a week. We are, clearly, still fascinated by the extraordinary life and death of Alexander Supertramp.

For more perspective, I spoke to Walt and Billie McCandless, Chris's parents, who've watched their son's death turn into a global phenomenon—Krakauer's *Into the Wild* has been printed in twenty-eight languages, Walt told me, and their own book of Chris's writings and photos, *Back to the Wild,* has been sold on six continents. I asked the McCandlesses what they make of the whole thing.

"We're still as amazed as you are," Walt told me. Billie offered a possible explanation: "I think everybody has this inner person that wants to have their own world, you know, and of course fulfill their own dreams, and would like to do it inconspicuously . . . especially young people. If they're interested in something, why does there have to be a rule about it? 'Why can't I just find out about it? Why can't I just experience it?'"

The McCandlesses—who get emails from bus-bound pilgrims, and from Alexander Supertramp fans worldwide—have visited twice themselves. They never encourage anyone to make the trip. If asked, however, the couple suggests that hikers make the attempt in winter, when the river is frozen, and that they consult with a local guide. And they have a message for anyone considering the trek. "If they are going to go out and fulfill their own dream," Billie told me, "they have to remember that their family, their loved ones, are part of their journey. They have to include them, they have to stay in touch. Don't abandon them."

Before we hung up the phone, I mentioned that I sometimes worry about the impact my own wilderness adventures have on my parents; the close call at the river still weighed on my mind. "Listen, young lady, I hope you call home," Billie said. I promised her I would.

৵৾ ৵৾ ৵৾

Eva Holland is a freelance writer and editor based in Canada's
Yukon Territory. Her work has been featured by Longreads,
Longform, *and* The Browser, *and was included in Byliner's list*
of "102 Spectacular Nonfiction Stories from 2012." Her stories
have also been listed as notable selections in The Best American
Essays 2013 *and* The Best American Sports Writing 2013. *She*
is a founding contributor to Vela *and co-editor of* World Hum.

⁓ ⁓ ⁓

Oh Captain, My Captain

A taste of the good life in an unlikely place.

It's nine o'clock on a sunny April morning, and my husband and I are scanning the parking lot outside the Dubrovnik Hilton. We're waiting for someone, though we don't know who. Suddenly, a smiling, mustachioed Croatian man approaches.

"This way, this way!" He cheerfully rushes us into his SUV, and without so much as an introduction, peels out of the parking lot. David and I glance at each other, wondering if we should have asked the stranger with a moustache where we are going, or at the very least, clarified that he's taking us on a wine tour.

"So . . . will anyone else be joining us on this wine tour?" I nervously call up.

"What? Ah! No. Is just us. Is still the off-season, you know."

"Yes. We know." We've been hearing this a lot.

"But I am happy to take you. I am Captain Nikola Lasic. I used to be sea captain." And indeed, Captain Nikola looks like a perfect child's drawing of a sea captain. He's all barrel chest and squinting eyes and is missing the tip of his pointer finger.

"I fought war for five years. Croatian War for Independence, yes? But now . . . now I all tourist industry. Normally there be much more people on tour. But today—just us. You will relax. We will enjoy fun."

As our Captain drives us high into the mountains, we gawk at the landscape—pale blue sky stretching brightly against soft white mountains, the sea blinking up at us like a giant emerald eye. The Dubrovnik roads appear to have been constructed by a building crew whose motto was "Que Sera Sera," and as we spike around curves, two wheels kissing the air below, the Captain gestures with his stunted pointer.

"See hills there? All fire! During war, all fire!" We nod. Apparently there are to be no casual descriptions of historical sites and local vegetation. We squint out the window while the Captain waves his hands, the van careening side to side as he indicates fields aflame.

"Where from?" he calls back to us. David informs him he's from Northern Ireland, and they exchange what looks like the universal nod for having survived life in a war zone.

"And I'm from Indiana!" I call up. I receive no such nod.

To the well traveled, Croatia isn't that exotic. But to the average imbecile, the name summoned vague imagery of bombs, Clinton, and the '90s. Then my friend Louisa—a seasoned traveler whose opinion I trusted—suggested it to me one evening while we shared a joint on her roof. At the time, I was sufficiently blazed that she could have suggested we time travel on her Stairmaster and I'd have eagerly begun packing my socks.

"You can do a wine tour!" She'd smiled at me, her pupils the size of cue balls.

My husband and I were living in Ireland at the time, and Dubrovnik wasn't that far—though when I mentioned it, he acted like I'd suggested we holiday in an abandoned mine shaft. Apparently he too had some outdated associations with the country. Thanks to the magic of the Internet, I was able to show him pictures of a sapphire blue Adriatic, and our flights were booked.

Now here we are, barreling through the mountains on our off-season wine tour. Before we hit our first winery, the Captain decides we should stop for a coffee and oysters. *Because what pairs better with an Americano than mollusks?* We sit at a plastic table by the harbor, where men in tall rubber boots pluck the shiny shells up right before our eyes. The Captain chats with his friend, the owner of the restaurant, and slides an oyster down as effortlessly as inhaling a cigarette.

"You! You must try!"

David sits motionless, and I know he'd rather throw himself onto the motor of a passing boat than eat an oyster for breakfast, so it's up to me to save us from appearing rude. I suck the slippery bit of sea back, and it is in fact delicious, if a shock to my stomach, which had been expecting an Egg McMuffin.

We make our way to our first winery, and the owner's teenage daughter saunters outside, blinking at the light, as if shocked to find idiots banging on her door this time of year. *Do we not know this is the off-season?* But she gamely invites us in and pours large, rich glasses of Plavac Mali—a wine so dark it looks like squid ink. Captain Nikolai picks up a glass.

"Just a touch for me!" He shouts, and glugs it back.

He then leads us across the road to a winery owned by his friend Slavenka. Slavenka is a round-faced smiling woman who warmly ushers us inside and around a large wooden table.

"Slavenka's husband was snake catcher. He catch rattlesnake. Caught three hundred! Then sold venom to make antidote. It was enough to buy new car, eh?" The Captain raises his eyebrows at David, as though suggesting a possible new line of work for him.

He explains that Slavenka makes brandy, as she pours us some bright red liquid from a tiny bottle. The concoction looks like it fell out of Professor Snape's pocket, and I eye my glass tentatively while Slavenka pours a bit for the Captain.

"I really shouldn't, but you know . . ." he says, as the brandy slides past his moustache and down his throat. Slavenka smiles and produces fresh figs for us.

It isn't quite noon, but David and I are tipsy. I'm also feeling as if my stomach is in a knife fight with my other internal organs. By now I've had strong coffee, two oysters, three dried figs, wine, and several brandies. Perhaps this is the Croatian breakfast of champions, but my American belly is crying mercy. There's no time to ponder any gastrointestinal discomfort, though according to the Captain, the best winery of all awaits! We bid Slavenka farewell and stumble back out to the SUV.

"Ah! Here we are! This is the place!" The Captain pulls up to the Grgic winery, famous for its triumphant chardonnays. I sit up in excitement, but the Captain slows before a locked door and a small sign with a single word: "CLOSED."

I patiently wait for the Captain to hop out and perform his "We're here to see the wizard" routine that he employed at the previous wineries, where he had only to knock, and the door would be swung wide, and we'd be welcomed and handed beverages. But apparently his powers will not work at Grgic.

"I am very sorry. Is off-season, you know." He swings the car out of the winery and drives us to a tiny fishing village, where he pulls over.

"Well, perhaps you will like to take walk, and I will do some thinking about our problem, and where to go?"

David and I stroll tipsily through the deserted village, woozily snapping photos of men untangling fishing nets. When we return, we find the Captain waiting for us, a tentative look on his face.

"There is winery I can take you to. Is run by my friend." He pauses. "We will go, yes?"

We nod enthusiastically and follow the Captain down a short path, until he stops in front of a ramshackle house. The front yard is littered with stray boat motors and plastic tubs. A bike tire hangs from a tree branch. The Captain calls up to an open window. The front door opens, and out steps an enormous, sweatpants-clad giant. He has wild gray hair, is at least 6'5" and looks like he's been napping inside a hollowed out log. His face, hands, and clothes are smeared with dirt, and he gives us a wide, toothy grin.

He and the captain shout happy greetings to each other in Croatian, and the Captain explains our sad tale of the closed Grgic winery. Andre the Giant (which is how I'm addressing him in my mind) laughs, then gestures for us to follow him. He leads us along the side of his house to a garage door. Hanging there is a small paper sign that reads "PRODAJA VINA." Quite simply: "We sell wine."

The garage is jammed tight with several large fermentation tanks. Rubber tubing and ominous metal instruments litter the shelves. Bags of corks lie asunder, and plaster droops from the low ceiling.

"It is like nuclear war in here, yes?" Andre grins. "Like Hiroshima?" he nods cheerfully.

The Captain follows us in, as does Andre's son, Matteo. Matteo is also 6'5" and also favors sweatpants. As the son pulls the door closed, David and I suddenly find ourselves dwarfed by three very tall, Croatian hosts, in what looks like a discarded set from *Silence of the Lambs*. My alcohol-soaked "stranger danger" antenna makes a wobbly attempt to lift itself from my brain and assess the situation. Three huge men. Many strange implements and tools. Small enclosed space in a deserted town in a foreign land. I glance at David and see a large vein standing out in the middle of his forehead.

He appears to be quietly flexing his muscles beneath his "I Heart Robots" t-shirt, but his expression reads, "I'm about to be murdered in a Croatian garage while on holiday."

"His wine . . . it win awards! At many festival!" The Captain reassures us. Andre fills a smudged glass with wine from one of the tanks and hands it to me, pouring glasses for everyone except Matteo, who declines.

"I do not like to drink," he explains from the corner, where he perches on a dirty stool. "It makes me act very silly. My father, he was born in a barrel of wine. He does not mind being silly."

At this, Andre roars with laughter. With his purple-toothed grin, Rudolph-red nose, and rosy-stained t-shirt, it's easy to imagine him entering the world via a cask of merlot.

We stand in the garage and sip, and the wine is in fact delicious. I turn to Matteo.

"And what is your line of work?" I politely inquire, as though we're all standing on a veranda in cocktail attire. Matteo shyly ducks his dark head and explains he is studying to be a seafarer. Upon learning this, I cannot help but think that were it not for Matteo's sweatpants and hoodie, he could have stepped out of a romance novel. With his wind-tousled black hair and handsome smile, I kind of want to watch him tie large ropes into knots or stare intently out at the horizon. Or whatever it is seafarers do these days.

"I also work in tourist industry, in hotel. It is O.K." He sighs. "But customers, they not have so much patience sometimes."

At this Andre rises from the upside down bucket he's using as a seat. "Fuck your mother!" He shouts to the room, the broad, friendly smile still on his face.

We look to Matteo in confusion, uncertain for whom this directive is intended. He rolls his eyes.

"Do not listen to him. His English is terrible." Matteo says something to his father in Croatian, and Andre plops back down onto his stool with a smile. He collects everyone's glasses and begins refilling them.

"He is giving you special wine now," the Captain explains. "It wins many prizes." Andre sloshes out wine from a different tank. My husband is now sporting his own purple-toothed smile. He's no longer worried we'll be murdered or is too drunk to care.

"I have band," Andre says. "Sounds of the Adriatic, it is our name. I play drums, drink wine, and fish. That is all I want to do. All day. Drums and wine. Life too short. People, they make life too complicated. Me, I want the good life." He dispenses this sage advice while passing around our glasses. Then, as though toasting this sentiment, he adds: "Fuck your mother!"

The Captain clears his throat and attempts to switch topics.

"Yes. Well. David here. He is Irish." He claps David on the shoulder. "He should move to Croatia, we will open Irish pub. We will serve Irish stew. Yes?" He turns to David and winks.

"Ah yes! Very good!"

Andre ponders this. "And our band will play. Sounds of the Adriatic. We will play at your pub." He nods with finality.

"Oh . . . uh . . . well . . . thank you." David nods back, politely accepting the offer for a free band to play his fictional Irish/Croatian pub.

After several more glasses of the award-winning tank wine, the garage door is cracked open, and the afternoon light spills in. We all stumble out shielding our eyes, surprised by the bright orange ball in the sky. Andre presents the Captain with the parting gift of a large plastic to-go jug of his special vintage.

Then we say our goodbyes and crawl back into the SUV, and the Captain navigates us back to Dubrovnik. His sealed jug of wine sits beside him, acting as co-pilot.

When he drops us off, we thank him for our unique, off-season tour. He's glad we are pleased, and our farewells are tinged with a maudlin merlot sadness. Our lives crossed here on this quadrant of earth for one sunny afternoon, but we know we'll likely never gaze upon his mustachioed face again.

Back at the hotel, we sit on our balcony staring into the sunset as it drops a layer of pink onto the old town like it's draping a sheer, rose-colored scarf along the fortress walls. I gaze out at the shocking blue of the sea and feel grateful that Grgic was closed. We didn't get to taste the famed chardonnay, and I wouldn't be able impress my wine enthusiast friends with talk of acidity or cedarwood notes. But we drank wine the way it was intended: with open curiosity and pleasure, in communion with new friends.

As my head nods into a nap, I daydream about our Irish pub in Croatia. I know this will be a good daydream to roll my mind back to later when I'm standing on any icy cold subway platform or pushing through a sweaty throng on a city street. I'll imagine this alternate universe where David and I serve plates heaped high with mounds of Irish stew and Sounds of the Adriatic play in the corner, tapping out a stirring beat. The barmaid will flirt with the seafarer while the Captain sits in a corner and captivates all with his tales of battle and bravery. The dark, heavy wine will flow, and the crowds will press in tight, smiling and sunburned. We'll raise our smudged glasses in thanks, and together we'll bellow a toast to the good life: "Fuck your mother!"

Johanna Gohmann has written about men who breastfeed and what it's like having a third nipple. She doesn't always write about areola. She lives in Brooklyn with an Irish husband who loves building things, and a toddler son who loves breaking things. She's a regular contributor to Bust *magazine, and her essays have been anthologized in* Every Father's Daughter, A Moveable Feast: Life-Changing Food Adventures Around the World, Joan Didion Crosses the Street, The Best Women's Travel Writing 2010, *and* The Best Sex Writing 2010. *www.JohannaGohmann.com*

🎵 🎵 🎵

Ashes Over Havana

One cure for grief, she learned,
was tossing the excess baggage.

*M*y father is flying to Havana with me.

This is not my father's first Miami-to-Havana flight. There were many before, in the fifties, when he and my mother would leave my sister and me in the loving care of my grandparents and return to the island bearing gifts: a Sears tabletop record player that folded like a suitcase and played "Take Me Out To The Ballgame," Thumbelina dolls with that happy, vinyl, new-doll smell, and other American things. But that was before 1959, when Fidel and his army of long-haired men and long-rifled women marched down the Sierra Maestra Mountains to the cheers of the crowd at El Malecón, Havana's pulsing seawall. The triumph of the Revolution, of free education, of health care and social justice for all. Color-blindness. Two years later, I followed my parents out of the homeland. I was eight. I had no choice. My father is flying to Havana with me one more time, fifty years after our emigration, and fifteen years after the last time he set eyes on his country. But this trip is different. My father is inside my carry-on. I am carrying his ashes back to Havana.

*   *   *

My father's body lay in the hospital morgue for ten days because his third wife, to whom he remained married for thirty-seven years, insisted on a Catholic burial, which is what she claimed he wanted even though she is a Jew-ban, as Cuban Jews call themselves in the U.S. A Catholic funeral is what she said he wanted, even though she hardly saw him during the last two years of his life. And she refused to pay for either the burial or the cemetery plot on Calle Ocho, in the heart of Little Havana.

I buried my mom seven years ago, and I knew I could not bury another parent—the morbidness of it, the closing of the coffin, the sliding of the corpse into a row of drawers, a wall of the dead. Besides, after two years of taking care of my father, I was broke. Broke and beaten. I could do a lot of things, just not bury my father. This much I knew.

The empathetic social worker at Mercy Hospital, who shared with me her grief at losing her own father, began leaving me daily voice mails on the fourth day following my father's death: We really need your father's body out of the hospital morgue. By the seventh day: We have no space for the others. Where would you like us to put the other dead bodies? On top of your father? By the ninth day: Remove your father's corpse from the hospital morgue, or else. The county morgue and a pauper's grave. After ten days, my father's third wife, who had denied him the right to live out his final years in the marital home and vehemently fought his living with me, signed papers turning over the body to me.

I asked my sister to pick up my father's ashes at the funeral home, ten minutes from her house and an hour from mine. At least that. My father's ashes remained at the funeral home longer than his body had remained at the hospital morgue. My sister will pick up the ashes, I reassured the funeral director

each time he called. Busy, my sister would say, just as she had
every time I asked her if she could fill in for me for a few hours,
with Dad. Once, I had to catch an early-morning flight with
my daughter for her semester of study in Lyon; just a three-
day trip to help her find housing, make sure she was safe. My
father was due to be released from the hospital after another
bout of MRSA pneumonia, but no, my sister could not fill in
for me, she could not be there the morning of his discharge to
talk to his urologist and pulmonologist and infectious-disease
specialist and physical and occupational therapist and take
careful notes of the nurses' discharge instructions regarding
his Albuterol and Plavix and Prednisone and Lorazepam.

My sister was busy, working, running her day spa. I am
alone, she would say, with no help from anyone. Her high
school-sweetheart-turned-husband had left her after twenty-
five years. That was seven years ago, I reminded her, and did
you forget that I was alone too, for eight years? I had left Paul,
my high school-sweetheart-turned-husband, a few short years
into the marriage when my youngest was thirteen months old.
I was alone for eight years, supporting our mother, our grandmother (my father's stepmother) and my three girls with no
help from anyone, not even—especially not—from Dad.

This last part I wouldn't actually say, but I thought it. Dad
with his-and-hers Mercedes, *tin marin de dos pingüey*, one Mercedes for him, one Mercedes for his wife. But could you *visit*,
I asked my sister? He was asking for her. He was more than
asking for her. He was saying *Tu hermana no se ocupa de mí.*
Your sister does not look out for me. This, I wouldn't tell her.
She has problems at work, I told him. The economy, Dad, you
know. The Republicans, they left a mess.

I wouldn't tell him I had stopped practicing law after
thirty-three years of frantically fighting to win clients fleeing
persecution for the right to live and work in the United States.
My fervor had already taken precedence over everything

else—over my five children, three with Paul, two with my second husband, Ira. I could not continue to manage my law practice and take care of my father the way I should, so I made a choice.

When I told my sister *this*, she paused for a long time. Then she said, He wasn't much of a father. Or a grandfather, either. So what? I said. He was our father. When I complained to my husband about my sister, he said quietly, Your father made choices in life. I said, not quietly, And what? He made his bed, now lie in it? And let Bertha—the wife of thirty-seven years—drop him on the doorstep of some nursing home? The Jewish Home for the Aged?

My father was a proud man. He was especially proud that in *el exilio*, he had worked his way up once again, from renting seat cushions at the Jacksonville Suns Baseball Stadium in upstate Florida to Senior Vice-President at a major bank in Miami. As an insider, he had access to information regarding the homes that the poor lost through foreclosure. He bought properties dirt cheap and resold them at top dollar.

He also left my mother a few years after we left the homeland, after a tumor in her pituitary gland made her face, her hands, her entire self grow to monstrous proportions. Along with my mother, he walked out on my sister and me. He married his second wife immediately; my sister and I never met her; the marriage was short-lived. But Bertha was different—he let her pull him toward her and her children and grandchildren and away from my sister and me and our children. And then he lost his fortune and once tried to put a bullet to his brain. I waited for hours outside his room at St. Francis Hospital's mental ward until he was finished with his shock treatments. Or rather, until they finished with him. *Papín*, I would say, what I called him in Havana. *Papín*, he would say and shake his head, your *Papín* is no more. And

I would feel the physical sensation of my heart cracking in two. Then he was discharged, and he and Bertha went back to driving the streets of Miami Beach in his-and-hers Mercedes.

Both in Cuba and in the U.S., my father's heart was in what he loved most—baseball. So it seemed appropriate that we should spread his ashes at the baseball field in Miami. I told my sister, Bring Dad's ashes when you come to Max's—my fifth grandson's—first birthday party and we'll spread them at the Bobby Maduro Stadium. By then, my father had been riding in the back seat of my sister's Mercedes for over a month. He likes riding in the Mercedes, she said, and where have you been? The Bobby Maduro Stadium was demolished years ago.

Bobby Maduro had been my father's boss in Cuba at El Gran Estadio de La Habana, the *Great* Stadium of Havana, the home of the minor-league team, the Havana Sugar Kings. The new stadium is all the way up in Miami Gardens, *en casa del carajo*—in the middle of nowhere—my sister said, and it's not even finished yet. We'll spread his ashes on the construction site, I told her. And if they don't let us in? she asked. Then we'll rent a helicopter, for chrissakes, and let him sail on down below us. Again, she said, He wasn't much of a father, you know. Again, I said, So what? He was our father. This time, she added, *¡Ay!* And I could see her throw her hands in the air. That's what you say about Cuba: *It's my country*. Here she mimicked what she presumed she heard in my voice every time we got on the subject of Cuba. My sister didn't come to Max's first-birthday party.

The last time I visited Havana with my father, fifteen years earlier, we stayed at the Hotel Naciónal, a big, historical landmark that sits atop a small cliff facing El Malecón with its crashing ten-foot waves. Built by the Americans in the thirties, the hotel is emblematic of Cuban culture and identity.

Black and white photographs of Hemingway with Fidel,
Mafia kingpins, and sex kittens from the forties adorn its
Hall of Memories in the basement. It was my father's first and
only trip after Fidel. We had laughed in a way I had never
seen him laugh before and in a way I had never laughed
around him. We took pictures on the breezy garden terrace:
rolling hills of translucent green, curlicued walkways and
Moorish-tiled fountains overlooking the Malecón blue. We
sat on the tippy edge of the small cliff, our feet up, freshly
squeezed mango juice in hand as El Cañonazo, the centuries-
old cannon that is regularly fired to commemorate the closing
of the city wall doors—nothing barring it, not Cuba's War of
Independence, nor coups d'etat of a string of presidents, nor
The Revolution—is set off precisely at nine P.M. Some things
never change, I started to say as my father looked at the pretty
girls on the seawall below us. Now I can die happy, he said.
When we returned to Miami, he called me. Bertha had left
the home. It wasn't just that he had traveled to Cuba, viewed
by many of my Cuban-American compatriots as a betrayal to
the exile cause; it was that he had returned to the motherland
with me. But all I said was: *¿Y eso?* and all he said was: *Bobe-
rias.* Silliness. I didn't hear from him for a while. But I heard
Bertha was back.

Flying time Miami-to-Havana: forty-two minutes. No sooner
are you up than you're down. I look down and there she is.
Havana. The red earth, the royal palms. On our last family trip here, my grandson said the royal palms looked like
birthday-cake sparklers. But I don't know if anything spar-
kles for me anymore.

During the descent everything rattles, food trays clang, the
plane shakes, but the landing itself is smooth and greeted, as
is always the case, with a burst of applause. Ladies and gentlemen, welcome to José Martí International. But you can hardly

hear the flight attendant over the clapping, in unison now, like tapped drumbeats on the beautifully glossed body of a *guajiro's* guitar.

Whoops of *¡Al fin!* and *¡Bendito sea Dios!*—At last! Blessed be God!—fill the air. A woman hollers, *¡Viva Cuba!* I lean forward in my seat to see who she is. She looks back at me. *Nadie sabe lo que tiene hasta que lo pierde.* Don't know what you got till you lose it, she says. She dabs dry her eyes and reaches under her seat for her bag. I reach under my seat for my father. The plane taxis toward the terminal. Everyone stands. I remain seated. The flight attendant says, Ladies and gentlemen, please remain seated until the plane has come to a complete stop. I want to pull the *Viva-Cuba* woman to me and cry with her. The passengers swarm the aisle, bang open the overhead bins. The flight attendant is losing her cool: Ladies and gentlemen, please *stay seated*. We'll have you there in just a minute.

Together, my father and I deplane and walk the hot, asphalted runway toward the Havana terminal. I walk, he rolls. Together, we sail through Immigration, then Customs. No, not through Customs. The young olive-clad officer asks me what is in the box. My father, I say. My father is in the box. He takes the box out of the shopping bag with its imprint of the funeral's logo, a tree of life. I haven't opened it, I say. The box is little and black. It is cute. It is the first time I have seen the box. Do I have documents? he asks. Yes, I say, and I do not lie. I do have documents, but I left them in Miami. Why, I don't know. I had opened the envelope, unfolded the Certificate of Cremation and set it aside. A supervisor approaches, an older woman. She sees my face. When she asks me when my father died, *tu papá*, I let out a wailing cry. Not a choked-up cry, a child's I've-hurt-myself-badly cry that surprises me. *Ay mi'ja*, she says, *es lo que Dios manda*. What God sends our way. And the documents? asks

the young fellow. No documents, she says, and sends my
father and me on our way.

My skin sizzles. It's supposed to be an air-conditioned room
here at El Hotel Naciónal, and the Turistaxi ride in from the
airport was air-conditioned but still, my skin sizzles. I call Ive,
my best buddy from those days of long ago, she and I *mataper-
reando* on the pretty new sidewalks of our Havana neighborhood. I needn't look up her telephone number on Avenida
Parque. Same house, same hill, same number. Unlike the jab-
berwocky in exile circles, Cubans who stayed in Cuba did not
lose their homes. As for those of us who left, whoever lived
in the home at the time, *la criada*, for example, the help, was
granted ownership of the home.

I tell Ive now that Dad is with me. I laugh, a forced laugh.
I needn't say *his ashes*; she gets it. I needn't ask her to go with
me. I needn't even say where it is that we will spread his
ashes. The stadium, she says, pick me up in ten minutes. And
I needn't say I cannot do this alone.

I can't go anywhere, I tell Ive as I bolt through her front
door, till I've had a *merienda*. I throw myself on her living-
room couch, splay open my legs, fan myself with my skirt.
I am hot and carsick. A fan, I say, bring me a fan. She will
make me a mango shake, she says. You're lucky it's mango
season and that I have a mango tree. The lights flicker overhead and *¡Le zumba la berenjena!* says Ive, flailing her arms
in exasperated motion. *Se jodió el batido*, says her son Victor Manuel, shrugging in a what-else-is-new? way. Another
apagón has overtaken Havana, another power failure of the
sort that leaves its residents in heat and darkness sometimes
for hours, sometimes for days, always when least expected. So,
no mango shake for me.

I take out the box with my father's ashes from the pretty
shopping bag with the pretty tree of life. Finally, I touch it.

Victor Manuel, I yell, come open the box. Neither your mom nor I can find our glasses. We did find our glasses; we just can't read what the box says. I touch the surface, black and smooth, a corner of it Braille-like. It has instructions here, I say. He peers at the box. Made of recyclable material, Victor Manuel says. *Caballero,* Ive says, *tanta lucha—la vida—para termimar es esa cajita.* So much struggle—life—only to end up in that little box.

She lays the box atop the living-room console, a mosaic of tiny mirrors. As a child, I marveled at the vast number of images of myself that danced and leaped before it. I sit unmoving now and stare at the mosaic of mirrors, its reflection dull, its edges black.

El Gran Estadio de La Habana, my dad liked to say, had a playing field and state-of-the-art lighting comparable to—no, better than—major-league stadiums. In 1947, a year after it opened, the Brooklyn Dodgers chose the stadium as their spring training site, as did the Pittsburgh Pirates in 1953, the year I was born. But in 1961, American professional baseball in Cuba was stopped, and the Great Stadium of Havana was renamed El Estadio Latinoamericano. That was the year I followed my parents out of the homeland, one small suitcase in one hand, my Thumbelina doll in the other.

Standing before us, the stadium slouches like an old movie star, faded and wrinkled, a flicker of what once was, except my sister and I never got to see what once was because my father never took us to El Gran Estadio de La Habana, only my mother. Wait for us here, I tell the cabbie. Ten minutes. He can't, he says. He has to drive clear across town to meet his last customers, who promised they would pay his fare if he came back. You're going to leave us here? I say. *¿En casa del carajo?* In the middle of nowhere? On the street, women wear *pantunflas*, rickety bedroom slippers, and their butts stick out like backwards Cs from fluorescent spandex miniskirts.

Ive taps the cabbie on the shoulder. *Mi Americanita* friend here thinks we're going to get assaulted, she tells him. Then she turns to me. You're in Cuba, *amiga,* remember? Not in The U.S. of A. This last part she says in English. So don't worry about crime. Worry about how we'll get back to the city. *Mira,* she says, in no time I'm going to see you doing this, like the rest of us. She sticks two fingers in her mouth, lets out a whistle, then moves her thumb back and forth in hitchhike-mode.

The cabbie drives a full circle around the stadium. When he starts the second circle, Ive says, You think if you go in circles long enough you're going to solve everything? We laugh, the three of us. I'll give you the fare you'll collect, I say, if you wait for us. Double the fare. In American dollars. *No, mi'jita*, he says, no need. He'll wait.

Out of the cab, Ive calls out to me, Where are you going? I am already midstreet, crossing to the other side. Two rifled young men in blue uniforms stand guarding the stadium entrance. To ask them to let us in, I call back. *¿Tu estas loca?* she asks. Things aren't done this way *en este país*. In this country. They're going to think we're doing *contra-revolución*, spreading white powder like that. I put my hand on her shoulder. She cringes. Her shoulder, she says, her entire arm. She's tried putting everything on it. She *can* find relief, the shots they give her at the local clinic, but they are $37 a pop. In American dollars. Before I can ask her, What happened to free health care? she says, *Lo unico que me falta es ponerme una gallina congelada.* The only thing I haven't done is wrap a frozen hen around my shoulder. And I wonder if she has a hen in her freezer but I don't say, You have a hen, in your freezer? even if I am sacrificing a shared laugh.

So we walk the perimeter of the closed stadium in the gray of dusk. She takes the plastic bag and spreads the first fistful of ashes for me, and I am grateful for that. I look at her, so far removed from the bouncing, sun-streaked ponytailed girl of years past, her dry, over-processed hair now cropped closely to her scalp, her weather-beaten skin giving her a worn-out, hardened look. So far removed from the ballerina leaping across the terrazzo of her living room floor doing arabesques and grand jetés before her mirrored console, her sequined costumes leaving swirls of pink and blues and greens behind her. And I wonder, when she looks at me, does she see my purple Nikes and cool asymmetrical haircut? The suitcases I bring full of clothes that my children discard, some hardly worn, that her children greedily don? Or does she see the sunken flesh under my eyes, the hard lines around my mouth? A wrung-out lawyer staggering under the weight of financial struggles, glob glob, a ship's anchor around my neck. A not-so-good mother begrudging all she gave up, time with her children. Like my father.

But my father never came to that realization.

After a while, I say, *Coño*, Ive, at least spread him on the grass. Even if it is littered with flattened cans, crumpled newspapers, and smoldering cigarette butts. Not on the sidewalk, with its raised slabs and wide deep cracks. It is when we turn the corner that I trip over a crack. One foot then the other, moving quickly forward, irrespective of me, my entire self on its way to the cracked sidewalk. The fall is fast but slow. But I don't complete the fall because Ive swoops a quick, strong arm my way and lifts me, my friend Ive. In two years we'll be like Mr. Magoo, she says, of the nearsighted, senile old man navigating his way through one calamity after another. I didn't know they had watched Mr. Magoo cartoons here. Now she laughs, a laugh of long ago.

*   *   *

We save some of the ashes for El Hotel Naciónal. Let's go to the long-stemmed flowers at the front of the hotel, I tell Ive. I stick my hand in the bag and grab a fistful of my father. We spread. We have gotten good at this. And then: El Malecón, I say. As we descend the big hill and head to the sea, Ive says, We buried my dad in pantyhose. I say, What? Pantyhose, she says. After three years of burial, the family receives a call: Remove the corpse to make space for others. And Cubans found a nifty trick: Bury your dead in pantyhose so the bones stay inside the pantyhose. Easier to scoop out the bones, Ive says. She holds up an imaginary bag, dangles it before me. And you did that? I ask. No, she says, she couldn't. Her son Victor Manuel told her, *Mami, I'll do it for you, I'll dig up Abuelo.* But when he arrived at the cemetery, he was told there were four corpses in the grave and was handed a bucket. His grandfather he easily recognized; he lay on top and his long, loose locks were still attached to his skull. Plus he recognized the suit in which his grandfather was buried. One of the suits you brought for him from Miami, Ive tells me. But as to the other three corpses, Victor Manuel couldn't figure out which head or which bones belonged to whom. So he laid out the bones in separate piles and went *tin marin de dos pingüey.* Ive pokes her finger at the air, eenie meenie miney mo. To decide which bones he would put where, she says.

Together, we cross the European-wide boulevard and head to the legendary seawall. Ive switches the bag of Dad's ashes to her outside hand. In case you start to fall again, she says and puts her arm through mine, like she did in those days of long ago. She tells me the problem is that I don't look down when I walk. In this country, she says, you always have to look down. One, so you don't fall. Two, in case you find ten *fulas*, American dollars.

She finds a small opening at the seawall and that is no easy feat, to find space among swarms of fathers fishing with their sons and young *enamorados* kissing and rubbing. I try to climb the seawall but I can't. I am stuck, neither here nor there; not strong enough to climb up, too scared to jump down. I think I am limber, with my daily bouts of hot yoga back in Miami, but I am not. Ive, I say, between uncontained laughter, when was the last time you peed your pants? Like those days of long ago when we hid in her dad's study and looked at pictures of naked people in his medical journals and laughed so hard we peed. Just now, she says, and now she's also laughing. Me too, I say. I told you, she says, Mr. Magoo. In two years. Less than two years.

But I make it. I stand on the seawall, Ive beside me, the Malecón waters a silvery black. I take the final handful of my dad's ashes. They are chalky and after each throw, they stay on me. The hard particles are bone shards, I know, maybe slivers of the pacemaker that was supposed to have been removed before his body was slid into the oven. I think of them as seashells. I throw my dad's ashes at the sea wind and at the waters that connect my here and my there, Havana and Miami. But the ashes don't fly in the direction I throw them. The ashes fly back inland, toward a pretty girl with brown skin kissing her boyfriend, a pretty brown girl covered now with my father's ashes. Ive and I stare at each other. *Ay*, I say to the pretty brown girl's boyfriend, as he wipes the white off her face, her hair, her blouse, *perdónanos*. It's O.K., he says, pronounced *O-kah*, the *anti-imperialista*, Revolutionary way. If they only knew, Ive whispers as we cross the highway, the slow groan of the crashing, ten-foot waves of the Malecón behind us. That's O.K., I say. *O.K.* Dad's happy, going home with her tonight. He always did like brown-skinned girls best.

ॐ ॐ ॐ

*Magda Montiel Davis emigrated to the U.S. from Cuba when
she was eight years old. She practiced immigration law in Miami,
Florida, for thirty-three years, at which time she packed her man-
uscripts, adopted three dogs, and moved to Iowa. Her essays have
appeared in* Bellevue Literary Review *and* Cimarron Review
and her articles and op-ed pieces in The Miami Herald *and* The
Sun-Sentinel. *Chapter One of* Kissing Fidel, A Memoir, *was
published online by WLRN, South Florida's NPR station. She is
currently an MFA student at the University of Iowa's Nonfiction
Writing Program.*

❧ ❧ ❧

The Siberian Connection

When just saying "*nyet*" gets you nowhere.

We had been warned.

Guidebooks, our travel agency, and fellow back-packers had all informed us that we'd meet roving sales-people on the extension of the Mongolian branch of the Trans-Siberian Railway. These traders, they said, tried to bring more than their share of salable goods from China to Russia, via Mongolia. They would probably ask us to carry an extra suitcase through customs for them.

"Just say *nyet*," everyone advised.

"*Nyet*," my husband had said, again and again, to the Mongolian woman in the Mickey Mouse t-shirt and her silent companion. But she just kept talking, and Erik squinted at her, trying hard to apply his four semesters of Russian to her hushed, rapid-fire speech.

Finally he'd turned to me, brow furrowed. "She says it's already in here. And now they want to take it out."

We had received no advice to prepare us for this situation—smugglers asking to retrieve goods they had already stashed in our compartment. So we stood at an impasse, four people nose to nose in the tiny compartment.

*   *   *

When we'd boarded the green, round-topped train in Ulaanbaatar the day before, we hadn't expected this leg of our trans-
Siberian journey to be eventful. Train rides were supposed to
be relaxing. My husband and I, twenty-four years old and married six months in the summer of 1998, had hatched the plan
to travel from Beijing to Paris overland, inspired in part by the
pajama parties on rails described in Paul Theroux's *Riding the
Iron Rooster: By Train Through China*. We pictured ourselves
sharing snacks with our compartment-mates, who would pref-
erably be Mongolian so we could practice the two phrases we'd
learned during two weeks of trekking in the country (*sain baina
uu*: hello; *bayarlalaa*: thank-you). We imagined that after a day
of cultural exchange, we'd climb into our bunks to read up on
the natural wonders of our next destination, Lake Baikal, until
we were rocked to sleep by the sway of the cars, listening to the
chuggeta-chunk of train wheels like a mother's heartbeat.

The Ulaanbaatar station, like most buildings in the Mongolian capital, is a pompous Soviet-era work of concrete,
uncrowded and orderly. After handing our tickets to a solemn woman in a pencil skirt and military hat, we climbed the
steps to find we'd been assigned to a four-bunk compartment
by ourselves—a luxury usually, but not at all conducive to
the kind of cultural exchange we sought. So we dropped our
packs in the room and hung out instead in the narrow corridor, watching the concrete blocks of Ulaanbaatar give way to
suburbs of round white *ger*, or yurts. Speakers in the hallway
walls played a nightclub-inspired soundtrack up and down
the carriage. "Ra-Ra-Rasputin" and Aqua's "Barbie Girl"
repeated numerous times as the afternoon wore on.

Whenever a passenger who looked Mongolian walked by,
we grinned and launched our best *sain baina uu*. But the Mongolians on this train were nothing like the friendly herdsmen

who'd continually approached us on horseback out on the grassy rolling hills, pantomiming requests to take their pictures. These Mongolians wore Western clothes instead of the long, jewel-toned silk or wool *dels* we'd seen on herdsmen. And they didn't speak to us.

The train was obviously still used by traders, as our guidebook had alleged; on my way to the samovar at the end of the car, where I would fill my big metal cup with instant coffee powder and water, I saw one fellow passenger in his compartment repacking piles of plastic-wrapped jackets into a huge duffel bag. Still, to our relief, no one asked us to carry anything through customs for them. Maybe Russian customs had relaxed, we thought, and traders no longer needed to worry about weight limits.

Once it began to get dark, Erik and I appreciated having our own private compartment. We slid the door closed and switched off the speaker set into the wall; with plenty of room to spread out, we left our bags on the lower bunks and climbed into the narrow top bunks. The rhythm of the train was as pacifying as we had imagined, and we were soon asleep.

Not for long, though. We had only slept a few hours when we woke to a rapping on our compartment door and opened it to find a Russian man in uniform who informed us that we were to take our bags and leave the train to go through customs. We blearily stepped into our shoes and shouldered our packs to head into the customs building, where we waited in line, feeling like wilting produce under the fluorescent lights of a state-owned grocery store.

Erik handed over his passport, which was bedraggled after riding in his back jeans pocket for two years of living in Beijing, where foreigners were required to keep their papers with them at all times. The Russian border agent, a thin man with a bushy brown mustache, eyed it as if it was a dead mouse dangling by its tail.

"This photo looks like you could just reach in and pull it out," the agent said.

He had a point—the passport had acquired moisture during rainy bike commutes and sweaty subway rides, and the plastic securing the photo was beginning to separate at the edge of the page.

The agent walked out of sight with Erik's passport. There is no five-minute period longer than the one in which you're standing at a border crossing far from home, with no passport.

He returned a few minutes later, the passport in one hand, a pair of tweezers in the other. The tweezers held Erik's passport photo.

"I had to check if the seal was intact. It was," he said, as if this would reassure us.

We could only stare miserably at Erik's mutilated passport. I imagined a life as a couple stuck between countries. I surveyed the customs building—it didn't even have a snack bar.

"Just a moment," the man said, and disappeared again. People shifted impatiently in the line behind us, and I thought longingly of our cozy train compartment. When he returned again, he was holding Erik's passport, this time with one finger on each side of the photo, tamping the layers back together. He patted it to demonstrate that it had been glued and then handed it back. Erik, open-mouthed and speechless, stood gaping at his passport, which now looked like a preschool craft project.

The border agent nodded in satisfaction—as if he had done us a big favor—and waved us along. "Go to an embassy and get a new passport as soon as you get off the train," he ordered, and we nodded like bobble heads as we grabbed our backpacks and quick-stepped out before he could change his mind and call us back.

*   *   *

That panic seemed like nothing more than a bad dream late
the next morning, as we lingered in the sunny corridor outside our compartment. Yesterday's grassy steppe backed by
low mountains and endless sky had given way to trees. We
were just thinking of checking out the Russian dining car
that had been added to the train at the border when the two
Mongolians stepped into our compartment, the woman in
her black t-shirt with Mickey on the front, the man in a plain
long-sleeved black shirt.

"*Sain baina uu!*" I said, wondering if they might be looking
for an English lesson or a game of cards.

Over the past two weeks, we had fallen in love with the
Mongolian people. We couldn't fathom how such gentle,
happy folks claimed as their most famous citizen the brutal
Genghis Khan, a warrior so bloodthirsty he wiped out 11 percent of the world's population with his army and reportedly murdered his own brother. The Mongolians we'd met
had shown us exuberant hospitality, sheltering us in their
gers during rain showers and serving us bowls of *airag,* sour
mare's-milk yogurt, and shots of *arkhi*, milk vodka.

Now we hoped we could return the hospitality by welcoming these Mongolians into our compartment. We followed
them in, smiling.

But the moment we stepped inside, the man slid the door
shut and pulled down the bar that locked the compartment
from the inside. As the bar scraped and clunked into place, the
light dimmed—the woman had closed the window curtain.
Then she began speaking intently to us in Russian, which only
Erik could understand.

I heard a voice in my head, as if I were already telling the
story to friends: "And that's when we realized we were about
to be robbed."

What would they take? I was suddenly very conscious
of the nylon money belt chafing my skin under my jeans

waistband. Our passports and most of our cash were secured in our belts. Could we get away with giving them only the few U.S. dollars we'd left in our packs?

Then Erik told me the one phrase the woman kept repeating: "It's already in here."

"*What* is already in here?" I asked, my voice rising in panic.

"I can't understand that part," he said. "But whatever it is, they have to take it out now."

"Oh my God," I said. "They hid something in here to get it through customs. While we were in there last night, the authorities were searching this train, and there was something in here."

Erik just nodded.

Meanwhile, the man and woman watched us, their bodies close, their eyes darting urgently between ours.

When the woman opened her mouth to begin again, I interrupted her. "O.K.," I said. "O.K."

This needed no translation; the man sprang to action. He climbed onto our little table, turned on the radio set into the curved panel over the window, and kept turning the knob to the right until the dogged beat of "Ra-Ra-Rasputin, lover of the Russian queen," drowned out everything but the rattling of the train. Then he removed the knob altogether and began unscrewing the bolts of the wall panel itself.

Hours passed, or at least it felt that way. In reality he might have struggled with the panel for five agonizing minutes. There was nothing for the woman to do but stand there with Erik and me. None of us sat down, so the three of us were still crowded awkwardly together like passengers in an elevator. No social protocol existed, I realized, for how to interact with a smuggler while waiting for her accomplice to reclaim illicit goods from your bedroom.

Her accomplice, meanwhile, was having a hard time removing the panel. Sweat dripped from his face and landed like raindrops on the table next to the tiny vase of fake flowers. At one point Erik half-raised his arms, as if ready to help the guy out; I jabbed him in the ribs with my elbow, and he dropped his arms. We held hands and watched silently while the man worked.

We wished ourselves a million miles away, and yet, at this moment, our fate seemed bundled with theirs—we all wanted this job finished quickly. And though my body remained still—petrified—my mind ran wild. I imagined police officers with German shepherds straining at their leashes breaking the compartment door open at any moment. Ransacking our room, dragging us off the train to an interrogation room in some old Soviet city that didn't even appear on the map. Would they believe we had nothing to do with this? My heart pounded so loudly in my ears that I thought I really did hear knocking.

Finally, the big curved piece was off, and he handed it down to the woman, who laid it on one of the lower bunks. Behind it was a long piece of Styrofoam, and as he pulled that toward himself, tiny foam balls showered the table around his feet.

Removing the foam panel revealed an orderly row of cylinders the size and uniform shape of artificial fireplace logs. They were wrapped in something like brown plastic or waxed paper, so we couldn't see what was inside. The woman started to hand her partner a white sack.

"No!" I hissed. I was convinced that she was holding our white laundry bag, and I didn't want drugs going into our bag.

The woman paused—she didn't seem to want to argue with me. I pointed to one of the pillows instead. She and the man exchanged a few words in Mongolian, then she removed two pillows from their cases and began loading the cylinders into them.

Once she was finished, the man started reassembling the wall. I didn't quite feel relief, but I felt that relief might soon be possible—like realizing a root canal is half over. We might actually survive this horror show. The re-assembly was smoother than the disassembly, and within minutes, the man was standing on the floor again, sweeping Styrofoam balls off the table and into the pillowcase with his hand. He had turned down the radio.

Finally they picked up the empty white sack, preparing to leave, and only then did I realize that it had been theirs all along—it only looked like our own white laundry bag. I felt embarrassed by my mistake, and considered apologizing, but it was clear that our visitors weren't interested in hanging around to chat.

The man scanned our compartment one last time, swept up a few more white balls with his hand, and opened the door a crack. He stuck his head out and peered up and down the corridor. Then the couple left, disappearing into the compartment next to ours.

I pushed our door shut, locked it, and collapsed against it, trembling.

And at first I almost giggled, flush with adrenaline and the relief that accompanied the end of an ordeal. Erik wrapped his arms around me, and for the next several minutes we stood clutching one another as hard as we could, muttering, "Oh my God . . . oh my *God*."

It took about fifteen minutes before we could really think, and then we began to talk seriously. What should we do now? Pack up our things and get off the train at the next station? What if these people were caught—would we be implicated? We had just witnessed a crime. What if they planned to kill us before the train reached our stop, to make sure we couldn't turn them in? Or did that kind of thing only happen in movies? But having just lived through the kind of thing that only happens in movies, we were confused about what was realistic and what was silly.

Just then a knock came at the door. I clutched Erik's hand so hard he winced, and I started shaking all over again. Erik gestured toward the door to silently ask if he should open it, and I shook my head, stifling a sob. The knock came again, and again. Finally, Erik cracked the door an inch, and there stood the woman in the Mickey Mouse shirt. She handed us our pillowcases, neatly folded.

"*Bayarlalaa*," I said weakly. *Thank you*. And she was gone.

Six more hours of the train ride stretched ahead of us. We no longer felt like visiting the dining hall—we were still too shaken—but we couldn't concentrate on reading, either. We sat in our locked compartment, holding our guidebooks open on our laps, our eyes returning again and again to the wall that we'd seen opened like a surgical patient's skull. We debated what those packages contained. Erik thought he had glimpsed leaves through the package, so he was convinced it was marijuana. I was sure the packaging had been completely opaque.

"It was probably heroin," I said, as we circled back for the thirtieth time. It didn't matter which of us was right. There was no way to prove each other right or wrong on that train, with no one we could ask and no literature available to research drug smuggling on the Trans-Siberian. But it passed the agonizing minutes as we sat and waited for something else to happen. Every so often, one of us would turn to the other and say, "Oh my God," and we would sigh or shake our heads.

Eventually hunger compelled us to unlock our door. I emptied a packet of instant oatmeal into each of our big metal cups and padded down the corridor to the samovar at the end of the carriage. There sat the *provodnitsa*, the fleshy-armed Russian woman whose job it was to keep the hot water flowing and lock the toilets when we came into stations. She was drinking tea at her tiny table, and across from her sat the woman in the Mickey Mouse shirt. I looked at both women and gave the tiniest of smiles, but neither smiled back. They continued their conversation in Russian.

Bizarrely, I felt snubbed, considering what the smuggler and I had just been through. I supposed that she *had* to act like she had never seen me before, but still. I kept my eyes on my hands, as if it required great concentration to hold one cup, then the other, under the spigot. Then I walked back to our compartment as quickly as I could without sloshing two cups of steaming oatmeal, to tell Erik what I had seen.

Now we understood that more people might have been involved. The *provodnitsa* was friends with the smugglers. She must have known what was going on. Being given our own compartment with no roommates had seemed like a stroke of luck, or maybe a courtesy to the only Westerners in the carriage. Now it dawned on us that we were probably assigned alone to that compartment *because* there were already drugs hidden in there. We were the designated rubes. Was the company that sold us our tickets—a China-based tour company—in on it too?

"What about that border agent?" Erik asked, removing his glasses and lowering his head to his cup to let the steam hit his face. Then he quickly straightened up and replaced his glasses, looking newly alarmed. "Maybe that's why he pulled the picture out of my passport! Maybe he's planning on us getting detained somewhere."

"Now you're just being paranoid," I said. In all likelihood, our ordeal was over—we had only to survive the anxiety of sitting on the train for five more hours, then we could get off and never see the criminals again.

"Or," I said, laughing with fake bravado, "maybe they're planning to shoot us just before we arrive, so there won't be any witnesses." I couldn't help thinking that the woman's unfriendliness at the samovar was a bad sign.

The hours dragged. The woods outside our little window deepened. I slid open our door again, and what I saw made me cry out: "Baikal!"

Erik came as far as the doorway of the compartment to look. Every window from one end of the carriage to the other was filled with Lake Baikal, bluer than any water I had ever seen and scintillating like endless fish scales in the sun, blending into the sky at the horizon.

I stood against the window, reading aloud to Erik that two-thirds of the plants and animals in this massive lake were found nowhere else.

"It's the world's deepest lake," I told him, trying to rekindle the thrill of exploration we'd felt boarding the train a day before. "It has a fifth of the world's fresh surface water."

We would be walking on those banks tomorrow—assuming we made it off the train alive and were not detained by authorities. We had no idea whether our fears were far-fetched or reasonable, but at 3:30 P.M. Moscow Time, when the relentless disco on the speakers finally paused and Irkutsk Station was announced, we speedwalked toward the door, our tall, overstuffed backpacks bumping against the window curtains and each other. We each held a smaller bag in one hand.

Then, just as I reached the train door, inhaled my first breath of air, and placed my foot on the metal stairway, someone took my bag and put a hand on my arm. I sucked in air and flinched, certain that I was being arrested. But the tall, blond young man now holding my bags wore shorts and a hooded sweatshirt, not a uniform. And he was smiling up at me.

"You are Carrie and Erik?" he asked in a Northern European accent, as he helped me down the stairs. He named our tour company—he was there to drive us to our homestay, he explained. I giggled madly, unconcerned by how strange my reaction must have seemed. When we closed the car doors, Erik and I took deep breaths, releasing them only as we pulled away from the station and into traffic, separated forever from two Mongolian businesspeople and their *provodnitsa* friend.

* * *

A few months later, I found an article describing the rapid spread of heroin use in Russia and showed it to Erik as support for my theory about the cargo. But Erik, having conducted his own research, countered that heroin was mostly grown in Afghanistan and would have come in through Central Asia, not Mongolia.

In the end we had to agree that we'd never know what manner of contraband we'd unwittingly harbored in our compartment. It could have been dinosaur bones or cigarettes or socks and underwear for all we knew.

"And we thought Mongolians were so nice," Erik or I would always end up saying, when we narrated the incident for friends.

Sometimes I imagined the fierce heart of Genghis Khan beating in the smugglers' chests, giving them the cruel willingness to off us if they suspected we might narc. Or maybe, I reasoned, they were just ordinary people pressed by financial need into an unsavory errand.

Then I thought of the woman standing at my compartment door, returning our neatly folded pillowcases. I remembered the man painstakingly sweeping up the little Styrofoam balls he'd dropped on our table. And I decided that, as smugglers went, these Mongolians were the nicest I'd ever met.

☙ ☙ ☙

Carrie Kirby is a writer, Monkees trivia master and frugalista who lives with her husband and three children on the suburban island of Alameda, California. Her work has appeared in San Francisco *magazine, the* Chicago Tribune, *the* San Francisco Chronicle, *and other publications. A former newspaper staffer and world traveler, Carrie spent the past ten years having and nursing babies and blogging. Now that the whole family is done with diapers and naps, Carrie has taken the show on the road, exposing the kids to America's varied beauty whether they like it or not. Carrie's new blog, about going places without owning a vehicle, is CarFreeMom.com.*

ℬ ℬ ℬ

For the Sake of the Sin

It was a fine setting for a murder.

*E*veryone on Malangen knows the story: In March 1733, Birte Olsdatter murdered her husband, the troll-man. Birte was a beautiful girl from the next fjord over, forced to marry Jens Olsen, who was twice her age and beat her. She escaped home to her family, but they insisted that she return to her husband; they sent her younger brother, Benjamin, to keep the peace. But the abuse continued, until finally it was too much to take.

One day, while Benjamin was out hunting, Birte killed Jens by bashing his head with an ax. Benjamin returned to find Birte covered in blood, sobbing. As he comforted her, she told him what she had done.

Together the siblings carried Jens's body down to the beach and loaded it into a rowboat. Benjamin rowed out into the middle of the fjord while Birte wept. They tied iron pots to Jens's ankles, then poured his body overboard, where it sank into the salt water and vanished. They cleaned the bloodstains from the farmhouse with moss, set the place on fire, and ran to their neighbors for help extinguishing the flames. Birte publicly mourned her husband's tragic death in the blaze.

Two months later, Jens's body washed ashore in the village. When Birte found out, she ran away into the nearby mountains, where she hid in a cave for three months. The local authority, the Master-Man, who was particularly bitter toward Birte because she had once refused to marry him, vowed to find her and bring her to justice; he caught her three months later, sneaking into her family's farm for food. Birte was jailed but escaped, hiding in her cave for the rest of the winter. During this time, a few sympathetic villagers brought her supplies, but she subsisted mostly on animals that she trapped herself and the few scant items she was able to steal. Come spring, she and Benjamin escaped over the Swedish border with a family of Sami reindeer herders.

The Master-Man, now twice thwarted, was determined to catch the fugitives. He sent a team of six men to Sweden. The men found Birte and Benjamin living in a Sami encampment and brought them home in shackles for a public execution. Folks rowed from hours away to watch the proceedings.

The execution was held on the rocky point of an island called Ryøya, clearly visible to boats entering or leaving the fjord. A crowd gathered; the siblings wore white. Birte sang aloud in her last moments, her pure voice rising like a curl of smoke through the cold air, though she stopped abruptly when her right hand was chopped off with an ax. Then the executioner chopped off the siblings' heads, in two strokes each; he was careful, for tradition demanded that if he missed three times, he too would be killed. As a final touch, Birte and Benjamin's heads were skewered on long poles at the edge of the fjord, left there to decay, so that anyone traveling by boat from Tromsø would see Birte's long blonde hair waving in the breeze.

So the story's told.

In some ways, Norway's Malangen Peninsula hasn't changed much since Birte's time. About two hundred miles

north of the Arctic Circle, it is home to tiny villages and
lone farms, with such strong local dialects that certain road
signs are spelled differently depending on which side of
the road you're on. Sharp white mountains soften near the
fjord, sloughing into low mounds like melted wax. On
Ryøya, now called Musk Ox Island, an increasingly inbred
herd of musk oxen now lives stranded, trapped between
currents that churn into maelstrom when the tide changes;
the next island over is called the Island of Rams, because
local farmers leave their rams on its rocky shore over the
summer. Unless they need a ram, nobody visits the islands,
so the fat rowboats along the shore are used mostly for cod
fishing. Men clean their catch on the beach and drape the
potent fish over long racks, where they hang to dry for
months. The cods' heads are ground into fishmeal and
sent to Africa, and their flesh reconstituted with brine and
eaten with bacon grease, a delicacy. Norway's wealth seems
only now to be trickling down in the form of city tourists,
who come to newly built cabins and a luxury retreat center
to get away from city life and remember, for a few days,
what Norway used to be.

It's a fine setting for a murder—part of the reason, perhaps,
that Birte's story has lasted so long, told and retold on candlelit
winter afternoons, or on bright summer nights with the midnight sun low and dim over the horizon. The story's been told
in two novels, a local musical, and a 1993 TV miniseries that
turned the core plot into a reindeer-herding love story. But it
remains fresh enough that an elderly woman might produce,
from a carved wooden box, a silver cup that once belonged to
Birte's mother, or Midsummer's Night might find three men
around a bonfire, their conversation shifting from Anders
Breivik's recent massacre in Oslo to a vehement argument
about whether Birte had a lover. Everyone has their favorite
details, or perhaps some conviction—such as that Birte and

her brother were romantically involved—that they're eager to share. But mainly, people find ways to tell Birte's story because they need her.

I first came to Malangen in 2006, when I was eighteen. I had just graduated from high school in California and moved to the Northland to attend the local folk school, a yearlong boarding school where students learned dogsledding and winter survival. That was the year I fell in love with the North—its light and darkness, its obscure dialects, its disregard for sentimentality, its incongruous warmth. I was in equal parts infatuated and terrified at all times.

When I wasn't shoveling snow or chopping meat in the dog yard, I wandered down to the village shop, which sold cheese, frozen pizza, wool socks, and other necessities. There, villagers gathered around a single table known as the Coffee Corner. The shopkeeper, a man in his late fifties named Arild, would set out a roll of expired chocolates from the shelf, or maybe a bag of tiny cinnamon rolls, and villagers would sit there for hours, leaning back in their chairs, drinking sour coffee out of plastic cups that grew soft in contact with the hot liquid. There was a tin on the table that said COFFEE: 5 KRONER, but no one ever paid. Arild busied himself, unwrapping stacks of newspapers or straightening tickets from last Saturday's gambling, and I'd hover by the candy rack to eavesdrop.

"Remember that time Sverre lost his polar bear in Tromsø?" the man called Trond might say, thoughtfully, to the table at large. "Sverre, he was glad with the drink. He was taking a ship down from Svalbard with the baby ice bear in a cage, and he put the cage out on the dock—"

"He was selling it," another man interrupted. "And he went back on the ship to get his spirits flask. But the bear opened its cage and ran off down the street—"

"A cop started yelling at him to get the bear," Trond continued. "So he Sverre, he handed the cop his spirits flask, and asked him to just hold it—"

"—and left the cop there, with his thumb in the mouth of the flask!"

At which point everyone laughed uproariously and refilled their cups of coffee, then settled back into quiet.

"Wait," I said. I couldn't help it. "What happened to the bear?"

Six heads swiveled toward me. "I don't know, girl," Trond said. "That's the end of the story."

I learned quickly that the stories rarely ended on a conclusive note, at least not the way that I expected them to. They started and stopped on the terms that decades of retellings had choreographed them to start and stop. A century-old tale was as fresh as yesterday, and yesterday's news well-worn as myth: Often, stories set two hundred years ago began with the words, "Remember that time—?" and people would nod, because, in a way, they did. In stories, as in place, time collapsed.

Which is why I might be forgiven for assuming, when I first heard about Birte Olsdatter, that she was my contemporary, or at least that her life had overlapped with those of the older storytellers, up here in rural Viking-land where I would not have been shocked to learn of beheadings seeping into the twentieth century. Few cues gave me historical context—or if they were there, I hardly noticed. It was only later that I recognized the real clue: Birte's tale had a rush of energy to it, an excitement. And something else: pride. If there was sorrow in the retelling, then the sorrow was a calculated accessory to the story itself. It was old, then—old enough that the grief and anger, along with the details, had long since been polished away.

I collected the story, and so many others, like stones to pocket and take home. Come May, I packed my duffel for a college dorm room in Maine and returned to life in the States.

Last summer, five years after leaving, I went back to Norway. I intended to report on the annual reindeer migration out of Kautokeino. But when I got to the Northland, I learned that the reindeer, with whose herders I had made plans to collaborate, had left without me, and nobody else seemed concerned about the change of plans. "You could try to find them on the tundra," another herder suggested, but he warned that the animals had a five-day head start, and hell if they were anywhere near a road. I reconsidered my options and decided to pay a visit to my old school.

The county had recently built a tunnel to Malangen, making it easily accessible by road, and I caught a bus from Tromsø. I disembarked at the front door of the shop, hesitated, and climbed the steps to see how much had changed. The villagers were sitting at the table. "Is that you?" said Arild. "I suppose you've gotten so old that you'll join us for coffee." He pulled out an extra chair.

I was only going to stay the night—then two nights, a week, another week. I found places to sleep in the woods, at the folk school, in an empty barn, and eventually in a spare room above the shop itself. Two months passed quickly. In the mornings I hiked along the shore, in the afternoons I joined the coffee table, and in the in-between times I took odd jobs, rounding up lost lambs or planting flowers in the graveyard for families who had moved away. Arild, who had once been a truck driver and rejoiced in long drives, invited me to join him on treks to pick up books in Storsteinnes or whale meat in Finland. He explained landmarks as we drove past.

One Sunday we were headed to the bank an hour away when Arild slowed his Volvo. "Yes, then," he said. "It's your turn to say what happened here." I looked around. The scenery had not changed; a broad green field sloped down to the edge of the fjord. A red barn stood in the field, and beside it a white farmhouse, where two kids were jumping on a trampoline.

"I don't know," I said.

Arild shook his head. "This," he said, "this is where she Birte killed her husband the troll-man." Troll-man meant abuser.

We drove on, toward the shallow end of the fjord, where the landscape smoothed out and a thin snow scabbed the ground under trees. A few molting reindeer trotted calmly beside the road, and a forest rose to our left. Arild stopped again, this time by a wooden sign with words painted red and an arrow pointing uphill: the BIRTE CAVE. A thread of a trail wound up through the trees. Arild cleared his throat expectantly.

"This's where she Birte hid in the mountains?" I asked. I'd begun to pick up a bit of a northern accent, with its slurred contractions and superfluous pronouns.

"You are correct," said Arild.

The gravity in his voice gave me pause. I looked up the trail, toward where it vanished up the slope. Although the mountains dominated the landscape, few people lived in them. They were the literal backdrop to everyday life, casting shadows over the red houses clustered at the shore, flowing with clear streams that tasted sweet as a kiss in your cupped hands but made your fingers and teeth ache with cold. It was in the mountains that people had hidden their livestock when the Nazis anchored their warships in the fjord; in the mountains, too, that the Sami had kept their sacrificial sites, and where cocky teenagers had summited on wooden skis, and then telemark skis, and now with snowboards that split apart into skis. There were bears in the mountains, and wolverine, and the occasional cabin maintained for public use by the Norwegian Trekking Association. People used the mountains for travel and play, not for living—but still they were possibility, a collective backup plan for Northlanders who knew well how vulnerable their strip of coastline could be.

So when Birte went to the mountains, I understood that she was acting on a collective fantasy—taking advantage of a communal backup plan, alone. As Marte Solum, a master's student at the University of Tromsø, described it, Birte was "a woman from the past with the modern ideal of female strength . . . the village's own feminist pioneer." Not too shabby for an eighteenth-century young woman, at least not according to our twenty-first-century eyes. And although in her court records Birte never claimed that her husband had abused her— rather, that he had had an affair with the elderly maid, which was embarrassing—then that's a detail that time can surely swallow and forget.

Last summer, while checking my email from the ancient computer in the back room of the shop, I came across a *New York Times* article about Norway. I read,

> Many Norwegians still like to think of themselves as the inheritors of a life of hardship and risk. But they live today in one of the gentlest, most protective countries on earth, and it is commonly agreed that the nanny state has replaced the state of nature as Norway's dominant reality. . . . Today the average Norwegian is a coddled creature whose folk memory, nevertheless, is a struggle against nature.

Fair enough—for urban, southern Norway. But folks on Malangen, and their neighbors, would lament that once again the Northland, in the tattered margins of Europe, slipped under the radar. Headline news in the Northern Light, Tromsø's newspaper, cover avalanches, bear hunts, mountain fatalities, lost reindeer, or, in a recent example, a $1,000 fine issued to a Sami man who cursed a police officer with an ancient enchantment. ("Up here," a neighbor told me, "there's more than one kind of darkness.") Coddled? In some ways, maybe. But anyone who couldn't see their ongoing struggle against nature was, in local parlance, dumb as bread.

But if the article's blind spot grates, it's because it follows a long tradition of southerners misunderstanding, or looking askance at, their northern neighbors. It wasn't long ago, Arild told me, maybe fifty years or so, that rental ads in southern Norway would specify "No Northlanders": "There was too great a risk that a northern roommate could come knocking on your door uninvited, wondering if you had an extra cup of coffee and some minutes to share it." Where Southlanders took pride in their restraint—they rarely made eye contact on the street, arrived exactly on time, spoke with eloquence and restraint, and adopted a precise dialect related to the more "educated" Danish—Northerners were loose, vulgar, and indelicate. They cursed, slurred their words, held an unsettling belief in witchcraft, joked frequently about sex ("keeping warm"), and gauged time loosely ("I'll meet you here Wednesday, after three cups of coffee," someone once told me by way of timing). The Northland wasn't just the Arctic: it was North of the Moral Circle.

But what Northlanders have, and maintain connections to, is wilderness—they have a heritage, a communion with nature, that the rest of the country is quickly losing yet still defines itself by. Even so, the cultures of wilderness and the larger society are blurring. One of the region's biggest events is the Northern Norway Wilderness Fair, held in Bardu each June. The fair, like most, is a maze of booths selling wares: reindeer-skin boots, fried seal meat, buttery potato bread, hand-carved knives, hunting rifles, discount Gore-Tex jackets, and woolen long underwear. There's a shooting contest, a kayak-throwing contest, a competition for the best carved wooden cup. More than ten thousand people drive from hours away, packing their cars with eager passengers, pitching tents, and parking RVs in fields around the fairgrounds. Girls dress up, wearing silver eye shadow with their woolen sweaters; men stay stoic until they reach the hunting wing, where rising voices give away their excitement. But there's a kind of irony to the crowd's enthusiasm, as if they were watching themselves on a reality television show. At its heart, the fair is an elaborate packaging of everyday life, a celebration of the details of Northern existence. But it takes the language of the Southland—commerce, advertisements, pop music blaring over speakers—to keep those details from being taken for granted.

I knew that Birte's song, which she sang en route to her execution, had survived the centuries, but everyone I asked declined to sing it to me, citing tone-deafness. (Despite the fact that most of them were members of the local choir, which had recently performed, for its Beatles-themed summer concert, such classics as "Norwegian Wood," "Hey Knut," and "Got to Get You Into My Leif.") So I didn't hear the song until several months ago, when I found a recording in an online archive of folk music. The song was not titled, as I had believed, "The Birte Song," but took its name from one of the lines: "For the Sake of the Sin I Must Suffer." Although I'd never been frightened by the story itself, the recording chilled me.

At first, I wasn't sure why I suddenly had goose bumps. The singer was an old man, unaccompanied, whose thin voice wavered along a chantlike melody; I would later learn that the tune was based on a hymn of the fifth commandment, Thou Shalt Not Murder. The melody felt slightly off, its silences held just a beat too long, with mouth sounds of saliva and breath whispering between the words. But none of that was bad, per se. Rather, it lent the song an air of authenticity that transported me far from the small pressboard desk in the corner of my studio apartment. No, there was something about the words themselves. I hit replay and listened again:

In all my days of youth and pleasure
I never thought it would be so
That Jesus would so come to plague me
And this is how my life would go
But fastened are my heavy shackles
For the sake of the sin I'll suffer slow
Oh what must my Jesus think
Who sees and knows how all things go?
At night, when the others sleep
I am overwhelmed with tears
And now the clear day is coming
When tears will be my only food . . .
I wish I was so far from the North
That nobody would know of me
Or else buried so deep in the earth
And my soul was, my God, with thee.

The song continued for several verses in this vein, as Birte expressed her longing to be dead, to be gone, to be punished. I didn't believe it for a moment. Would a woman who hid for so long in the fierce mountains, and escaped even after her first capture, have sung of her desire for punishment? How could the songwriter even have thought that?

Music historian Ola Graff believes that the song does, indeed, date to Birte's lifetime. He suggests that a community member wrote it, and that Birte probably heard the words before she died, an idea I found upsetting. I was disturbed at the thought of someone putting words in Birte's mouth, the idea that control of her own voice was another loss she had to endure.

And I wanted to defend Birte's violence, which was so often, in the retellings, secondary to her escape and gruesome execution—or at least, I wanted to defend her right not to regret her violence. Nobody else could decide her sorrow. I was surprised at how indignant I became at the thought of it.

It was, I realized, because I envied Birte. I envied her defiance, her self-sufficiency, even the fact that she lived on Malangen. Murder aside—and that's a big aside—she was the kind of person I want to be. I doubt I'm alone; for a few centuries after her death, the name Birte fell out of favor, but in the past century, she's become a popular namesake for local girls. With time, murderer has become hero.

But perhaps I'm an easy fan, already enchanted with the idea of northern women. At nineteen, I wanted nothing more than to be one. The female teachers at the folk school braided their hair around their faces and moved with agile confidence as they repaired a motorboat or slaughtered a reindeer. I watched one grab a snarling husky by the skin of its neck and flip it onto its back, then sit on its writhing chest, lean forward, and bite its ear hard, rumbling from her throat all the while. The dog went limp; the woman stood up, plucked a few hairs from her tongue, and rearranged her shawl. Yeah. She was my hero, too.

It was early November, during my year at the folk school, that I first tried to camp by myself. I wanted to stake my own place among these northern women. I packed my backpack, snapped on my skis and skins, and tromped uphill from the school to a mountain lake known as Sick Water, which, contrary to its name, was clear and full of fish. I brought with me a four-month-old husky puppy named Condoleeza, a shovel, a Primus stove, and lots of powdered hot chocolate. I wanted to prove to myself that I could spend a night alone in the wilderness, but planned to stay for two, just to make a point.

The first night, at midnight, shaky and afraid to sleep— afraid to be vulnerable outside, alone—I crawled out of my snow cave, stuffed my backpack, whistled to Condy, and skied home.

I was embarrassed, and told the few classmates who inquired about the trip that everything had gone fine. But the failure hung over me. I felt that my yielding to fear betrayed that I was not, in fact, the kind of outdoorsy person I imagined myself to be.

In December, the Time of Darkness came. The Darkness was a period of fifty-seven days when the sun never rose, the outside world lit only by campfires, headlamps, and pulsing green aurora. Time passed slowly, an endless dusk punctuated by sleep, so that even I forgot what we were waiting for.

It was nearly February, early afternoon, when the sun crept back over the southern mountains. I was in the dog yard, shoveling snow, and it took me by surprise. In an instant, the white landscape caught like a candlewick and blazed up around me, brighter than anything I'd seen. I thought, *If I can get through the winter all right, I can get through one night alone, too.* I took Condy, who was taller and had developed somewhat better control of her limbs, and returned to Sick Water.

In the evening I built a fire by the frozen lake and sat up late feeding it. And I surprised myself by thinking of Birte, alone as I was, in these same mountains. She'd been twenty when she escaped, just two years older than me. It was funny to think of her as all right out there, but I imagined she had been. In the wilderness, at least. It was people that were her problem.

Sitting there, I wasn't frightened at all. I knew that I had been before, but I couldn't even quite remember what it had felt like. Probably my new confidence came from experiencing the Time of Darkness, that longest of all winter nights, but I smiled to think that invoking Birte had something to do with it. I felt Norwegian, then. I felt tough.

But if I was particularly Norwegian in that moment, it was not my toughness but my use of Birte that aligned me with the locals. After all, people in the area had a long tradition of using her for their own purposes. The Master-Man used her to serve a warning, and the songwriter for a morality lesson. Even her execution served another's purpose: Her punishment was so severe because the northern courts were trying to prove their competence and stringency to their skeptical counterparts in the south.

But more than anything else, Northlanders need her, and use her, for wilderness.

If that means swallowing facts, so be it. Who knows? But the more I learned about her case, comparing historians' accounts, the more it seems that Birte never really lived in the mountains.

She never hunted animals over the winter, never even set foot in the Birte Cave. Most likely, she ran away to another village, or hid on her family's farm. But just as her story, in its time, served as a warning against sin, her story now takes her to the mountains because that's where any Northlander would go, or at least what they need to believe. Because in today's version of the story, Birte is the Northland itself: an underdog, as the North to the South; violent, in a land whose natural violence is a constant; dangerously beautiful and misunderstood, punished unfairly despite her ferocious competence; and taken, finally, to the wilderness—to prove her place there, surviving, looking down on the petty urbanites below. Locals are proud of Birte because they're proud of themselves.

Not long ago, I made it to the Birte Cave. I brought two young girls with me, restless and solemn city children I'd met at the shop, and we followed the thin trail together. It had rained that week, and the ground was soft. The girls had not heard Birte's story before, so I told them as we walked, glossing over the execution to fill in details of my own—that Birte was an avid fisherwoman, that she liked to tuck a sprig of yarrow behind her ear. I looked for yarrow to show them, but it grew mostly by the shore.

The trail climbed steadily, passing the tree line. We stopped to drink from streams, and then to throw snowballs in a small snowfield. Blueberry plants covered the ground like moss, but the berries were still pink dots among the leaves. Finally, we came to a mound of boulders, jutting up like a tower on the slope. Beneath the tower, a crack opened into the mountain.

We turned and looked at the fjord shining white below us, its beaches traced with green farmlands that rose into dark woods. There were boats on the water, ripples threading behind them, and the specks of seabirds coasting on the breeze. The sun was low over the northern horizon. It would not set that night.

"Oy," the older girl said. Then—"It's so much." She didn't need to explain.

Blair Braverman is a journalist and dogsledder currently living in northern Wisconsin. Her first book, Welcome to the Goddamn Ice Cube, *is forthcoming from Ecco.*

JAYME MOYE

ℬ ℬ ℬ

The Road Not Ridden

What would you risk to ride a bike?

*A*t dinner in Kabul, my colleague Shannon pulls out her phone. On the screen is a press release from the Taliban that she'd picked up on Twitter. It details what they are calling the spring offensive—a series of coordinated attacks around the country. The targets? "Foreign invaders." That's us. To the Taliban, any American—a journalist like me, or even a humanitarian doing work in Afghanistan, like Shannon—is a foreign invader.

Listening to Shannon read the release from her phone, it's hard to say what's more difficult to digest: the fact that the Taliban use Twitter, or that we could be in mortal danger. I'm no war zone reporter; I'm an adventure travel and sports writer here to cover the first Afghan women's cycling team with a small group of filmmakers and photographers. Besides Shannon, none of us have any experience in Afghanistan.

But we do have a groundbreaking story. Under Taliban control in the late '90s, women weren't permitted to go to school, let alone play sports. Even today, most Afghans disapprove of women doing activities outside the home, not to mention activities that require the obscene act of straddling a saddle. Afghanistan remains one of the worst places in the

world to be a woman due to lack of human rights and tar-
geted violence.

Against these seemingly insurmountable odds, eleven
women currently ride with the Afghan National Cycling
Federation. The team is the first and only of the country's
twelve bike racing clubs to allow women. Coach Mohammad
Abdul Sediq taught his teenage daughter to ride to inspire
other females to give the sport a try. He has the support of
Afghanistan's Olympic Committee, which is working to
increase participation in sports in schools, for both boys and
girls. In March, three of Sediq's young female cyclists participated in a major international race—the 33rd Asian Cycling
Championships in New Delhi. It marked the first time in history that Afghanistan fielded a women's bike racing team.

For me, the story is particularly powerful. I was an ama-
teur female bike racer in Colorado in 2008. During that time,
some of my most significant personal growth occurred, from
switching careers to ending a failing marriage. The bicycle
has since become my catalyst for change. I decided to take this
trip because I was inspired by the idea that the bike could also
have a positive effect in Afghanistan—a place where women
so desperately need change. But now that I'm in Kabul on
the eve of the Taliban spring offensive, I realize I may have
underestimated the risk.

We spend the next couple days interviewing the Afghan
women cyclists in their homes. Meanwhile, the Taliban spring
offensive ramps up. Schoolgirls are poisoned in the Takhar
Province in the north. A hotel in the same neighborhood as
ours in Kabul is raided, and an American woman staying
there is raped. I experience firsthand what it's like to live with
fear on a daily basis. Each night, I pack a small getaway bag
and sleep fully clothed, in case our hotel is invaded.

The day we interview Mariam, twenty-two, one of the
Afghan National Cycling Federation's top riders, the local

paper reports that, in the south, the Taliban slaughtered dozens of people working in the fields. I expect the mood at Mariam's house to be somber, but it's not. She's bright and animated, dressed in a Western-style pantsuit with the requisite hijab, or headscarf. I wonder if violence is so commonplace that it doesn't affect her. Or maybe she doesn't know—like Americans who don't pay attention to the news because it's "too depressing."

During her interview, Mariam tells the story of the road bike crash that fractured her lower back. It happened earlier in the year on a training ride on a highway north of Kabul. A man on a moped pulled up beside her and verbally harassed her for riding. When she kept going, he rammed her with his moped. She tells the story matter-of-factly, as if being attacked for riding a bike is normal. I realize, as a female cyclist in Afghanistan, that's exactly what it is—an everyday, ordinary risk. If you choose to be a woman athlete, violence and harassment are part of the deal.

I put my head down and scribble into my notepad, hoping no one can tell that I'm rattled. As part of my story, I'm supposed to ride with Mariam and the team on the same highway where she was attacked. But after hearing about her assault, combined with the Taliban spring offensive, I'm no longer so psyched about the prospect.

One of the filmmakers asks Mariam if she is afraid to ride. I look up to see her reaction. Mariam smiles and says her attacker was put in prison. Then she pauses, as if considering the question further. I feel like she's looking straight at me when she says, "Riding a bike is not possible with fear."

I voice my concerns about riding to Shannon over dinner. I imagine that, to the Taliban, an American woman on a bike, blond ponytail flying, would be like waving a red flag in front of a bull. I'm torn. I want to ride, it's a big part of what brought me to Afghanistan, but I'm afraid. And not just for myself. If the Taliban see me—a foreign invader—with the Afghan National Cycling Federation, it could put them at even greater risk.

Shannon agrees that riding would be risky, not just for me, but for the team. She doesn't want to spoil my trip, but, at the same time, she knows how dangerous it is to piss off the Taliban. She suggests I sleep on it.

After a long night, I decide to leave my bicycle—which made the trip crammed in a bike box—at the hotel. On the morning of the training ride, I show up at a gas station on the outskirts of Kabul with a notepad and a pen, and watch six women of the Afghanistan National Cycling Federation prepare to ride. I'm distracted by the fact that we're near gas pumps—it seems dangerous to be close to explosive fuel. I keep checking over my shoulder. For what exactly, I'm not sure. I feel like a chicken shit.

The women—girls, really, as most are in high school—don't appear concerned. They're amped up on adrenaline, just like my team was before a big ride. As they make their final gear checks, they giggle and tease each other. The language is different, but their tone is familiar from my days as a competitive cyclist. At the same time, their clothing gives away a cycling culture that American bike racers wouldn't recognize. The women secure their helmets and sunglasses over a hijab. They wear full-length pants and long sleeves under their jerseys, no matter how warm the temperature. And despite these precautions, they risk inciting violence every time they ride.

I load into the follow bus with the coach, the filmmakers, and the photographer. As we trail the team, I notice that the road has recently been paved and is in relatively good shape, with a wide shoulder for riding, which surprises me. It appears that the Afghan countryside, with its sweeping pasturelands set against the backdrop of the Hindu Kush

Mountains, is actually a decent location for a road bike ride. The Afghan culture is another story.

The bus pulls over so that the videographer and photographer can jump out and position themselves on the side of the road to film the team pedaling by. I stay in the front-most seat, watching out the window for suspicious activity—cars that drive too slowly, mopeds that get too close, leering men in beards and turbans. I observe several brightly painted semi trucks traveling past. They are ornate, with lavish murals, beads, and bells. Coach says that truck drivers decorate them as a source of pride. I'm surprised again. In my mind, Afghan men are not the type to lovingly adorn anything, let alone a truck.

After the team rides by, the film crew returns to the bus and the driver accelerates to catch up. As we get closer, I notice that Selma, one of the younger riders, is way ahead of the rest of the pack, and riding in the middle of the lane. How'd she get so far out front? Then I see it. She is getting a free ride, holding onto the back bumper of one of the brightly painted trucks.

Suddenly, Selma lets go and pedals furiously in the truck's slipstream. She must be going 30 mph. She rides as long as she can, probably fifteen seconds, then re-grabs the bumper just before she starts to fade back. As she catches her breath, she pumps her fist in the air toward the truck driver's rearview mirror. The driver sticks a thumbs-up out the window in return. I know exactly what they're doing—interval training, Afghan style. As we start to pass, Selma goes for another interval. I can't help but cheer for her out the window. Watching her pedal at top speed, a giant grin on her face, I forget to worry about the Taliban.

An hour later, the women pull over and pile into the bus to join us for lunch. They're sweaty and rambunctious. Selma dashes to the front in order to crank the radio volume.

Bollywood pop blasts so loud that it cuts off all conversation. With the music, the women become even more energized. They remove their helmets and headscarves and start to dance in their seats and in the aisle. They clap and sing and laugh and shout, twisting their arms and hips in the serpentine movements of a belly dancer. Suddenly, they are no longer the vanguard of change in post-Taliban Afghanistan—they're simply teenagers enjoying life.

Selma notices that I'm the only one not moving and starts a chant, "Jayme, Jayme, Jayme." I hesitate for a split second and then slide out from my post against the window into the aisle. The women whoop. I throw my arms in the air and mimic their motions, swaying my hips in a figure eight and twirling my hands from the wrists. They shriek their approval. Dancing in a bus somewhere between Kabul and Charikar, I stop feeling like a chicken shit. I realize it doesn't matter that I didn't ride. What matters is that they did.

Award-winning travel writer Jayme Moye didn't journey beyond North America until she was thirty years old. But once the travel bug bit, it clamped down hard and didn't let go. She eventually left her career in the technology sector to become a full-time travel writer. Since then, Jayme's travels have taken her from Afghanistan to Iceland in pursuit of the greatest stories ever told. She's written hundreds of narratives for more than fifty publications including National Geographic Traveler, New York, National Geographic Adventure, Women's Health, Men's Journal, *and* Fodor's Travel Intelligence. *In 2014, the North American Travel Journalists Association named her Travel Journalist of the Year. Visit her at jaymemoye.com.*

JILL K. ROBINSON

❧ ❧ ❧

Milagros and the Underworld

Not all is lost in darkness.

On my first day in Akumal, I was given a heart.

Milagros—or miracles—are tiny metal votive offerings. They're created in the images of animals, people, food, or body parts to honor a wish about health or welfare. My new milagro, forged of gold metal and hung from a red string, made me uncomfortable from the beginning.

A woman with long, raven-colored hair offered the charm as I walked through the small Mexican beachfront town. "*Necesita esta*," she said, holding the gleaming charm out at arm's length, the crimson string dangling from her fingertips like a thin ribbon of blood.

I looked around, thinking the day must be some sort of *milagro* celebration, when strangers handed them out on the street like flyers for happy hour specials. But I didn't see anyone else displaying the petite gifts for other passersby.

"I do?" I asked.

Under the sunlight of the summer day, already hot by eight A.M., the woman looked into my eyes. Hers were coffee-colored and flecked with gold, the same color as the heart milagro. Crow's-foot wrinkles radiated from her eyes, although she couldn't have been more than thirty. She brushed her hair out of her face with her silver bangle-bedecked arm, which still stretched in the air between us. She smiled kindly, as one might for a confused child.

"You need this," she repeated in English, this time more slowly. "You may not think so, but you do."

Hushing my internal jaded traveler—the one convinced she was selling the charm—I politely accepted it and thanked her, forgetting to ask why it was meant for me. The unexpected gift had shocked me out of my normal travel mindset, allowing me to relax in my new surroundings. Still, being told I needed it was slightly unsettling. Even I didn't always know what I needed.

That week, all I thought I needed was my SCUBA Open Water certification, the very reason I was in Akumal, on Mexico's Riviera Maya. I had two days scheduled for diving in the warm Caribbean water to see the coral reef just off the coast, full of sea turtles and brightly colored fish. But I'd really come to dive in a cenote, something I'd wanted to do since learning about their importance in Mayan folklore.

Xibalba, the Mayan underworld, was described in the *Popul Vuh* (an ancient sacred text) as the parallel unseen Otherworld, a place of fear where the dead had to traverse an obstacle course of bats, jaguars, rivers of blood, and rooms of sharp knives. Cenotes, the deep limestone sinkholes scattered throughout the Mexican Maya world, were the gateways to this aqueous, hellish underworld.

While I was intrigued with the Mayan idea of Xibalba, I'd also recently found myself drawn to boundaries of all kinds: cliffs, canyons, caverns, deep-water drop-offs. Not some fatalist fascination for me, those thresholds represented the feeling of "here I'm safe, and there—who knows?" The exhilarating uncertainty of the unknown soothed those moments when life felt clunky and full of sharp edges, or even worse—mundane and tedious.

As a travel journalist, my trips had become increasingly frequent, and for months, I'd returned from one assignment only to do laundry and repack for another. In prior years, my beach house near Half Moon Bay, my husband Doug, and my chocolate Labrador Marley had been the tethers that pulled me home between journeys—to a place where I could breathe the salt air slowly, sink my toes in the sand, and recharge. But the road had become more comfortable over time—maybe *too* comfortable. It was more exciting to plan my next journey than to stay stagnant.

Was I running away from some problem I couldn't acknowledge, or just unable to balance my work and home life? I'd grown increasingly confused about where my cornerstone really was, as home became a perch where I'd alight briefly before flitting out into the world again.

Though Doug knew I was conflicted, he'd never stop me from doing something I loved. "Do you need a ride to the airport?" he'd ask, whether my flight took off at noon or in the middle of the night. His generosity gave me freedom—but also intense waves of guilt. The ease with which he enabled me to travel left me feeling as if I was having an affair with the road. I was living two lives, often forgetting about the one I had at home when I was immersed in a new destination.

As I drove with my dive guide Jose through the thick jungle to the Dos Ojos (two eyes) cenote, just south of Akumal, he listed all the things I'd have to keep in mind once we were underwater.

"Use your flashlight to signal me in case you have a problem with air," he said, drawing his flashlight across his throat in a cutting motion, to illustrate. "Don't stir up the sediment at the bottom with your fins, or we won't be able to see," he added. But absolutely, under all circumstances, I had to follow the yellow string line through the cavern to keep from getting lost, staying behind Jose the entire time. There were no exceptions.

We were to enter the gateway to Xibalba at the East Eye, follow the line through the Bat Cave, and then through the West Eye to what was briefly described by Jose as the "crocodile cave."

I raised my eyebrows.

"No," he answered my nonverbal question. "There are no crocodiles there."

Even after the West Eye, we'd still be underwater for some time, as we'd have to retrace our path back to where we began. The entire dive, he estimated, would last forty-five minutes—an average dive time, but it seemed somehow more daunting without the opportunity to swim straight up for air. In many places, the cave's ceiling touched the water's surface.

I didn't think about Xibalba as we walked toward the gaping limestone maw from the dirt parking lot. Children played near the cave entrance. Their screeches bounced off the undulating stone and through the jungle. The delighted squeals were far from what I imagined the tortured screams of the dead would sound like. They weren't scared. Neither was I. Aside from the gruesome images in my mind, courtesy of *Popul Vuh* stories, there was nothing to fear.

At the East Eye, the limestone walls were illuminated by sunshine and underwater lighting that caused the water to glow turquoise. I sat down on a small, wooden stairway that disappeared into the liquid, breathed in slowly to calm my pounding heart, and made sure my tank's air was on and all my equipment safely connected. I tied my flashlight onto my wrist, slipped beneath the surface, and everything changed.

In the three weeks leading up to that moment, my brain had been nonstop chatter. Hardly a minute passed when I wasn't resolving some problem with my work schedule (and wondering why I so willingly let it dictate my life), or trying to quiet errant song lyrics, or writing articles in my head. My heart raced, making it difficult to catch my breath. Some nights I sat up in bed at three A.M. gasping for air but trying not to wake Doug. In the middle of writing about a country I'd recently visited, I became teary for no reason. Instead of searching for the solution to my anxiousness, I took medication to help me sleep through the night.

But when I entered the gateway to Xibalba, the internal chaos lost its claim to my body. For the first time in weeks, I couldn't feel fluttering in my throat. My slow, steady heartbeat echoed in my ears like heavy footsteps in an empty hall. It felt like I was awakening from a deep sleep.

The silence in the underwater cavern was far different from the Caribbean, where I'd taken my class the day before. There, the *whoosh* of the tide surging through the reef and the constant clatter of triggerfish crunching on coral provided a rich soundtrack. Here, in the motionless cavern where pale fish occasionally swam across my path, all I could hear was my own breathing.

I'd never been good at meditation. I could sit motionless and silence my mind for a handful of moments, but it rarely lasted long. My brain—like the proverbial monkey jumping through the trees, jabbering at anything that moved—would not allow itself to be quiet. But in the cenote's deathly stillness, it was as if that monkey mind finally shorted itself out. The endless loop of ideas and anxiety sank somewhere into the depths and disappeared.

I hadn't been running away from home but adjusting (poorly) to my husband's waning travel schedule at a time when mine was becoming more active. We'd taken countless trips together in the past, but now we struggled to find a balance that allowed our paths to intertwine in our beach-town haven. While he loved to travel, his work and a daily surf session occupied his days. Mine were spent writing about faraway places—when I wasn't occupying them. Our daytime lives were so comfortably separate that it was hard to shift into home life when we were off the clock. Even then, an evening surf or late-night travel research sometimes kept us from spending time with each other.

In Dos Ojos, once I was past the East Eye, everything became dark. The beam of my flashlight served as a spotlight on stalactites and stalagmites, fossils, and tiny fish. Glowing through the water far ahead was such a serene shade of blue that I found myself holding my breath in astonishment. Below me were huge fissures in the limestone, which made me wonder about the Mayan underworld. If Xibalba was a hellish place, the pathway there was quite the opposite. Was the idea to calm the dead, to prepare them for what was ahead?

Ahead of me, Jose continued following the string through the cenote. I fingered the surprisingly thin twine. Except for the color, it was identical to the cord that held the gold heart, safely tied at my wrist. The underwater string connected the chambers of the cavern and remained tight—a tiny demonstration of tenacity in an enormous world. Despite the trip it took in the sunless underwater realm, it led me safely to the same place without falling slack.

I thought about Doug. From transforming our backyard garden while I was gone to cooking dinner when I was tired, to taking our dog to the vet and depositing checks for me when I was on the road, he maintained our lives at home so I'd always find it easy to return.

I fingered the twine again and grabbed a little tighter. Sometimes the strongest bonds are easy to overlook in the darkness. And sometimes, that's where you find them.

*   *   *

When we finally neared the end of the line and approached the East Eye again, I wanted to trace the route backwards to stay in the quiet azure water as long as I could.

Jose quickly climbed the stairs out of the East Eye and looked down at me as he peeled off his fins and mask.

"Do you need more time?" he asked. He hoisted his weight belt over his shoulder, indicating that he was ready to walk back to the parking lot.

"I'll be right there," I answered.

He disappeared along the jungle path, and I was alone at the gateway to Xibalba. The children from earlier were gone, leaving me with a peace not dissimilar to the one I'd found beneath the surface of the water. I floated in the luminous cenote, with only the haunting *whoop-whoop* sounds of a mot-mot echoing in the cavern. The bird suddenly flew out into the open, the stunning color of its cerulean tail matching the cenote water. I followed it, ready to go home.

Before carrying my diving gear to the van, I pulled back the sleeve of my wetsuit and took the heart charm from around my wrist. Then I walked over to a young ceiba tree and left the bracelet hanging from a branch, where someone who needed it would find it.

Jill K. Robinson is an award-winning writer and photographer whose work has appeared in the San Francisco Chronicle, AFAR, National Geographic Traveler, Saturday Evening Post, Every Day with Rachael Ray, American Way, Coastal Living, ISLANDS, *and in other print and online media. Her travels never last as long as she wants them to, and her six-week Cuban honeymoon leads off her list of all-time favorite trips. She lives in a tiny surf town on the California coast with her husband and dog, and even when traveling, she can be found at www.dangerjillrobinson.com.*

❧ ❧ ❧

Why Did the American Cross the Road?

To get to the other side.
Sometimes it really is that simple.

"Let's move to Vietnam together," Sam suggested over breakfast one morning.

"Yeah, O.K.," I responded.

What can I say? I was in love. It leads to hasty decisions.

A month later we arrived in Hanoi on a sticky hot Wednesday afternoon, and after languishing for a week in a $10-a-day guesthouse, we found an apartment on a busy side street teeming with sizzling food stalls. It was incredibly romantic, if you relished the constant scraping of a metal wok, the pungent aroma of fish oil, and the inevitable drunken bottle-smashing brawl at three A.M.

Sam eagerly set about exploring the country with his infectious curiosity and ability to befriend everyone from the giggling, cellphone-wielding teenaged girls to the local town tailor, and I got accepted into a teaching program. While Sam discovered the joy of a custom-made shirt and a bowl of *pho* sprinkled with lime, chili, and cilantro, I managed, one evening, to choke down a chicken's asshole—I didn't want to offend my dinner hosts who'd undoubtedly served me the choicest pieces. About the only thing that still proved a challenge was crossing the street unsupervised.

Roads in Vietnam are scary. They remind me of that old video game Frogger, except without the fun hopping sound effects and the fact that you might actually die—there is no second frog life to fall back on. Most Vietnamese don't own cars. You'd think this would make it easier, but it doesn't. Cars I can deal with—they tend to maintain some semblance of order by restricting themselves to specified lanes. Motorcycles and scooters—motos, as they're called here—are another beast entirely. They're not confined to lanes, so anything and everything becomes a lane: sidewalk, back alley, stairwell, train track, storefront, or wherever you happen to be standing. Millions of motos chug, sputter, and rev their way through the city, with no pedestrian-safe zone in sight. Even Frogger got a lily pad.

One morning a few weeks into our new Vietnamese life, I realized I needed to do some shopping. There was only a can of beans in the cupboard, and I was sick of street food and accidental anus eating. I was excited by the prospect of going to the local market—it was nothing like a supermarket back home, where you pushed a cart through sanitized aisles and sorted through boxes of prepackaged foods under buzzing fluorescent lights. I wanted bright and colorful, hustling and bustling, vendors shouting, customers haggling, fruit and veggies tumbling off tables, beans and rice busting from their sacks. I wanted to have my own "tomato guy" and "bread guy," and I envisioned myself carrying all my purchases in my own thatched shopping basket.

Unfortunately, I didn't have a basket, and Sam wasn't home to walk with me. I wandered outside to look for Chop Chop. He usually loitered around my apartment, sleeping soundly atop his moto. I'd met Chop Chop our first week in Hanoi. He saw me exiting my apartment and followed after yelling, "Mam! Moto, moto! Chop chop!" When he smiled, his faux gold tooth glinted in the sun. I'd assumed Chop Chop was his name and started calling him that. He was actually just explaining how he could drive me places really fast. He quickly appointed himself my personal chauffeur. I paid him quadruple what a local would, which allowed him more leisure time to nap on his moto, and in return I didn't die trying to walk somewhere. This seemed a fair arrangement. Sam felt Chop Chop and I were enablers, however, and that it wasn't good for either of us in the long run.

It wasn't good for me today, anyway, because Chop Chop wasn't around, nor was his creepy minion who sometimes gave me a ride. "I love you," the little perv had pulled me close and whispered into my breasts. I had no choice but to go alone, a terrifying thought.

I waited at the first intersection.

And I was still waiting fifteen minutes later. The constant flow of honking, sputtering traffic never receded. I longed for a button to push and a kindly flashing green man to aid my crossing, but crosswalks hadn't been invented yet. Instead I watched three motos transport a rather large in diameter, thirty-foot-long metal pipe. They rode in a synchronized train, each driver holding the pipe hoisted to his shoulder with one arm and driving with the other. It was impressive.

Sam and I had passed many a muggy evening sitting on tiny blue plastic stools at *Bia Hoi* Corner, sipping thirty-five cent lukewarm "beer" and watching the motos pass. The first one to see a family of five riding on a moto got to sucker punch the other in the shoulder and yell, "five on!" Larger livestock like pigs, goats, or dogs counted as family members if they were alive. Watching the motos was a favorite pastime of ours; however, my inability to navigate through them on a daily basis had become a point of contention between us.

"You're a rock and they're the river," he'd preached the other day while we were walking into town. "You just have to move slow and steady, and they'll part around you like a river. Here, take my hand." He reached out and started pulling me into the motorized current. I took a few tentative steps under the steady tugging of his hand. *I am a rock. I am a rock*, my head chanted. A few feet in, though, I realized I didn't *feel* like a rock. I felt fleshy and breakable. I tried to bolt back, but Sam wouldn't let go.

"Just keep walking," he'd urged.

He continued to drag me across; I continued to resist. The motos didn't know which way to sway. They teetered back and forth, unable to predict our course. By default they aimed straight for us.

"I'm a bad rock!" I screamed, ripping my hand from Sam's and leaping back toward the relative safety of the nonexistent sidewalk. Sam had continued crossing as if he were The Chosen One, deflecting death with his steady gait and utter lack of concern.

"Chicken shit!" he'd yelled from the other side.

It turned out beginning a new life in a new country with your new boyfriend wasn't as uncomplicated as it had seemed that morning over bowls of oatmeal. Sam was faring better. In the same sure way that he charged into oncoming traffic, he'd leapt into our relationship. We'd been together only a week when he first told me he loved me. Six months after that we were on a plane to Hanoi. He believed that whatever roads life laid down before us, we'd make it to the other side unscathed. I, on the other hand, didn't want to become roadkill. I'd moved all the way to Vietnam to stand on the sidewalk of our relationship.

The three-man metal pipe-moving motos were long gone, and I was still on the wrong side of the street when a teetering stack of illegally photocopied books approached me. Behind the stack was a small twelve-year-old Vietnamese boy I knew all too well. He found me everywhere.

"Lady, you buy book," he said. And so it began.

"I don't want to buy a book."

"Lady, funny book." He was relentless. "Look pig on moto." He displayed the grainy cover for me to see. It was indeed a pig on a moto.

"What's so funny? I see pigs on motos every day. Look around, kid."

"So, you buy?"

"I'm not interested," I responded in the most uninterested tone I could muster.

"Oh, lady. You funny," he laughed.

I'd already bought two of this kid's books. The first was missing twenty pages in the middle, and the second gave me a nasty paper cut. Granted, that wasn't his fault, but his presence was making my finger throb.

I was still working out my plan of escape when I felt a delicate hand grab hold of mine. I looked down to my side and saw an old, slightly hunched lady holding my hand. She looked up and smiled through her wrinkles with a charming stained-tooth grin. Even at 5'3" I felt tall in this country. Was I so helpless that an elderly Vietnamese woman had to assist me? She motioned for us to cross. Apparently, I was. Or maybe, just maybe, this woman was a spirit guide. She had clearly crossed a few roads in her life. Maybe she was here to teach me that sometimes you just had to suck it up and risk a moto to the heart if you ever wanted to get anywhere worthwhile. Or perhaps it was just a fucking road I needed to cross to get to the market, so let's get on with things.

I took a deep breath and gave her frail hand a gentle squeeze. Without looking or hesitating she pulled me off the curb. It might as well have been a cliff.

"Hey, lady. You buy book!" Book Boy would not be ditched. He tagged along to the other side of me with his tower of books blocking our line of vision to the left. So there I was, amidst a sea of high-speed motorists, acting out some sort of relationship metaphor with a probably half-blind and possibly deaf senior citizen, and a persistent kid with no regard for copyright laws. I wondered if Sam would eat the can of beans for dinner, since my death felt imminent.

Of course I'd heard the old cliché that before you die your life flashes before your eyes. Mine wasn't doing this exactly, but I did get to thinking about Sam and our relationship. Things hadn't been going well. We'd been fighting a lot, growing distant. We blamed it on Vietnam—or at least I did—but really, it was my fault. I had never fully committed to us, just as I couldn't commit to crossing this damn street. I always kept one foot firmly planted on the sidewalk, just in case. But Hanoi didn't have sidewalks, and neither did love. Armed with this realization, I suddenly felt ready to take the next step—though still convinced this could all end badly.

Yet, miraculously, my life wasn't ending, which might have had something to do with the fact that the motos were actually *going around us*. Maybe three rocks were better than one. Together we were more like a boulder. We were definitely moving at the pace of a boulder, anyway, since the old lady couldn't hobble very fast, and the kid had to keep squatting down to pick up fallen books.

The motos zipped past, their wind fluffing my arm hair, beeping horns filling my ears in surround sound, and gasoline fumes hanging thick and heavy in my nostrils. We kept crossing, and the motos continued to artfully weave and dance around us. It was like choreography; you just had to trust your part. And perhaps be holding the hand of your newly adopted Vietnamese granny.

Before I knew it, I'd done it. I was on the other side of the road. Some people heal the sick. Others pen award-winning novels, advance technology, or lead nations. I crossed a road. I wanted to hug my granny in victory, but in true spirit-guide fashion, she had vanished into the crowd, never to be seen again. Book Boy was still there though, so I bought the one with the pig on the moto. I'd give it to Sam, our version of a love story.

Sarah Katin has been a television host in Korea, professor in Japan, treehouse dweller in Laos, house painter in New Orleans, sangria swiller in Spain, dragon hunter in Indonesia, and fishmonger in Australia. Her travel essays have been featured in The Best Women's Travel Writing series, Leave the Lipstick, Take the Iguana, *and various print and online magazines. These days she can be found in her Southern California office (the cushy chair by the window at—insert café du jour) where she writes for film and television. Or in Costa Rica bathing baby sloths. You never can tell about these things. Find out by following @SaresKat on Twitter.*

❧ ❧ ❧

Waiting for the Sun

Not a complete washout.

I hadn't considered the rain.

If I had been thinking, I might have figured out that the email promotion for the plush beach resort on Vieques was dirt cheap because it was for the earliest days of the off—that is, wet—season. What did I know? We are a two-artist family, and for us a Caribbean respite consists of take-out Jamaican beef patties from a bodega in nearby Waterbury, Connecticut. My children, a girl and a boy, attend the kinds of schools where many if not most of their friends bolt for Telluride or Costa Rica or at least Orlando over spring break. Some years, when we have room on our credit cards, we haul off to Tucson to visit family and fill up on guacamole and those saguaro-studded vistas that wipe winter from the brain. We're used to any sort of getaway being a wing-it affair and have grown—in some undeniably defensive way—to like it that way. Even my kids claim to genuinely love downtime at home, our freezer stocked with Heath Bar Crunch and their mother willing to sling up eggs to order pretty much any time of day.

It had been a tough year, even aside from our Leaning Tower of Unpaid Bills. By March, I was on the upswing from a leave of my senses that had nearly derailed me. For almost eighteen months I'd been unable to discern any strip of daylight above the sea of regret in which I found myself suddenly adrift at midlife. It was the riptide of hormones that eventually took me under, until one spring day I crawled out the other side and loaded up a few vases with tulips I'd planted in the darkest moments the prior November. I was exhausted but hopeful, bursting with apologies I wasn't sure I could ever articulate. What was I supposed to say to my beautifully unscathed children?

What we needed, what I needed most of all, was to get out of town, for an absence to sweep the melancholy from my house. I wanted to force the kind of togetherness only a vacation can allow and for my kids to see me as I was meant to be: smiling, at peace, the get-it-done, multilingual, at-ease-anywhere journalist. The rock-solid foundation of the family. The person who wasn't a basket case.

What we needed was a white-hot beach. To scour tide pools for shells or drape myself along a patch of sand and watch the children leap around the turquoise waves. And then my solution arrived, courtesy of the Inbox and my American Express card: a five-star hotel opening in Vieques. Forty percent off rooms, free this, complimentary that, on a gemlike little Puerto Rican island studded with sparkling beaches and a sprawling nature reserve one tiny plane hop from San Juan. Sold! We would leave when the kids got out of school and return tanned and whole, the family tighter than ever.

Securing the cheapest flights meant that my daughter and I needed to leave a day early, and so we set off with our books and carry-ons, luggage crammed with filmy sun dresses and quarts of sunscreen in every SPF. On the plane, we riffled through the Vieques research I had dug up: food trucks and coves to explore, the bakeries and drives and promenades we'd insert between our beach expeditions. My daughter pored through an article about the bioluminescent bay on the island, caused by billions of small organisms that glow when the water is disturbed. I read about the history of the U.S. Navy's weapons testing on the island, which the Pentagon had ceased in 2003.

"Otherwise, I'll be happy just to hang on the beach all day and body surf," Ava said.

"You're my daughter all right," I said.

When we changed planes in San Juan, the sight of pineapple juice carts and vendors dispensing *café con leche* signaled a singular delight: Tropical Brain Suspension was imminent. When our little Cape Air Cessna flew into chunky, black clouds, though, I was less worried about the plane being banged around by lightning than about the weather and my looming disappointment. When we landed, the rain was driving with force enough to pummel my shoulders, bared optimistically upon takeoff in anticipation of our midday arrival in Vieques. My daughter and I braved the downpour in our flip-flops and ran across the tarmac where we found our way to our hotel's welcome lounge off to the side of the tiny airport. It was air-conditioned to suit a much dryer day, and under our soaked clothes, our skin prickled from the chill.

"Welcome to Vieques!" the man beamed, holding forth two glasses of juice.

"Was this rain in the forecast?" I asked. The forecast I never bothered to check. If he gave me the wrong answer, the hope in my voice was poised to leap into panic.

"Yes, the rain is now here to stay, but we like it when it arrives," he said. "It was beautiful until yesterday!" The man's good cheer was so close to infectious that for a minute I thought he was delivering good news. Instead he handed down a death sentence on my beach vacation fantasy. All that money, all that anticipation: all out the window.

"Ava, let's call the boys," I said, meaning my husband and my son Ray. "We're going home."

"Mom, that's not funny."

"You heard him," I said, pointing to the picture windows that shook from the pounding storm outside. "It won't stop raining until October."

"Something like that," he said, still grinning.

"My God," I said to him, my bloodless face clearly alarming my daughter, who looked as stricken as I felt. I wished he'd lied to me, shooed off the downpour as a passing squall, assured me of blue skies in a mere five minutes.

I suddenly became aware that my daughter had witnessed quite enough despondency in the not-too-distant past. I needed to find a way to shroud my sense of misfortune and keep it together. But it was the beach—not a soaking one—I thought we needed as the antidote to all. I took the forecast personally, as a true betrayal. My high hopes had blurred what should have been obvious (or at least, easily researchable), but I nevertheless felt tricked by this man, the whole conspiratorial island of Vieques, and in fact, the entire Caribbean Sea.

We attempted a nibble on a biscuit, finished our juice, and slogged through the hurricane to the van and then, the hotel. The reception staff greeted me with similar bonhomie, as if there wasn't a river where the driveway once had been, as if my heart wasn't bruised from my foolish oversight, as if I was ecstatic about arriving on the first day of the rainy season. *Monsoon* season.

"So you don't want to go home, where at least the weather's nice?" I asked Ava as we made our way to our room along the hotel's flooded walkways. In my mind were the great, candy-striped peonies I had left behind in Connecticut, and the waning light of a summer evening on our back porch.

"I swear, Mom, I don't care about the weather and neither will Ray and Dad," she said. "And neither should you."

Now that my thirteen-year-old daughter was parenting me, for her and all of our sakes, it was time for me to buck up.

Our room was refrigerator cold, and I marched straight into the tub to blast it full of hot water.

"Look, the beach is right there," said Ava from the porch. I went to join her in my robe. The sky seemed as dark and thick as putty, and the air bore close upon our skin. The sand lay ghostly under the mist, and we listened to the swish of the waves below. "The palm trees look so green," she said.

After my bath, I perused the contents of my suitcase, devoid of any shred of rain gear. It would have been easy to stick a plastic poncho in among my bikinis and cover-ups. I have dozens of them, purchased over the years for camp and overnights and soggy track meets. "I guess I won't be needing this," I said, brandishing the bag full of sunscreen.

My daughter shrugged. "You still might," she said.

While Ava napped, I paid a visit to the front desk. As much as I could fake it for my family, I needed people trained in hospitality to bolster my spirits. I approached them near tears, and one woman touched my hand with tenderness. I apologized for my state, but I felt foolish for being so surprised by the turn of the weather.

"You need to take your family to El Resuelve, the best place to eat on the island," she said. "You need to do the Bio bay and drive around the old military barracks, and visit the beaches, even if it's not sunny. You will still find Vieques beautiful."

"Promise?" I said.

"You will want to come back," she said. "There is more to the Caribbean than sun."

Not for a girl from Boston.

In a few hours, with borrowed hotel umbrellas in hand, we hopped a taxi to the capital, Isabel II. We strolled along the soaked streets looking for signs of life. Streetlamps glowed yellow light but illuminated nothing on the sidewalks. I took note of a bar on the main plaza that I'd check out when my husband arrived. A shopkeeper pulled the metal grate over the door of his haberdashery, and the mannequins in pressed guayaberas and straw Trilby hats vanished for the night.

From the startled look on the owner's face, we were not expected at the fancy restaurant in town. Apparently, no one was. It was on the second floor of a pink stucco building on a side street. Ava and I perched at a table by the wide-open window overlooking the desolate town. Rain pounded on the tin roof above the second whir of two stationary paddle fans. Our murmured conversation was the only other sound, but hardly audible with the double-drilling above our heads. A margarita was cold and sweet, and Ava and I shared crispy cod fritters and devoured an order of mofongo, served with a fan of sliced limes.

The boys arrived the following day during a respite from the showers, and the van splashed through puddles on the airport road to the car rental. In the office, I pulled my husband to one side and gave him my woebegone best as the sky darkened for a fresh downpour.

"Are we just going to pretend it isn't pissing down rain all over our first vacation in years?" I asked.

"Actually," he said, "we are."

"You don't think this is a huge waste of money?"

Mark jingled the keys to our new PT Cruiser, and his smile both confused and buoyed me. "No, I think this is perfect," he said. "Who the hell cares? It's just rain."

Just rain? My daughter, my husband, and everyone I had met so far on this island kept repeating these same words since I'd arrived. Perhaps it was my childhood in New England, where beaches turn charcoal dark in summer storms that cast gloomy reminders of shipwrecks and lonely widows. I spent one waterlogged summer on the seacoast of Maine, my hair frizzed up under the hood of my rain slicker, feeling heartsick for the empty restaurants with lobsters milling around the tank and for the hopeful owners who prayed for nothing more than a passel of sunburned tourists.

Now that the boys had arrived, the stakes seemed even more perilously high. We had to keep two teenagers busy, and we had to make the family (and myself) whole again. Under the circumstances, there was little to do besides eat, and as much as he loved the manicured grounds and heated pools at our hotel, my son wanted to venture elsewhere for meals.

We took the car across the island south toward the beaches and on the way stopped at El Resuelve, which was shuttered for the day. The rain fell steadily, but we parked the Chrysler and ambled along the perimeter of the marina to settle upon a food truck for *pinchos*—finger food. The odor of roasting meat and hot cooking oil wafted our way as we waited for sizzling chicken skewers, *pastelillos* filled with spicy meat and green olives and crispy *papa rellenas*. We strolled along the avenue through the tourist town of Esperanza. It should have been packed with vacationers, but it was almost deserted. We decided to wait out the shower at another restaurant on our list, a tropical wooden structure with the most Fort Lauderdale of names, Bananas. Mark and I ordered a beer and chomped on a tasty mound of homemade potato chips while the kids wandered off, content to be in each other's company and explore alone. The air was tranquil and, perched on the patio with my husband, watching my nearly grown kids wander off together conspiratorially, so was I.

It wasn't even two P.M. by the time we drove slightly east to the beaches, first to Blue Beach, which shimmered invitingly in photos I had perused while planning our trip. It was too wet and so we turned back, noting the location to place our towels should we return. Next we headed for the place I'd craved the most in my dream of Vieques, Secret Beach, or Pata Prieta. As we cruised the road leading to its hidden coves, we passed herds of feral horses, some with white seabirds perched on their backs. We scaled a small hill, and Pata Prieta revealed itself before us, the electric blue water from the photographs now steel gray. Mark and the children wanted to swim and had worn their bathing suits in anticipation of a spontaneous dip. The water churned under the black sky, and they ran with whoops and yelps headlong into the surf. I walked the semicircle of the cove, back and forth, wading in periodically to let the water swirl around my ankles to wash them clean. I repeated this as if it were a ritual, and for a moment the clouds parted and I saw the seat of my daughter's bright pink bikini pop above the wave as she dived.

"Mom, you've got to come in," Ava cried. "The water's fantastic!"

"Thanks, I'll stay right here," I replied.

"But you can't feel the rain when you're floating in the water," she said.

It made perfect sense, and maybe one day I'd believe her.

The next morning we ate our breakfast at a *panadería* in Isabel II, with *café con leche,* donuts and fried eggs. I hadn't bothered with sunscreen because although it wasn't pouring, the rain loomed above us, relentless and threatening.

"Isn't this great?" my husband kept asking, or saying. The kids were excited for the Bio Bay excursion, which we planned to make that night after dinner at El Resuelve.

Instead of waiting pointlessly for the sun to appear all day, we took a drive along the military road to see the old naval bunkers abandoned when the Navy left the island. In time we began to see eerie-looking doorways buried into soft shapes under the hills, barely visible through moss and vines. My husband was intrigued enough to stop and photograph each one we passed. We were alone out here on this abandoned road, and the structures had a strange and neglected beauty that could inspire both fairy tale and horror story.

"Are we near the beach?" Ava asked.

I sighed and gazed around at the mist, indistinguishable from the sky. "I will never dry off after this week," I said.

Ava made sandcastles and Ray ran sprints along Red Beach while I went to sign up for the Bio tour and fetch lunch from a food truck. I walked past the horses to the car and envied them for their peaceful countenance. We had four days left. I wondered how long it would be until the children started making noises about ditching this wet island.

We sat on towels on the damp sand for spicy jerk chicken and massive Cuban sandwiches from Sol Food, a truck painted with blue sky and white clouds. For the briefest moment, the sun flashed through as I sipped on a cold Presidente. There was no avoiding it—the island was sinking into me and I felt it all: the quick toasting from the sky, the closeness of my family through these al fresco meals, the pleasantly growing distance between this beach and my home.

El Resuelve was closed again, the patio furniture stacked up on the drenched terrace and the neon lights turned off in a scene of utter dejection. Sheets of rain made the driving treacherous, and so we stopped at Al Meson Criolla, a café with an orange metal roof. It was not on our or anybody's list of things to do in Vieques, but it was clean and the chicken smelled glorious. We all ordered pollo asado al carbon, and I volunteered to drive to the launching site of the Bio Bay tour to see if the weather would thwart us. In truth, I wanted a few moments alone. I was all too aware of the destructive power of an unhappy mother, no matter how gamely she tries to hide it, and my family deserved better than I was giving.

As I headed east, the rain got so dense that I could no longer see the road. I kept driving, believing in the sanctity of landmarks I might recognize. The PT Cruiser slipped beneath me, even at five miles per hour, and when I plunked into ditches along the perimeter of the road, or veered into swales, I jerked out of them, praying that this low-riding pleasure mobile would stay intact. It was June 20, the second longest day of the year and though it was six P.M., there was only the vaguest hint of daylight. My hands clutched the wheel and as I breathed, I felt panic coil in my stomach. I pictured my cellphone where I'd left it on the table at the restaurant, believing I'd be gone for fifteen minutes. I had been driving for an hour. I could see no hotel signs, no roadside attraction, no other person, even, who might have ventured outside and to whom I could ask directions. I didn't know if I was on the north or south part of the island, but I knew I had to stop, so I parked on a dead end on a tiny patch of road hugged by a cluster of jungle. I took the keys from the ignition and perched barefoot in a soaking shirt and blouse on the hood of my car. I let the rain soak into the pores of my skin. I listened to the broad leaves of the kapok and mango trees shake overhead. I waited. All winter, I had sought solitude and believed that in order for my crisis to pass, I needed to distance myself from the people I loved. How wrong I had been.

Within ten minutes, I hopped back into the car. It was night and there were still no people, and not even a goat or a chicken to guide me home. But in time, I spotted a few semi-familiar signs, one to a hotel and bar, one marking entrance to the National Wildlife Refuge that covers much of the island. Onward I crept, grasping onto anything I recognized as a crucial knot in a lifeline. Finally I pulled up to the restaurant, where my family stood on the porch.

"Hi Mom," Ray said.

"I guess the bioluminescent tour is canceled tonight?" Ava asked.

"Um, guys?" I asked, "Were you a little worried that I'd driven off a cliff?"

"We figured you needed a little break," Mark said. "And no, we weren't too worried." He carried a brown bag, which contained my roast chicken.

"Tomorrow is the first day of summer," I said.

The skies opened up again the next morning. When it halted, for an hour here or there, with the air misty and thick, we bolted for the beach, and when I closed my eyes I heard the waves and my children's voices. It was unlike any Maine day I had ever known. I was far away—we all were. We snacked on *carnitas*, *chicharrones*—fried pork rinds—and gritty bottles of lemonade, sharing everything and getting similarly stuffed, as if it were Thanksgiving dinner.

Later, on the way to the launching point of our tour, we stopped at El Resuelve, whose cheerful sign seemed like a relic from better, sunnier days. None of us was really hungry but by now it was a ritual.

"Are you open?" I asked a man who appeared with a quizzical look from behind a kitchen door.

"No, not tonight," he said.

"They say it's the best restaurant on the island," I said. "Will you be open tomorrow?"

He gestured across the drenched patio, raised his arm skyward and shrugged. "Come back," he said, not specifying when.

After meeting up with our guide and the rest of the group, we bumped along in a van to Mosquito Bay where we covered ourselves in bug repellent. We paddled out in our kayaks to see the mangrove swamps, whose decomposing roots allow those unicellular protozoans, called dinoflagellata, to proliferate. It is these micro-organisms that, in some strange alchemy, glow when the water they inhabit is agitated.

Eventually we got the go-ahead to clamber into the water, and I saw it at once. The more I waved my hand, the greater was the micro-organisms' excitement and the brighter was the swoosh of strange green light. The four of us swam a bit from our boats. We knew we had to share this discovery, this astonishment, this bit of sorcery practiced in these tropical waters. As I stirred the area around my arms and feet, I was probably aware that the eruption of light in my movements' wake had a greater reason on the planet than to make me feel alive and unified with the people I loved. You can't look at one of life's mysteries and think it exists for you. Right?

Ava was correct. I could barely feel the rain when I was in the water. It began to fall softly then more urgently, warm Caribbean rain, the same temperature as the sea.

"Mom, you've got to see this," said Ava. "Go under and look up."

When I submerged, I looked up to the sky. Somewhere beneath the vast blanket of clouds, the planet and the sun were aligning into perfect order for summertime. Just under the surface, the cool, clear water erupted with ghostly flashes of blue and green light. Individual raindrops that caused a downpour that caused an unknowable and dazzling phenomenon for a girl, her brother, his father, and his wife to see. Together.

やや や

Marcia DeSanctis is a former television news producer who has worked for Barbara Walters, ABC, CBS, and NBC News. She is an award-winning essayist whose work has appeared in numerous publications including Vogue, Marie Claire, Town & Country, O the Oprah Magazine, More, Tin House, *and* The New York Times. *Her travel essays have been widely anthologized, and she is the recipient of three Lowell Thomas Awards for excellence in travel journalism, as well as a Solas Award for best travel writing. She holds a degree from Princeton University in Slavic Languages and Literature and a Masters in International Relations from the Fletcher School of Law and Diplomacy. She worked for several years in Paris, and today lives in northwest Connecticut with her husband and two children.*

♨ ♨ ♨

An Hour Like Water

Another city, another clock.

*A*lfonso is half an hour late. He doesn't call to tell me this, nor does he apologize when he finally shows up where we've arranged to meet, on the corner in front of the convenience store. He just smiles, kisses me on the cheek, and asks me whether I like Arabian food. He asks it in Spanish, and I have to get him to repeat the question two more times. *Árabe* is the word I'm not getting, not with the way he crushes the *r* and turns the *b* into a *v*.

"Should we be talking in English?" he asks me in English, after the third and final attempt. I pout.

"It was just that one word!" I protest, and he laughs and unlocks the car. The door on my side scrapes the edge of the sidewalk as I pull it shut.

"You sank the car!" he says, but he's not angry. He's used to the screech of the door against the high curb, and jokes that if I weighed just a little bit less, the car wouldn't sink so bad. I know he is teasing, though, because he told me the other night that I should eat more and ordered us both desserts.

I decide, as we drive down Bullrich, past the horseracing track and the massive banyan tree, past the lime-green Chinese restaurant and the tiny gas station, that I won't be mad that he showed up late. Even if I said something, he'd just remind me that it wasn't his fault—"I don't have a watch, remember?" he'd say. And I'd have to admit that I've used the same excuse. Anyway, I tell myself, leaning back in my seat and watching the lights of Palermo flicker past, isn't the strange slow movement of time the sweetest thing about this place? I traveled all the way from Guatemala to get to Buenos Aires, riding buses through Central America and Ecuador, Peru and Bolivia and finally Argentina's northwest frontier. And yet I found no other place that treated time the way Buenos Aires does. With each mile I crept farther from the States, time loosened—stretching in the dripping heat or altogether ignored, clocks an hour off and watches lost. Yet only here, in this massive, layered city, can you really let the minutes collect; they sit like honeyed drops on your tongue, drawn out and savored, inhabited fully.

Alfonso turns up the music as we cruise down Jorge Luis Borges, a street I love for its name and its graying apartment buildings with their green awnings and creeping vines. This street, as it stretches into Palermo Soho, gives way to tiny, dim bars, and to clothing shops with doors propped open late, spilling pink light onto the street. Alfonso tells me that the man's voice that comes through the stereo is that of an Alaskan guy who grew up in Buenos Aires. We listen to his raspy, folky song as we cruise up and down the nighttime streets. I've been seeing Alfonso two weeks; we always drive like this, up and down, before going to a restaurant or once the movies. "I like the lights," he told me the first time he picked me up. "Buenos Aires is magic at nighttime."

The bars we speed past are crowded with trendy twenty-somethings who smoke and kiss, making the night sultry. Knee-length stiletto boots; tight jeans and leather jackets. The girls have this hair, this amazing long hair that reaches down so far they have to move it to sit down, and their boy-friends hold them at their waists and draw out the kisses. We drive down the series of streets named after Central American countries—Nicaragua and Costa Rica, Honduras. I tell Alfonso, in Spanish, that I like this part of town because the streets remind me where I started my long trip south.

"Which one's your favorite?" Alfonso asks, and I tell him, without hesitating, "Nicaragua." I tell him I liked the heat there, I liked the poets, I liked the blue waters of the Corn Islands and the way, in the late Granada evenings, the sun made everything pink.

The Arabian restaurant, when we arrive, is so jammed that we have to add our names to a long list, a list that a bald man holds with importance at the door. He is smoking and ushering couples in and out, and there must be thirty or forty people waiting for him to call their names, standing there beneath the plastic awning in the sweet, unexpected warmth of this springtime night.

"Let's go for a beer," Alfonso suggests, after he puts our name down.

"How long is the wait?" I ask, and he tells me it's enough time to have a beer. I don't push it. This is like him ringing the doorbell late and not apologizing; time works like this here. Argentines don't use the word *ahorita*, as the Peruvians do, and the Ecuadorians, and the Central Americans, whose meals are churned out like clockwork at the same time each day. *Ahora* means now; *ahorita* means *right* now, this very second, let's go, *vamos entonces*. It's a word I've heard a million times, a word I still can't pronounce quite right, not with the way the *ah* becomes *or* becomes *eat*.

The absence of *ahorita* suits Argentina. Nothing ever happens *right now* anyway, and if you even suggest it you'll be met with surprised looks and a possible snort of laughter. "Now?" the person will say, and blink at you. "Right now?" And then everyone will order another drink and the minutes will slip into hours, and when you look at your watch again you won't believe the time it reads. Here, 9 o'clock means 10:30, breakfast means brunch, coffee means an early dinner and meanwhile, your bedtime creeps into the *madrugada*. You cannot help but get swept up in the way time advances here; 6 in the evening ceases to be a viable dinner hour, and you drink coffee at 9 without ever worrying about whether you'll sleep that night.

Although the Arabian restaurant was jammed inside and out, the streets around here are empty. Alfonso and I peer into the windows of bars that are silent, the stools and counters gleaming and unused.

"Spooky," I say.

"It's a vicious cycle," he tells me. "The place is empty, so no one goes in. No one goes in, and the place stays empty."

I practice saying "vicious cycle" in Spanish; Alfonso makes fun of my accent, then takes my arm. "Here," he says, and points to a little pizza joint with a couple of outdoor tables and a few waiters standing around smoking.

I have let him do this since the beginning—choose the places, pick the plan. He's the one who selects our restaurants and decides what time we'll meet. I know I'd be better off long-term if I stepped up to the plate a little more often, but the truth is, I like sitting back and enjoying the night. He chooses nice places, after all, and I always like his plan. So far, he's only been late the one time. I like how he kisses me, softer than you might think, his hands gentle. On our first date, he rode in a taxi home with me but didn't hint at an invite inside. I woke the next morning to a message from him on my phone; I left it unanswered, and he called a day later. He has nice hands, hands that take mine, but not possessively; hands he puts on my waist to pull me closer.

He orders a big bottle of beer, which comes with little dishes of chips and peanuts and crackers. "I'm starving," he admits, pouring the beer into squat jelly jars and then reaching for a handful of peanuts.

He asks if I've eaten, and I tell him I have—"Hours ago," I say. "I can't wait until midnight for dinner," I joke, and he shrugs.

"Is it midnight already?" he asks, and checks his wrist for a watch that isn't there. Then he laughs and grabs for another handful of peanuts, tossing one at me, aiming for my shirt's V-shaped neckline. We finish our beer, he chats with our waiter. We sit for a moment. Then, "our table should be ready now," Alfonso says, and helps me with my coat when I stand.

And it is. We go back to the Arabian place and wait just two minutes at the door, the patio still jammed, until the man with the list and the cigarette calls our name. He doesn't show us in, just directs us between a row of tables and up the stairs. "Take the table with silverware on it," he says, and checks his list to call out the next name. After we sit, Alfonso orders without consulting the menu. He does this; I like it. He hasn't let me down with his choices yet. He rattles off a list of dishes and orders a bottle of white wine. Hot, thin bread arrives in a napkin-covered basket, and sparkling water, and then the plates come, one after the other, now stuffed grape leaves, now falafel, now a type of meat pie and a type of cheese casserole and a tart, lemony salad. The wine is cold and tastes like flowers and oranges both. We eat and eat, using our fingers and not our forks, and after a while baklava arrives for dessert, and possibly the best coffee I've ever had. It's sweet without being sugary, grainy and rich without being cloying. Every bite requires you to close your eyes, because with them open, your senses are overwhelmed. I am stuffed, I am sleepy; I'm in heaven.

Just before we leave, I check my watch. It's three A.M. The restaurant remains full; the waiters hurry around. I catch Alfonso looking at me; he shakes his head. I pull my shirt-sleeve down over my wrist to cover my watch.

"Time is a different animal here," Alfonso says. "It's another thing altogether, than what you know." He pulls me closer as we make our way though the restaurant, toward the door, squeezing between tables and chairs, diners and servers and the man with the list. "So forget it," Alfonso whispers, and hustles me out the door.

And he is right. Here, time's a river, and because it moves like water, it would be stupid to try and cling. On the sidewalk, Alfonso stops walking, takes my hand, leans in and kisses me. I love that he's led me to this night. Above us, one of Palermo's weeping willows drips down, nearly touching the pavement, and the air is sweet with springtime. *Time,* I think, Alfonso's mouth on mine. Here, the sun setting down doesn't mark another hour; the thing is the glimmer, the long shadows of the trees. This night is not the minutes; it's not the morning growing closer. It's the moonlight, it's the coffee, it's the not-so-distant summer on the wind.

Kate McCahill teaches English in Santa Fe, New Mexico. She uses writing as an excuse to travel, and her projects have taken her to Asia, South America, and, most recently, Hawaii.

ℬ ℬ ℬ

Snow in Mongolia

Forgetting, she remembered.

*W*hen I phone Amaglan in Mongolia, the first thing I
want to tell her is that it's snowing here in the U.S.
But I can't find the words for it. This shocks me. I sit there,
holding the phone, watching the snow falling onto a triangle
of lawn at my parents' house in suburban New Jersey. I listen
to the cadence of Amaglan speaking in Mongolian, carefully
enunciating words as language teachers do, as she did when
she taught me.

The snow is falling thick and fast, I want to say. But I can't.

Instead, I say other things. I say Happy New Year and she
says the same; she says it's freezing cold all over Mongolia,
especially in UB. But a few weeks ago, it was warm enough
that she got together with some of the other teachers at that
place near her house, that café where they have the good tea,
do I remember?

Yes, I say. I do.

Really, she laughs, you really remember after all these
years, that one café we went to once?

It's only been five years since I left, I say.

Long enough to forget, she says.

Actually, it's the opposite, I say. It's long enough to remember. She hears the defensiveness in my voice. She changes the subject. We continue talking. The snow keeps falling. I mourn those missing words.

In 2007, when I first get to Mongolia, it is New Year. The Year of the Pig. I've arranged to live with a city family before heading off into the countryside. The city family lives in UB or, as no one ever calls it, the capital, Ulaanbaatar. The city is crowded with blocks of old apartment buildings, Cyrillic signage, new skyscrapers, and fashionable restaurants, which reflect Mongolia's past as a Soviet satellite state and its present as a capitalist democracy.

The name Ulaanbaatar begins with the "*oo*" sound, as in "who." As in "who are you, where are you from, why are you here?" The answers I repeat until they are rote because then, even I have to believe them. I've had Mongolia on my mind for years, I say, since Bombay where I was born, and the U.S. where I now live. Don't ask me why. I just know I saw a photo of the steppe in a geography book when I was ten, and that was that. Maybe it was a city girl's longing for space; maybe it was something in the blood, kin stirring to kin as if I knew those spaces of old. It felt like a calling, I say, and so I conspired to make it possible. I've come on a yearlong Fulbright research grant. I'd like to see the steppes, live with families and record sounds.

Of what?

Anything. Everything. Stories and songs and sounds of everyday.

Norov, the mother of the family I stay with in UB, says, *there is so much I wish I could share with you but I don't have words, I'm sorry*. But Onika translates. She is thirteen, slim as a willow and quick in English, which she learned in her Russian-medium school. She loves Justin Timberlake, Harry

Potter, and above all, American Idol, which I watch for the first time in Mongolia. On International Women's Day, the father, Choijamts, cooks fish—the go-to dish for special occasions in a landlocked land—and we eat Russian torte. Onika plays Beethoven on the piano. We sip Mongolian wine. Then, with her father accompanying her, she sings a song about four seasons on the steppe.

Spring comes like the beloved, softly to the steppe, they sing. *Spring comes newborn to the steppe*. Except that spring is not gentle. It is fierce and windy. I can only encounter people in the present tense. No other time frame exists. Whatever words I manage to string together in one phrase are blown into another phrase. My "hello" becomes "goodbye," my "how are you?" becomes "who am I?" and I keep confusing hair—*oos*—with water—*os*—which causes terrible confusion when I am thirsty or need a comb. But somehow, Monjago understands. She is in her thirties like me. She has a broad open face and light brown eyes, far seeing, intuitive. She finishes my sentences, sometimes even starts them.

I spend a month with her in the countryside proper, in a *ger* proper. In that round, white, felt-covered home, we are five: Monjago's husband, their two kids, and me. And in a ger next door, her husband's brothers. And around us, hundreds of cows, sheep, goats, and horses doubling in number every minute during calving season. And beyond that, a hill, and beyond that, the flat yellow steppes of the eastern province of Hentii.

This is the *yag hoodoo*, the famed Mongolian steppe where nomadic herders live with their families in clusters of ger homes. Most make a living off their livestock—though this has become increasingly difficult with overgrazing and a recent spate of severe winters called *zuds* that scientists attribute to global warming. There is an ongoing exodus from the steppe to Ulaanbataar, which now houses the majority of Mongolia's population of three million.

In Hentii, spring is all about births—*horocks* (lambs), *ishigs* (kids), *togals* (calves)—and winds: fierce winds, soft winds, dry blustery winds, moist winds, winds that bring smoke from distant forest fires, and winds that hit the ger with full force so that bits of plastic on the roof make a flapping din, and people raise their hands and yell, "*Holdorei*" so the wind hears and knows to move far away.

I feel like a child. I speak when spoken to. Conversations fly above me, and I strain to catch words, ecstatic when I hear one I understand, or better still, my name. Then I raise my voice and try to speak. I am tiptoeing on a cultural boundary of my own making—they put up none, I am welcome everywhere—but I am wary. I especially don't want to step right on the threshold of the ger—that is bad luck, Onika told me before I left. So I step over gingerly, holding my breath.

Monjago sees this. She takes me in hand, and I become her shadow. I go where she goes, milking cows in the morning, cleaning out pens, gathering manure for the fire, herding goats, running after stray calves. I follow in earnest, I listen, and spring becomes a season of bearing witness and tentative steps.

In the stillness of summer, I find my words more easily. Heat loosens the tongue, and I navigate the present and the past with ease; sometimes, even the future. Ulaanaa and I talk for hours. He is twelve, and nicknamed for his red cheeks. For about a month, I stay with his family in the northern province of Hovsgol.

At seven every morning, we let the cattle out of the pen, and saying, "*duuch duuch*," lead sheep and goats through valleys and forests, and up and down the sides of mountains. Sheepherding involves a lot of walking and sitting and watching sheep, watching the sky, watching the breeze blow over the grass, picking flowers, letting your mind wander, shouting loudly after goats when they go where they shouldn't, and running after them when shouting isn't enough. It involves, every day, the experience of sun, wind, shadows, brown butterflies, the buzzing of cicadas, the persistent symphony of flies.

Ulaanaa slides down the slopes of mountains on rubber boots; he opens his mouth to catch the rain when it comes; he gets on all fours and growls after goats who flee; he breaks off tree branches and brandishes them at sheep; he drops his jacket on them and laughs as they trot away with it bouncing on their backs.

He won't be a herder like his father, he says. He'll drive a Russian jeep fearsome enough to take on Mongolia's roads. He already knows the route he'll travel; he'll take the road that goes along the eastern shore of Lake Hovsgol, what some call the worst road in Mongolia.

I understand, I say. In language, we are the same age. I follow him as he follows me; we get to the ends of sentences, syntax intact except for when I am distracted by a butterfly or a yellow flower that everyone says is good for colds.

One afternoon, he sings a song, and asks me for one. I've been expecting this because most people I've met either ask me for a song or offer up one. On a slope, surrounded by goats and sheep, I sing one verse of "Que sera sera" and another of a Hindi song about the full moon.

Chaudhvin Ka Chand Ho, Ya Aaftaab Ho. Jo Bhi Ho Tum Khuda Ki Kasam, Lajawab Ho.

Are you full moon or the sun? Whatever you are, I swear, you are beautiful beyond compare.

I pity the cattle, but Ulaanaa grins and says they're strong, they can take it and they've heard worse.

By the time I leave Hovsgol, I'm running with him down the green slopes. Who tiptoes across grass?

* * *

In the autumn, I stay with Sainaa and her husband Demee in the South Gobi desert. They live in a small ger surrounded by an expanse of reddish brown earth covered with tufts of low green bushes. They have a small herd of goats, camel calves, and camel mares.

My first morning there, Sainaa is impatient. She rattles off directions quickly.

"Gather the dried dung, and use it to tend the fire while Demee and I milk the goats. Keep the fire going, don't let it go out! And then later, in the afternoon, go and gather the camel calves—see them, right over there about a quarter mile away, go round them up and bring them back near the ger. Got it?"

I do get it. This amazes me.

"What's the hold up?" she says as I stand there, dazed.

"First of all," I say, "there's this shock that I understand everything you're saying. And second of all, there is what you're saying itself—you realize that I've never done any of this before?"

"So what," she shrugs. "*Yav*, go."

I try tending the fire, but it goes out. Sainaa sighs and shows me. I have better luck with the camel calves. It turns out that they are obedient. I make clicking sounds. They respond. But their mothers, the camel mares, do not. For them, I must learn a new language: camel-speak.

The most important word, says Sainaa's husband, Demee, is *Haa*. It means stop. In the evenings, when the camels are milked, he says, they must be organized into a line so they can be led off, one by one, and milked. I am a camel shield. I must say *haa* to any camel that moves out of turn.

So I stand in front of a line of camels, usually at sunset. I say *haa*. I yell *haa*. I sing *haa*. I even plead *haa*. Once in a while, the camels listen. Mostly, they don't. Sainaa and Demee don't seem to mind so much. Since it's just the two of them now— their teenage daughter is back in school in UB—they seem to appreciate the company. Or maybe they just appreciate the chance, every evening, to watch my shielding attempts and laugh their heads off.

Winter takes me to Bayan-Olgii province where people speak Mongolian slowly and clearly because it is their second language. I revel in almost full comprehension; it is dizzying to fully understand a sentence with all its nuances and reply in kind.

In this westernmost province of Mongolia, ethnic Kazakhs are the majority. Some came from Kazakhstan and some from Xinjiang in China. With a mixture of Turkic-speaking groups like the Uighurs and Kazakhs, Xinjiang has always been a volatile region for the Chinese. In the late 1930s, after it was further destabilized by a Soviet invasion in the Xinjiang War, many Kazakh nomads began looking toward Mongolia. Their exodus started in earnest after the Communist takeover in 1949. But Doldabai's family left earlier than most, in 1942.

I hear his story one winter afternoon. His relatives, with whom I am staying for a few weeks, bring me to his house for a visit. Just to say hello, they say, just for some tea. Tea turns into a feast. For hours, we sit and talk in a white adobe house, eating roasted meats and toasting with vodka. There are deep red tapestries on the walls, and in a room to the side, a wooden cradle built by one of Doldabai's nephews for his daughter. She is asleep in it, gurgling quietly as we talk loudly. Small square windows frame a landscape of brown steppe and patches of ice, frozen rivers, forests of elm and Siberian larch, and in the distance, immense snow-covered peaks.

"Bear with me," Doldabai says. "I have a bad leg, a bad ear, this eye doesn't open so well anymore." His voice is deep, scratchy, and full of feeling. He speaks of unrest in China, especially when the Communist party began gaining power in Xinjiang: how his family lost their property, how his parents decided on a new life in a new land. It was autumn when a procession of men, women, and cattle left Xinjiang on foot. It took months. Many died along the way. Many more became sick. That first winter in Mongolia was so cold they dug holes in the ground and slept in them. But they endured, and they have been here, in this very village of Aag Araal, since that time.

Everyone is quiet. Doldabai smiles. Slowly, he stands. He begins to sing then, a melody I've never heard before. When he is done, his niece says it's a song he made up on the spot called "kharaoling." It's in their tradition, she says, to improvise a song to fit an occasion, and this song is "about you, my daughter who has come from far away, may you travel well, may you live well."

I sit there, struck into silence by the grace of it all. I sit there, humbled as a grand old man who has undertaken such a long and difficult journey raises his glass to me.

Now, years later, I am on the phone with Amaglan, thinking about all I stand to lose by forgetting. I am reeling from those words I have lost and how she was the one who helped me to find them in the first place.

When we met, she had no English except for hello, and I had no Mongolian except for the Mongolian version of hello, *sain baina uu*. But she mimed, pointed, gestured, and taught me my first words of Mongolian. My first class, she walked into the room where I sat waiting—and walked right out. Then she walked in again, saying what I later understood was "I am walking": *bi yavaj baina*. She sat, saying *bi bosoj baina*: "I am sitting." She smiled widely, *bi ineej baina*; she shook her hips, *bi bujiglig baina*: "I am dancing." Every class became a game. With the help of other teachers at the language school where she worked, I got to phrases and sentences and tenses.

Inexplicably, rapidly, I took to it. It baffled me. I have some Hindi, and I studied French in school, but this was an Altaic-Turkic language written in a Cyrillic script. I had never heard anything like it.

Except for a few weeks in the spring, I traveled everywhere without a translator. In between trips to the countryside, I came back to the city, took lessons with Amaglan and other teachers, and fortified by more phrases, more grammar, I went back out. Often I was utterly lost, but I absorbed what I could, when I could, in increments. What I didn't understand in April, I understood in June. And even though it was gradual, the shock of comprehending was tremendous.

Suddenly I could talk to Norov, my Mongolian mother, without needing Onika to translate; suddenly we were speaking to each other. Some afternoons, we would sit in the kitchen and have *suu-tei tsai*, a milky tea with salt, and talk. *Bor ohin min*, she would start, *my dark daughter*, and ask me questions like how did the day go, when was I going next to the hoodoo—the countryside—what did I think of Mongolian men, what did I remember about India, was Bombay like UB?

There were times I forgot we were speaking Mongolian. It was like that feeling you get when you're reading a good book, and the world it describes is so vivid that you forget you're accessing it by reading. You forget what separates you.

Mongolia changed everything—how I live, how I see the world, how I see myself. When you travel, you tend to cultivate a persona different from that of your everyday life. You're open to everything, and you take better care of yourself emotionally. Because you know you're out of your comfort zone, away from home, you work on letting go of whatever you can so that you can move with ease.

At different points during my time in Mongolia, I remember thinking: one, what if I lived with the same persona I traveled with, and two, if I could manage here by planning only one step ahead instead of ten, instead of trying to see the whole road—well, couldn't I manage my life like that too?

And that's really what I've done since Mongolia—followed what calls. It's led me to New Mexico, where I now live, and into a period of creativity that I would never have imagined for myself and that only came about because I was able to let go and fully follow what moves me. This has felt like a revolution. For me, it is.

But just when I have processed my experience in Mongolia and realized how it has reverberated, the language that found me so quickly is beginning, in bits and starts, to leave. Every day I find it easier to write about Mongolia; every day, I have to work at remembering Mongolian.

Perhaps my facility with the language had less to do with having a "good ear" and more to do with being open: without buffers, so that everything around me in Mongolia came right on in. Did I go there without buffers or did the buffers disappear when I arrived? Is it the place that opens the traveler or the traveler who opens because she is traveling to that place?

I know there are ways to compensate for losing language: practice more, study more. And I know loss of words does not have to equal loss of memories. Except for me, they're connected. Those moments when people offered up something true and unguarded were in a language common to them, rare to me.

What to do? I write. I share what I can, while it is vivid. I write to honor the generosity with which people made themselves known to me. In retelling their stories, I feel I'm continuing a process in which our connections expand, the world contracts, and far away becomes close.

"Well, O.K. then," Amaglan is saying, "you stay well. Happy New Year again."

I hesitate, looking at the snow, mourning my lost words. And then it comes to me. "*Tsas orj baina*," I yell. I point to the falling snow as if she can see it. "*Tsas orj baina*."

"Here too," she says. I can almost see her smile. "It's snowing here too."

♬ ♬ ♬

Shebana Coelho is a writer and director, once a nomad, now rooted. Her documentary work has been broadcast on BBC Radio Four, NPR, PBS, and the Discovery Channel; her writing has been published in Vela, Chronogram, Madcap Review, Lummox, Sin Fronteras, *and* Word Riot, *among others. She received a U.S. Fulbright Research grant to Mongolia. She has also traveled in South America, Mexico, and India. She likes going far away, to places that feel like the ends of the earth. If you asked her why, she would refer you to the city motto of Ushuaia, Tierra del Fuego, which is:* fin del mundo, principio de todo, *the end of the world, the beginning of everything. Visit her at www.shebanacoelho.com*

CHRISTINA AMMON

❧ ❧ ❧

Juan's Jukebox

Don't judge a man until you've
walked a mile in his flip-flops.

I landed my paraglider on the beach, turned to the bar, and
gave Juan the signal: forearms pressed together and hands
split into the Y-shape of a cocktail glass. This was the cue for
Juan to start making our margaritas. He knew the details:
Allison's without salt; mine with. Both on the rocks.

A rumor circulated the Mexican village that Juan washed
the cocktail glasses in the dirty lagoon behind his restaurant.
We didn't care. His bar was closest to where we landed, and
after the steep climb to launch our long flights, we were too
lazy to shoulder our gliders another step. So what if just a few
trudges away, crisp-shirted waiters served up meals in pretty
carved-out pineapples?

Like most pilots here on vacation, we had a routine. The
top launch was good at noon, and the windsock straightened
out on mid-launch around two P.M. We'd take a couple flights,
then wash the adrenaline down with a margarita. Sometimes
two.

I shook the sand out of my paragliding wing, packed it up,
and slogged over to a beach chair. Juan flip-flopped toward

me in his dirty apron with our two margaritas balanced on a tray. He set the glasses down side by side.

"*¡Gracias!*" I said, lifting my glass. I took a sip. The rock salt abraded my lips. Juan's margaritas were the best in the world—cold, salty, gritty, like the sea embodied in a cocktail glass. Allison trudged over, dropped her glider, and stretched out on the chair beside me. Out in the bay, fishermen threw nets from their boats and a flock of birds fluttered over us like a fresh white sheet. Never in my life had I felt a more uncomplicated happiness.

We drained our margaritas, and I took the empty glasses back to the bar. I fished a five-hundred-peso note from my wallet—the smallest bill I had. Juan slammed the cash box down and glared at me.

"No change!" He went on to berate me in Spanish.

My mood dropped like a shot pheasant.

"Fu-fuu . . . forget this place!" I yelled.

While most days Juan was pleasant, one out of ten times he would mysteriously erupt like this. At first I was bewildered, then angry.

It seemed unfair. We were his best customers, dropping eighty pesos a day for a month straight. We put up with his grimy bathroom facilities—the seatless toilet and the lockless door, the scummy hand-washing barrel. We endured the lovesick ranchera riffs that wept nonstop from his jukebox. Other pilots had given up on his place long ago, swapping their flight stories next door at Domingo's instead.

"We're never coming back!" I yelled.

"*¡Adios!*" he said, waving me off. Juan pandered to no one.

This wasn't the first time we'd tried to boycott Juan's bar. Usually, by day four of the boycott, our laziness would exceed our anger, and we'd end up back in his beach chairs enduring the ranchera music and quaffing his fantastic margaritas. Juan pretended nothing had happened.

"*Margaritas, señoritas,*" he'd say, placing our glasses on the table. In a matter of days he'd blow up at us again, and the cycle would continue.

* * *

We didn't know much about Juan, but he seemed to have a soft side. Like a crusty version of St. Francis of Assisi, he tended a variety of animals—a stubborn mule, a brood of chickens, a few caged parrots, a dog that fetched rocks, and a cat with a freakish nervous tic. He'd even endeared himself to a wild pigeon by pouring a small pile of seed on the end of his bar each day.

Unlike the other bar owners who closed up and went home for the night, Juan lived with his two teenagers and wife in a large canvas tent behind his bar. The local villagers patronized his place in the evenings, often staying into the night playing cards and plunking pesos in the jukebox.

Sometimes, when standing at his bar, Juan would pull the canvas door aside and we'd glimpse his private world. Inside, an old television crackled on an upturned crate, his wife watching Mexican soap operas. She never spoke. Never came outside.

This second season, I began to joke with Juan about his moods, ordering "*¡Dos margaritas simpaticas!*" Two friendly margaritas—as opposed to the mean ones. He'd laugh and play along. I began to like a few of the ranchera tunes that played from his jukebox. One evening a lover and I spun around sun-drunk to the Vicente Fernandez song *Estos Celos—what pain, what love. . . .*

Juan sat in a chair, his head tilted slightly back, watching us dance.

"*Los Jovenes,*" he said, seeming wistful. "The young ones."

* * *

It wasn't until our third flying season that we learned about Juan's wife's cancer. Behind that heavy canvas door, between mixing our margaritas, he'd been tending to her illness. We only found out because he'd sometimes close the bar altogether and take the water taxi ride to the hospital in Puerto Vallarta where she received treatment.

His temper still flared, but we were more patient. Now we understood he had bills to pay. His jukebox was gone that year, replaced by a small handheld stereo. The owners of the nearby bars had been complaining that the loud ranchera was putting off the tourists. Juan's expression grew hard and serious.

He seemed to emigrate between two worlds that season—the one outside his door where we lay in the sun drinking margaritas, and the dark dank insides of his canvas hut, which might as well have been a different country. The geography of our paradise—the palm trees, the macaws, the cocktails—was the geography of his real life. Our vacation was not his vacation.

We returned for a fourth season. Juan was there as usual, tending his brood of chickens, the now-tame pigeon, the caged parrots, the stubborn pack mule, the stone-fetching dog, the nervous cat. But something had changed. Weeks went by and he didn't yell. We didn't boycott.

His wife had passed away that winter. Though he'd cared for her with great love and fidelity, it was obvious that his burden had lessened. Now he laughed with patrons, drank Pacificos, played rowdy card games into the night, and I finally got it: he hadn't been moody. Just struggling.

"How could we not have known his wife was so ill?" I asked Allison, hurling a stone into the surf for Juan's dog to fetch.

With the Godlike panoramas afforded by our paragliding wings, it sometimes seemed like we knew everything about that place. We knew how thermals formed over the first-blooming primaveras in March, how wind spilled over certain ridges at noon, and how to decipher wind lines on the ocean. We could see straight down into the village and all the way across to the Marietta Islands. But a big view isn't always the clearest view. Minor details get lost.

What wasn't lost on us, that fourth season, was how good it was to see Juan happy, and the understanding, at last, that behind a scowl is often a story that deserves compassion. We landed our gliders and gave him the cue. He disappeared into the darkness of his hut and returned with a handful of shiny green limes to make our best-in-the-world margaritas.

"¡Dos margaritas simpaticas!" he said, laughing, and set down our glasses.

Christina Ammon has penned stories on a wide range of topics, from paragliding alongside raptors in Nepal to exploring the underground wine scene in Morocco. She received the Oregon Literary Arts Fellowship for Creative Nonfiction, and her articles and photos have appeared in Hemispheres, *the* San Francisco Chronicle, *the* Los Angeles Times, The Oregonian, *and many other publications. Visit her at www.vanabonds.com.*

SIMONE GORRINDO

ೂ   ೂ   ೂ

An Unwanted Guest

Deep in the Javan rainforest,
a relationship is put to the test.

I didn't see the jellyfish, but I felt it—a searing pain at my
ankle that shot up through my leg, bringing me, in a matter of seconds, to my knees in the sand. That's when I spotted
the creature—a limp, blue body floating away down the rivu-
let I'd stumbled into when the sand along its border collapsed
under my step. It had gripped me with its tentacles for just an
instant before letting go, leaving a ribbon of angry red burn
blisters wound around my ankle and lower leg. I didn't know
what kind of jellyfish it was, but our guide had warned us to
avoid them, and the pain was so excruciating that tears welled
up involuntarily, stinging my eyes. I could almost feel the poison moving through me, my chest growing tight, my heart
beating hard and fast as though it wanted out.

"Simone?" I heard my boyfriend's voice behind me.

He knelt down to my level, saw my leg, and then glimpsed
the departing jellyfish. He breathed in sharply.

"Can you stand up?" he asked, reaching for my hand.

I took it, but he practically had to drag me the first few feet
before picking me up and setting me down several yards from
shore.

"Is it painful?"

I nodded, my mouth clenched.

"It's O.K.," he said. "Don't panic."

I couldn't help it. The pain was traveling at an incredible speed—up my thighs, to my groin, and now, my hips. I looked out at the expanse of Indian Ocean and the hard reality of our situation: Guides didn't carry radios in Indonesia. And even if they did, where could one get us? The dusty village of Taman Jaya at the entry point of the Ujung Kulon rainforest didn't have a fruit stand, let alone a hospital. This national park on the westernmost edge of Java saw few visitors because of its location—starting from Jakarta, we had spent eight hours on two different sweltering bus rides, two hours on a motorbike down a deeply rutted road, and three hours on a boat out to the island of Panaitan, where we finally began our hike. My father, an expat in Indonesia, lived on North Sulawesi, an island a plane ride away from Jakarta. After four months of traveling through the country, this was the most remote and alone we'd been. The horizon had never looked so unreachable, and the familiar had never felt so far away.

Andrew fished our pocket-sized health guide from his pack and scanned the images of jellyfish, little black and white drawings on the page.

"Is it a man o' war?" I asked, straining to see what he was reading.

I recognized these symptoms, remembered reading about their progression when I'd briefly glimpsed a write-up about Portuguese man o' war, which are technically not jellyfish at all but siphonophores—a colony of multiple organisms. A sting started on the skin as a scalding burn but could travel to the lymph nodes, causing heart palpitations and shortness of breath. The most extreme cases led to shock and cardiac arrest.

"Is it?" I repeated, my voice shaking with effort. It was becoming difficult to breathe.

Andrew looked up, shifting his eyes toward our guide, who was laying out our dinner on plastic plates.

"No," he said, shaking his head. "It's not."

He returned to the book, a tough, tired sorrow in his face. I knew, instinctively, that he was lying—Andrew was a terrible liar—but I also knew that, if only to calm myself, I should try to believe him. He closed the book and shoved it into his back pocket as he combed his fingers through his dirty hair, his whole body a knot of tension. I could feel his frustration like a third presence around us, sucking all the oxygen out of the ocean air.

"Jesus, Simone, how could you have let this happen?"

I looked up at him, stunned. Andrew was a natural caretaker, someone you could count on to remain calm in crisis. But over the past few weeks, I'd watched as his patience had worn away, revealing something hard and guarded, a barricade that made him impossible to reach. We spent every waking moment together, but I'd never felt so far from him.

We hadn't slept well since we reached the rainforest, and we were both worried about making it through Jakarta with just nine dollars and fifty cents between us. And then, of course, soon we'd be back in Maryland where we had no jobs, no savings accounts, no car, and no apartment, our belongings packed tightly in a storage unit. But we were accustomed to living like this; his new remove was about something else.

I cursed myself for taking on too much yet again. A month ago, Andrew and another guide had to push me up the side of a volcano for the last steep half mile of a difficult hike. What made me think I could do this? I'd been sick for years, and when I tripped into that stream, I was bleary with exhaustion. It wouldn't have happened to a healthy person, I told myself; it wouldn't have happened to Andrew. Beneath the waves of pain, I felt something else surging through me: anger with myself for trying and failing to be the person I wanted to be. I wondered, as I studied the hard clench of Andrew's jaw, if he was feeling the same about himself.

Three years before, I'd been diagnosed with Interstitial Cystitis, an autoimmune condition that inflames the bladder but can also transmit pain throughout the body. It's a condition that tends to take years to diagnose: I was twenty-one when I finally found out what had plagued me since I was seventeen. As my condition degenerated during that time period, my whole body became a crucible of suffering, a trail of fire making its way to my thighs, legs, and lower back. Symptoms of related autoimmune conditions compounded this torture, too: swollen joints, fevers, and aches that would come and go, a brain so foggy it was sometimes impossible to hold on to a single thought for more than a moment. And I often experienced a symptom common to almost all IC patients—extreme pain during sex, like sandpaper tearing at my insides. Afterwards, I sometimes felt as though I'd been punched in the gut, and the feeling would linger for days.

The story of my illness and the story of Andrew and me are, in some ways, inextricable. After I was diagnosed, I left New York City and returned to the Bay Area where I'd grown up. Andrew and I had been childhood friends, intermittently in touch across states and continents during the previous four years. There were missed connections: a love letter he wrote me from a bunk bed in Beijing that never arrived at my Brooklyn apartment; an aborted kiss one summer night when I was visiting California but was dating an older man I didn't love; a chance encounter at a café where he worked, his eyes glimmering beautifully in the sun, his heart jumping— "She's here!"

He had apparently been willing me to reappear ever since I'd left for New York at seventeen. He was in a short-lived, destined-to-fail relationship when I returned, and though the undercurrent of romantic tension was strong, there was something comforting about building a friendship first. I'd take the bus from Marin County to San Francisco, and we'd sit on the wharf drinking coffee and watching the ferry unload and reload, feeding stale bagels to seagulls, birds that were, for him, the sound of home.

One night that winter, we drove out to the coastal back roads of Mill Valley with a six-pack. Sitting on the hood of his car, a universe of stars above us, we came within an inch of kissing, but Andrew stopped us.

"I should do this right," he said.

I was touched. Later, after he had broken up with his girlfriend, we kissed just as we were getting off a MUNI bus in the middle of the night, our mouths and bodies coming together almost by accident, or instinct—later, he would say I'd kissed him, and I'd insist he kissed me. Our audience was a homeless man drinking from a paper bag. "Now, that's love!" he announced.

A week later, we stumbled drunkenly along Market Street to his studio, kissing in doorways, the world a blur of lights and color. We passed out in his loft bed before we could do much beyond kissing, folded into each other, limp as the sheets tangled around our warm bodies. We were just kids, twenty-one and twenty-two.

In the morning, the sun streaming in through the blinds, we attempted to have sex, but instead of "Oh, yes," there was a lot of "Oh no, ow, stop, sorry." It lasted ten minutes. He didn't come. My pelvis was on fire. I rolled on my side into fetal position, wanting to disappear.

Frustrated men had told me it was my fault. Some of them I had loved. One jerk decreed that I was not a real woman—as if there were a second category of women altogether, the false, make-believe ones—and another left me curled up on my futon after the first and only time we had sex because he figured I "wanted to be alone" with my pain. Instead I ended up in the emergency room, surrounded by patients. He called to check on me; I never called him back.

But Andrew did something then that would tie him to me forever. He held me to his chest and said, "You're going to get better, Simone. I'll help you." I didn't believe it was possible— every doctor I'd seen had told me I'd only be able to manage my condition for the rest of my life—but it meant something to know that he did.

Andrew viewed both me and the world with a kind of X-ray vision. His green eyes, flecked with gold, made the world feel small and close around me, and it terrified me to be seen so clearly. I was accustomed to men who found it difficult to see past their own reflection. I was accustomed to remaining hidden.

It took me a month to call him back after that humiliating morning. I withdrew into my life across the Golden Gate in Sausalito, where I worked early morning shifts as a barista at an Italian restaurant and shared an apartment with my father, who was back from Indonesia for the year. I ignored Andrew's calls and tried dating a straightedge vegan from Italy who possessed an innocent and all-around wrong vision of who I was. It died a quick, quiet death. I walked along the bay after work. I sent away for Ayurvedic herbs, and I saw specialists. I tried a slew of medications and different forms of yoga; I quit drinking alcohol and coffee and cut out all the foods that exacerbate Interstitial Cystitis—a litany as long as a week's grocery list. I smoked high-grade medical marijuana and did so with a little too much enthusiasm. Still, I felt stuck.

How, at twenty-one, had my existence become so small? Debilitating pain had interrupted the narrative of my life, and I didn't know how to write the pages that would move it forward and give me momentum; I was frozen, without climax or resolution, the same dull scene on repeat. And what are we without our own stories? It seems trite, but I learned that year that they do, in fact, mean everything.

The narrative of me and Andrew did continue to move forward, though in stops and starts, shot through with bursts of beauty: He moved to Maryland for a late go at college; I returned to New York, found work as a technical writer, and proceeded to plunge into a deep underwater depression, profoundly out of sync with my old friends who were still drinking in bars until four A.M., snorting coke off their apartment keys in grungy bathroom stalls. Andrew and I wrote each other letters—handwritten and snail mailed—and when I came up for air, I'd shoot straight to him, taking the train to Maryland on gorgeous fall weekends, ending up warm in his bed, safe from both the outside world and the interior one in which I struggled to stay afloat. He came to see me in the city on snowy weekends, in wool mittens and a thick sailor's coat, holding my hand on the ice skating rink at Central Park, where I fumbled to mirror his graceful steps. One desperate night I called him at midnight and asked him to come, and he did, no questions asked, boarding a one A.M. train because I needed him, the dark streets of Brooklyn covered in snow.

That morning in his San Francisco studio, Andrew had gone straight to my soft spot, the place I'd tried to hide in the crook of my body as I curled up against his stomach. Shame. A disease of its own proportions, it had grown quietly inside me over the past four years, and he had been the only one in my life to see it up close for what it was. I'd continue to apologize for sex that wasn't always successful, and he would delicately admonish me: "There's no need to apologize, Simone." And just hearing him say my name drove out my shame like an evil spirit.

Andrew came to New York when his first year of college ended, bartending to save up money. We stayed up late on work nights, lying on the wooden floor of his sublet in

Harlem and talking into the night, forgetting ourselves to the point that we'd neglect to turn on the light until well after the sun fell. We drove up to Bear Mountain, lying in the summer sun sharing Häagen-Dazs and reading books to each other. We argued fiercely about politics, raising our voices in Polish cafes in Greenpoint. We walked miles through Brooklyn on "Expedition Sundays," discovering new corners of the borough. One afternoon I went to a concert with a friend and returned to a bedroom of books shelved in a new bookshelf, flowers, and a note on my bed. I'd been meaning to get one for months, and he'd carried the eight-foot-tall bookcase up Greenpoint's Manhattan Avenue in the brutal summer heat.

But at the end of August, I couldn't find it in myself to go back to Maryland with him, though I had nothing keeping me in New York. I had seen the summer's end as an expiration date, a built-in ending that had allowed me to relax into being with Andrew. In his airy sublet, we lay that last evening on a stranger's futon side by side, untouching.

"Separation is always painful," he'd said. "But this just doesn't feel right."

He was right, but I was employing every defense mechanism I possessed not to acknowledge it. It was so wrong, so against whatever grain I should be going, yet the leap seemed utterly impossible to make. I lay mute and queasy, everything sharp-edged and wrong, refusing the tears that wanted to come.

Our separation lasted a month—until I called in sick to work one Friday morning, boarded a Greyhound bus and showed up at his apartment in Maryland telling him that I wanted to leave my job and the city and move in with him. I'd been filled with regret since he'd left. For the first time, he had, with very good reason, been trying to forget me.

"You can't come in and out of my life like this anymore," he said, standing at the threshold of his front door. The bitter cold outside stung my cheeks.

Something tired in his voice made my heart break a little. "I'm so sorry," I said. "I'm in." He pulled me to his chest and kissed me on the head. And then, to my relief, he let me in and closed the door behind him.

The entire bus ride back to New York, I felt like I was vibrating with life and also like I might throw up all over my seat. This was living, wasn't it? Making decisions, moving forward, unsticking my stuck life, allowing myself to love and be loved without a safety net?

But now, deep in the Javan rainforest, eight months after making that terrifying move, I felt a new kind of fear. I wasn't afraid that he'd stopped loving me—Andrew's love for me had always seemed an incontrovertible fact of life, as consistently true as the light of the sun. I was worried, instead, that he'd buckled beneath the burden of my body, that he'd just plain burned out. I watched Andrew as he sank the tent stakes into the hard sand. Despite his natural grace, he looked beaten down, like something irreplaceable had been taken out of him, and he was too tired to care or even notice that it was gone.

Three years on, Andrew's hopeful predictions had been wrong. I hadn't cured myself, and he—a young, idealistic man once so sure of his capabilities—most certainly had not cured me.

When we'd first reached the cove where I met my jellyfish misfortune, it felt like the brink of the world: huge waves beating against the jagged faces of cliffs, expanses of dirt and grass around us as flat and lifeless as the moon, only a few strange trees reaching jagged branches into the startlingly close sky.

Since daybreak, we'd been marching through winding rainforest, dark and close and wet, stopping only briefly for lunch. It was a relief to be in the open air of the coast, the constant whirring and rustling of the rainforest gone, surrounded by a beauty that reminded me so stunningly of the California coast where Andrew and I had grown up that it pulled at something ancient and buried in me. The violence of the waves against the rocks—so much like the roiling Pacific below the cliffs of Big Sur—nearly managed to dissolve the border between me and the landscape. I wasn't just small and insignificant as I was beneath the tall trees of the rainforest—I was obliterated, the closest I'd ever get to being free of my body. A slight breeze snuck up under my soaked linen shirt, soothing my chafed hips and dirt-glazed skin. I eyed a swampy stream just at the edge of the cove with longing, but knew enough to avoid its dark waters. For now, this cool air would have to be enough.

I hadn't anticipated the intense darkness of the rainforest, the constant sensation of something lurking nearby. I'd been on edge since the morning we'd entered it, my senses heightened to a point of near pain—I could practically hear the trees breathing, as alive as the long-tailed macaques swinging on their highest branches. Anytime we stepped into a moderate clearing, bits of sun peeking through the leaves, I felt as though someone had turned down the volume, and I relaxed in the relative silence. We walked in a line down the narrow trail—first the guide, then Andrew, then me, of course, dead last—but that line could split up in an instant, and had many times, Andrew disappearing around a sharp corner, and I, left to feel my way, calling after them to wait up.

There was a time I would have savored being alone in the wilderness, a time when I'd hang back deliberately from a group to experience the trail on my own. But at the ripe old age of twenty-four, I was lagging behind for new reasons, reasons that made me feel fragile and alone.

Andrew had never treated my illness as a burden or hardship, though it lived with us every day, an unwanted guest.

For him, it had certainly required sacrifice—evenings out cut short; endless stops at public restrooms; weekends holed up at home; weeks and months of pained, cautious sex; days I disappeared inside myself, unable to do much beyond curling into myself and breathing deeply, keeping tears at bay.

Getting sick when you're young—or any time, really—can radically derail your life. For me, it was like taking a wrong turn in the dark, the map flying out the window as I lost my way. I'd never been much of a planner, but there was a basic direction I thought I was heading, a vision of what I wanted my life to be. An integral part of that dream was travel, physical work, and new, raw experience. But the illness had blurred that vision, and, over the course of those first years, I stopped being able to see where I was heading. This backpacking trek—and the whole island-hopping trip through Indonesia—was, in part, an effort to get that sense back.

Though it had been some time since I tested myself, the five-day trek had sounded manageable. But forty-eight hours in, it already had begun to feel interminable. Every part of me screamed in pain, my joints aching and inflamed as I walked shakily across logs situated precariously above crocodile-infested swamps. My bladder was sending me to the sidelines of the trail every thirty minutes to pee, crouching in the darkness, the weight of my pack threatening to tip me over. I was suffering, and not the good, holy kind of suffering earned through hard work; it was a more desperate and pointless kind that damages instead of restores. I felt like the youth had been worn out of me.

But what about Andrew? Had this trip—my slow pace, my evident pain—brought him to his limit? I'd frozen mid-trudge on the trail earlier that day when this question occurred to me, the thought so scary and sad I could barely hold it in my mind. And yet it was clear that my needs and my fears were wearing him thin. Our first day out in the forest, he'd stopped when I called. Now, he'd given up on waiting for me—he'd quit replying in any way at all.

As we began unloading our packs, our guide Agus unpacked the pots and pans from his own bag to start cooking dinner, which was the same paltry meal as lunch and dinner the night before—ramen, fried rice, and an egg fried in coconut oil to inedible toughness. Ignoring *Lonely Planet*'s instruction to come prepared, we'd figured we'd stock up on food in the village at the entry point of Ujung Kulon, but there was nothing there. Even the small, poor village where my father's wife had grown up had a *"pasar tradicional,"* but this village felt like an Indonesian version of the Wild West, dusty and empty, with no sign of authority or government. The man who operated the guesthouse for backpackers had the only "market" in town, an aluminum-sided stall with only the goods we were eating on offer. I was starving, but just the smell of the burning coconut oil made me nauseous.

"You wanna set up right here?" Andrew asked, plopping his bag down several yards from shore. He began to unpack our cozy little tent, and I walked to the water's edge and took off my galoshes and filthy wool socks, the air a sweet relief against my soggy, red, blistered toes, oozing and faintly yellow from the Betadine I'd applied to them that morning. I walked slowly into the very edge of the tide, the salty water first stinging then numbing my feet.

Andrew looked up. "Hey, remember to watch out for those—"

"Jellyfish. I know."

The previous day we'd covered fifteen miles, twelve of it coastline, the equatorial sun relentless and unforgiving against our backs. The blue jellyfish had littered the beach, and many floated out in the ocean like tiny, incandescent buoys, their bodies without gravity or movement of their own, going wherever the current carried them. They were otherworldly, beautiful creatures; I'd never seen anything like them. Later, I'd learn that beaches in Australia close entirely when they wash up onto shore, en masse. Agus just told us to try not to step on them.

"Wait a second," I said to Andrew as he started to unfold our tent. "Agus," I yelled, "is it O.K. if we sleep down here?"

Our guide looked down at us not exactly blankly—he always looked like he was hiding *something*—but with a gaze as maddeningly impenetrable as ever. Agus spent more than half of his time out in the forest of Ujung Kulon and seemed to be in closer communication with the trees than with either of us. It was his burden to guide curious, unprepared hikers like me through the rainforest, and, to a lesser extent, entertain their bizarre whims.

"Is it safe?" Andrew asked in Indonesian, pointing to where he was setting up camp.

In much of Indonesia, the poorest of the poor reside on the water's edge, living at the mercy of unpredictable weather and earthquakes, so our choice to sleep closer to it—instead of under the primitive man-made shelter where our guide had laid out his sleeping bag—probably seemed misguided and stupid.

He squinted his eyes as though doing so would help him to understand what it was we wanted, and why. He shrugged.

"Yes," he said, and returned to the boiling rice.

Andrew resumed setting up camp while I rested on a log watching him move with an ease I'd always envied. Andrew was everything I was not—capable, agile, physically resilient, an athlete from the time he could walk—but he often said I was the strong one, fierce and independent and unwilling to take any shit. It was that fierceness that first attracted him to me, he said, but it was also what scared him.

And that was where my strength bled into my central weakness, of course—the barrier I'd put up against the world that, since I'd first gotten sick, had become nearly immovable. But over a period of three years, Andrew had changed me, little by little, weakening my resistance with his inexplicable insistence on loving me.

Had other parts of me become weaker, too? I did not feel so fierce anymore. This summer had been harder on me than either of us had anticipated—it was the first truly long-term travel I'd undertaken since getting sick, and we both wanted to believe, on some level, that more than six years of chronic pain hadn't changed me, or at least had not defeated me. At home, my condition and his abilities had, somewhat magically, never been at odds, but here, the difference seemed stark and divisive. He belonged to the land of the healthy, where people move easily, their arms and legs vehicles that get them where they want to go. And I was on another island entirely, a place that, no matter how many times I circled it, offered no way off.

The sting itself was some of the most acute pain I'd experienced in my life, but it got worse. A lot worse. The searing morphed into a deep, throbbing ache, digging deeper and deeper into me. My chest felt increasingly constricted, and my heart continued to thump so fast and hard it almost hurt.

Andrew had put his pack beneath my head so I could recline and was talking with the guide across the beach. I couldn't hear what was being said, but I could see that Andrew was doing most of the talking. Finally, after what felt like an hour but may have only been five minutes, Agus approached me with a small plastic cup.

"Drink this," he said, bringing it to my lips. I took the cup without glancing and tossed it back into my mouth, then choked, spitting up what was left of it.

"Sea water?"

"Good for you," he said with certainty.

I looked up at him, wanting to get angry, but his face, which had been so difficult to read since we'd set out, was no longer suspiciously serene. There wasn't exactly concern on his face—at least as I read it—but something looked like it had woken from its hibernation, something I recognized as familiar and comforting.

"Thank you," I said and lay back down on my pack.

When Andrew and I started spending time together as adults in the Bay Area, we'd trade books. In the summer, he gave me Tolstoy's *The Death of Ivan Ilyich*, a novel I read in a single night, unable to look away. It was about a middle-aged man who was suddenly dying from something his doctors could not pin down—an experience far different from my own, and yet the story struck something deep within me, some chord that until that moment had been vibrating but silent. Death, fortunately, did not lie before me—at least beyond the extent that it lies before everybody—but his experience of loneliness described my inner landscape, the limbo of living between one world and the next. There is no lonelier place in the world than the island of invisible suffering, though its population is varied and huge.

Andrew, unlike anyone I had ever known, willingly met me in that world, slowed to my pace with such nuance and grace that I didn't even notice he had done so. On the beach now, I felt like I was caught in that in-between place, except this time, Andrew wasn't there with me. He sat next to me, leafing absentmindedly through Jon Krakauer's *Into the Wild*, but he didn't offer any comfort, in words or body language. His mind and heart were somewhere else. He was unyielding, a stone wall.

Every relationship has a point when it develops its first fissures, which either heal and mend or continue inevitably toward breaking, like an unfixed crack in a windshield. How and why those fissures develop is unique to every relationship, but even in the strongest ones, there are little betrayals, ways we quietly break each other's hearts—or our own—without knowing it at the time.

I could already sense our first fissures, could feel them surrounding us in the dark clamminess of our tent later that night. The pain had begun to recede, and I was pretty sure I'd be fine, but I was unable to sleep. I took out my flashlight and my journal, something I only kept when I was traveling, a time when writing little missives to myself didn't feel entirely absurd.

When had it begun? I scrawled. *When we first stepped on the trail? When he pushed me up the side of that volcano? When we landed in Jakarta nearly four months ago, a new world of palm trees and rice fields coming at us as we plunged downward?*

Or was it months and even years ago, all those times I had pushed him away? Was it all that time I could never get back? That last thought was so shattering I couldn't bring myself to write it down. I watched him in his sleep, as free and vulnerable as he ever looked, and I felt, for just a moment, the crushing weight of what it would be to not have him breathing beside me.

We woke in the middle of the night to the sound of waves crashing—against our tent.

"Shit," Andrew said, bolting up. He unzipped the tent and stepped out, a cool rush of wind and spritz of saltwater coming into our muggy little world before he zipped it back up.

"Simone. Give me the flashlight," he said, his voice muffled by the sea and the tent between us. "But do *not* step out here."

I looked down at my leg in the dark. Stepping pretty much anywhere was not something he needed to worry about. Some swelling and pain had gone down, but the blisters around my ankle were still throbbing and inflamed.

I fumbled for the flashlight next to my sleeping bag and unzipped a small opening in the tent, handing it to him as I stuck my head out. He shone it against the side of the tent, an eerie light revealing this tiny section of the world—it was covered in sand, bits of seaweed, and a countless number of the beautiful, terrifying washed-up blue bodies of jellyfish, clinging to the nylon.

"Holy shit," I said. The ocean was up around Andrew's ankles. Which meant those things could also be around his ankles.

"We gotta move this thing *now*," he said. "Be careful." He didn't seem too worried about himself, but I could practically feel him holding his breath as I hobbled out of the tent and into the surf. When I reached dry sand, I looked out over the water: The moon was so bright that I didn't even need the flashlight to see the ocean and the little uninhabited islands around us. Andrew picked up the tent and began to beat its sides with a dirty shirt, getting the jellyfish as far away as possible—even dead, they could deliver a serious sting. When he was finally done, he walked up beside me and looked out at the ocean.

"It's beautiful," I said. He nodded, the moon lighting his face too.

That winter in California when we'd first fallen in love on the wooded back roads of Marin County, he'd taken me out on a cold, steep five-mile hike that he used to go on by himself in high school. Rain was falling hard on us by the time we reached the top, and the mud was thick and slippery as we pulled ourselves up by roots and rocks to a small swimming hole he'd swum in many times before—but never in the winter.

"Time to jump in!" he said.

"Are you nuts? It's January!"

But I jumped—maybe to prove that I was still the girl I envisioned myself being, the one who'd hiked the Sierras and jumped off cliffs and swum against the strong current of the American River. We peeled off the muddy clothes pasted to our bodies. My limbs went numb and immobile the moment I hit the icy water. I could barely speak it was so cold, and Andrew had to drag me out because my arms stopped working. I shivered the whole way back, chilled to the bone but more alert and alive than I'd felt in a long time.

"Have you been able to sleep?" he asked me now, after a few moments of silence.

"Not really."

"How's the leg?"

"Better, I think. Tomorrow should be O.K."

There was silence for a moment, just the sound of the waves.

"You scared the shit out of me today," he said.

I looked at him.

"Don't ever do that again," he said. But he was smiling.

"You were lying, weren't you?" I said.

"Yeah," he said. "It was very clearly a man o' war."

I laughed.

"You know, I asked Agus if it would kill you."

"What did he say?"

"Probably not."

We both laughed then, and he reached for my hand. I took it, feeling the callous that had grown between us soften.

"It's not your fault," he said. "That sting could've happened to anyone. And this trek, it would be hard on anyone." The statement felt like a peace offering.

I sat on the sand to rest my leg and he joined me, putting the flashlight down in front of us. In its light, I could see his torn up, battered feet.

"Dude, your feet are worse than mine," I said, a little triumphantly.

"I know. They hurt like hell."

I got up and limped to the tent, returning with our first aid kit. I laid it on the sand and took out the Betadine, staining his feet yellow as I applied it to his open blisters. After, I delicately swabbed the wounds with antibiotic ointment, protecting the sores on top of his feet and at his heels with small pads before wrapping both of them in gauze.

"Thank you," he said, peering down at me as I fastened the bandage with tape.

I looked up at him and smiled. His face looked young and alive in the glow of the moon.

"They'll be on the mend soon," I said. And then, I lightly kissed the toes on both of his wounded feet.

Simone Gorrindo is a writer and editor currently based in Columbus, Georgia, where she lives with Andrew, who is now her husband and a soldier stationed at Fort Benning with the 75th Ranger Regiment. Her writing has appeared in The New York Times, The Huffington Post, Tablet, *and* Vela, *among others. She is a contributing editor at* Vela *and the former senior editor of Kindle Singles. Recently, she was awarded an International Women's Media Foundation fellowship to report on government and democracy in The Democratic Republic of the Congo. She holds an M.S. in journalism from Columbia University and has received writing fellowships and grants for her writing from the Vermont Studio Center and the Hambidge Center for Creative Arts and Sciences.*

∫∂ ∫∂ ∫∂

Indian Ocean Commotion

She closed her eyes and cursed her sense of adventure.

"YOU WANT TO GO WHERE?" The manager of the Galawa Hotel shouted his shock at me.

"I want to visit one of the other islands," I repeated.

"But *why*? Nobody goes to the other islands!"

"Well, I want to."

He stared at me, astonished, but must have read determination in my gaze. "Where is it you want to go?"

"Anjouan." It was the prettiest, most populous of the Comoro Islands, four tropical specks scattered off the north coast of Madagascar.

The manager sighed. "It will be expensive."

"Fine."

Next morning, I was en route to the airport. The road ribboned along the jagged, volcanic coastline, pounded by the breezy turquoise breakers of the Indian Ocean. The hotel driver sped along, happy to have the open road ahead.

"Car!" he shouted excitedly. Traffic was rare, but sure enough, a white van was approaching, its occupants flagging us down. As it drew level, I noticed "Comoro Tourist Office" painted badly along the side panel.

A squat man stuck his head in the window. "You the one going to Anjouan?"

"Yes."

He thrust an envelope at me. "Can you take this to Mr. Kamal?" I was to stay at Mr. Kamal's hotel in Anjouan.

"What's in it?" I asked suspiciously.

"A check," the man said. "A *large* check."

"Why do I have to take it?"

"Only local people go to Anjouan, and they can't be trusted. We are taking advantage of you."

I put the envelope in my bag.

The plane, dismissed as "unreliable" by the Galawa manager, succeeded in taking off, and I was just admiring the view of Mt. Karthala simmering at the main island's southern end when we banked sharply. Snatches of white, blue, and green veered by as we lifted and dropped and cantilevered crazily above the ocean. Through the open door of the cockpit I could see the pilot grappling with the controls with one hand while restraining a baby with the other. It lent a whole new meaning to "Let's get this baby off the ground." I closed my eyes and, not for the first time, cursed my sense of adventure.

A lifetime and forty minutes later, the plane descended through low clouds and bounced to a halt on a tussocky landing strip. Once outside, I swatted away the transit card offered by a small man wearing a large badge that read "airport manager" and set off across sparse grass toward a small concrete building. There was no sign of Mr. Kamal, so I waited beside a red earth road that was overhung by dripping palm trees. Two women in bright batik sauntered along, banana leaves held over their heads in guise of umbrellas. The only sound was that of the rain and the flip-flop shuffle of the women. For being the Comoros' most populous island, Anjouan seemed unusually dead.

"Are you looking for a hotel?" A middle-aged white man had materialized at my elbow. Crumpled of face and clothing, he came accompanied by the smell of unwashed hair and alcohol. I recognized his accent as Belgian.

"No, thanks. I'm staying at the Al-Amal."

"The Hotel Al-Amal?" He sounded skeptical.

"Yes."

"But Madame . . ." He stepped round to face me, dull eyes searching mine. ". . . the Hotel Al-Amal is on Anjouan!"

We stared at each other, eyes and mouths rounding in horror, realization sudden and synchronized.

The Belgian unfroze first. "Stop the plane!" he roared, arms waving like a wind turbine gone haywire.

Half-panicked, half-laughing, I started to run, the Belgian panting at my heels. The plane was accelerating. We tried to run faster, but I was hampered by my bag; my companion by alcohol. We stumbled on, tripping, cursing, closing in. The pilot could see us, but already at the point of no return, he had no option but to get his baby off the ground.

"Too late," the Belgian said, needlessly.

We trudged in silence back to the concrete building. Suddenly, I stopped.

"I hate to sound inquisitive," I said, "but can you tell me where I am?"

The Belgian assumed a grave expression.

"Madame, you have arrived on Mohéli."

It was the smallest, least developed Comoro island. I was just digesting this information when the airport manager came huffing up.

"*Why didn't you take the card?*" he cried, inserting himself clumsily between the Belgian and me, brandishing his handwritten "In Transit" cards accusingly.

"Nobody told me the plane made a stop before Anjouan," I said.

He recoiled, shocked perhaps that anyone could be prey to such incompetence, and adopted a gentler tone.

"The plane will not return today."

I shrugged.

"What to *do*?" His cry was directed heavenwards.

"She needs a ride into town." The response came not from God, but from the Belgian.

Satisfied at having received guidance of some sort, the manager set off briskly to accomplish his mission. Once again the Belgian and I stood beside the red earth road.

"I could take a taxi," I suggested.

"There is no taxi here," the Belgian said, gloomily. It was a while before he spoke again. "Mohéli is good for three days only."

"How long have you been here?"

"Too long."

His response seemed to depress him, and he fell silent, watching a column of ants negotiate his dilapidated shoes.

A 4x4 pulled up then, spraying mud. A young Frenchman jumped out, introducing himself as Roland.

"Our agriculture expert here will drive you to town!" the manager shouted, bustling up to effect redundant introductions, officiate at the stowing of my bag, and put the stamp of authority on my departure. As I prepared to climb in the jeep, the Belgian suddenly grasped my hand, making a sandwich of it with his own.

"Thank you," he said, his voice thick with emotion. "Every morning I come to see the plane, and in twenty-three years I've never had excitement like it. I can't thank you enough." And giving my hand a final squeeze, he turned and hunched off slowly into the rain.

It was a short drive into town. Along the road, thin women wielded picks, breaking the stones that would serve as its paving, their spirits seeming as broken as their backs. I averted my eyes. The rain grew heavier as we drove into a large village where goats and chickens foraged on towering rubbish heaps. Huts of woven palm and thatch straggled along the road.

"This is Fomboni, the capital," Roland announced.

I opened my mouth but could think of nothing to say, so shut it again. We stopped at the far end, outside a long one-story building. No sign indicated its status, but it was the hotel, as in the *only* hotel. Inside was dim, but I could make out a linoleum corridor gleaming faintly and emptily.

"Anyone there?" Roland called into the gloom.

A shape materialized at the far end and shuffled toward us, manifesting eventually as a bored-looking young woman.

"Do you have a room available?"

"All rooms are available." She jerked her head toward a selection of large keys behind.

"Number five," I said.

Room number five contained a bed and a table boasting a damp mosquito coil and eighteen cigarette burns. At least there was a bathroom. Checking the water supply, I watched the few drops that emerged bring to life an impressive variety of insects resident in the drainage hole. I decided that showering could wait. The girl hung by the door.

"Fine," I said.

"Then I will send you the chef."

"The chef?"

"You will tell him what you want for lunch."

After settling on grilled fish, sticky rice, spicy cucumber and tomato salad, and melon for dessert, I sat down on the bed and sank into the sag in the middle. I idled in the hollow, watching the torrential rain sweep in over the ocean, the horizon lost in grey. I smiled to myself, feeling a deep sense of contentment. I was having an adventure.

Lunch, served on the back lawn among grazing cattle, was an exquisite feast of freshness and flavor. The sun had come out, transforming the setting from drab shades of grey to parrot-bright blues and greens. I sat back in the gazebo, thrilling to the magnificent sweep of chocolate-colored sand fronting Fomboni. A beat-up car raced the length of the beach, delivering thick bunches of bananas to cargo boats. Clanging sounds came from a dhow under construction, its wooden ribs stark against the new blue of the sky.

Suddenly, shouting erupted in the hotel. I heard my name mentioned and "Galawa." After a few minutes, a handsome middle-aged Indian crossed the lawn. He bowed slightly, introducing himself as the hotel manager and handing me a note.

"A runner has come from the post office with this message for you."

I unfolded the cheap paper on which a hand had laboriously written, "Phone Galawa. Two P.M. URGENT."

It was then that I remembered Mr. Kamal. He must have phoned the Galawa, frantic to know what had become of me. I laughed out loud.

"You must telephone isn't it?" he asked. There were no secrets on Moheli, it seemed.

"Yes."

"Then I will speak to Banana."

"*Banana?*"

"Banana is a useful boy. He will drive you to the post office."

Banana was a brash twenty-year-old with greased hair and eyes permanently narrowed in suspicion. I climbed into his rusting, windowless Peugeot, reaching for a seatbelt that was not there. He spat out the window in greeting. I decided I didn't care for Banana.

Outside the post office a donkey dozed. I skirted it and entered a spacious room shaded haphazardly by broken blinds. The clerk was writing slowly in a ledger with the stub of a pencil. I waited for him to finish, aware of his need to feel important.

"You have come to telephone?"

"Yes."

He produced a phone card from which an orange-eyed lemur stared. I paid for it and he indicated a cabin marked "International" behind me.

"Do you know how to operate a telephone?"

I offered him my coolest stare. "We do have telephones in Europe, thank you."

I disappeared into the phone box with my lemur. Within minutes I stood again in front of the clerk.

"Yes?"

"I don't know which button to press when and for what reason."

"I understood you knew how to operate a telephone."

We eyed each other levelly.

"I was mistaken."

Pressing Button B (hard) to make myself heard, I got the manager of the Galawa on the line.

"WHAT THE HELL ARE YOU DOING ON MOHÉLI?"

"YOU DIDN'T TELL ME. . . ."

"The pilot said someone like you got off there. *Why did you get off the plane?*"

"*You didn't say there was a stop before Anjouan!*"

"Oh."

A silence.

"Mr. Kamal is very upset."

"I suppose he is."

"Do you still have the check?"

"Of course."

"Look, the pilot will fly you to Anjouan tomorrow, although it's not his normal route. Mr. Kamal will meet you at the plane. Anjouan is the first stop!"

I hung up and went outside, wondering what to do next. Banana leaned against the car, arms folded.

"Would you like to pay me to drive you round the island?"

It was the perfect meeting of supply and demand.

We drove south first to Nioumachoua Beach, perfect as a travel poster, and got out for a walk. Banana told me that turtles came here to lay their eggs, although it was not the season. "The local people shoot the turtles, you know, to sell the flesh. Not for much, but we're poor here. Not like you in Europe—and Mayotte."

He spat at the mention of Mayotte. In the independence referendum of 1975, Mayotte had been the only island that voted to remain French, so its inhabitants enjoyed advantages, such as EU passports and unemployment benefits that were deeply resented by those on the other islands.

"Can't you move to Mayotte?" I asked.

"I'm banned," he said proudly, "for smashing a local with a broken beer bottle."

"O.K., let's go."

"Already?"

"Yes."

"Pity it's not the time for turtle eggs—they make great omelettes."

We continued north. With one ear half-tuned to Banana's whines about the islands' political situation (chaotic), the employment situation (nepotic) and the economic situation (catastrophic), I tried to concentrate on the beauty unfolding outside the space formerly occupied by a window. Leafy English-type lanes gave way to dense, magnificently forested hillsides. The valleys and lower slopes were luxuriant with exotic blooms, coconut palms, coffee and cacao trees. Every bend in the road offered some new delight—a waterfall thundering into the sea, a makeshift ylang-ylang distillery. There were no other cars, the road populated only by women walking, as they do all over Africa, vibrant splashes of color against tropical green, flashing shy smiles as we passed.

After the two-hour tour, I took a walk along the Fomboni beach. Towering clouds in the west had turned deeply pink, reflected in the wet sand. A long line of villagers hauled in a cargo dhow newly arrived from Anjouan. The cooking fires had been lit outside the huts at the back of the beach, and the women were grilling fish brought home by their men. I sat on the warm sand and closed my eyes, wanting to reflect on the good fortune that had brought me to this gem of an island.

"Please."

I opened an eye. An elderly man stood in front of me, extending a shriveled arm festering with sores. His eyes pleaded for help. I had nothing to give, so I shook my head, gesturing regret as best I could. He turned away, but not before I had caught the look of hopelessness in his face. There was no time to brood on his ills, however, because all of a sudden I was amid an excited group of sparkly-eyed small boys, and a soccer game with a deflated ball then required all my concentration. When night fell, my companions dispersed homeward, but the smallest boy took me shyly by the hand and with great seriousness as to the responsibility of his mission, led me safely along the beach to the hotel.

Dinner was served under a panoply of stars. I had never seen the southern constellations before, and they whitened the sky, glittering to infinity. Some hung low like fairy lights; red, yellow and diamond bright, so big and so close, seemingly, that I involuntarily stretched out a hand to touch them. Shooting stars streaked across this shimmering backdrop, leaving their evanescent trail. Only the mosquitos spoiled the beauty and magic of the night, and so I retired, along with the electricity, at nine P.M.

Twelve hours later, I finally arrived on Anjouan, which looked pretty in pastels and palms, and handed Mr. Kamal his long-awaited check. Obsequious in his gratitude, he expressed loud dismay that I had missed out on the charms of Anjouan.

It was clear he included himself among its attractions, and as I prised my hand from his clammy grip, I felt great relief that the plane had delivered me to Mohéli rather than into the welcoming embrace of the perfumed Mr. Kamal.

Back at the Galawa, the manager pulled me into his office. "What a commotion you caused! People will talk about it for months to come! Of course, I will reimburse part of the ticket and the hotel to make up for your dreadful experience."

"Yes, it was too bad," I lied.

"So tell me—how is Mohéli? I've never been there."

"You wouldn't like it."

"I thought not."

I smiled and walked out of his office. Mohéli would be my secret.

Although Judith Campbell has written all her life, this is her first print publication. She lives in the French-speaking part of Switzerland and is both a teacher and the manager of an English language program for foreign (mainly Chinese) students. She writes when she can, and continues to travel even when people insist she should not (which is why she found herself in North Korea when it exploded its first nuclear device).

ॐ ॐ ॐ

Private Lessons

A journey into the louder, later Cairo.

She rarely gets out of bed before noon. She sounds on the phone like Jennifer Lopez: nasal voice, sassy tone, Latina accent. She fills her living room every afternoon with foreign women who want to make their bellies roll, their hips vibrate. When Egyptian neighbors ask about her profession—her reason for living in Cairo—she says nothing about dancing, just calls herself a teacher.

Her subject material is ancient. Before there was a single mosque in Cairo, before Muslim invaders had even touched Africa, Egyptians were belly dancing. Traditional as it may be, *raqs sharqi*, or "oriental dance," remains scandalous today. Good Muslim women cover their heads and almost everything else; belly dancers bare their bellies and a lot else. Mohammed Ali went as far as to banish belly dancers from Cairo in 1834, worried they'd scandalize foreign guests. In the 1950s the dance was banned outright. Nowadays, certain pelvic movements are restricted, and belly dancers have to cover their midriff. Some comply with a translucent nylon swatch.

Still, Cairo is the belly-dancing capital of the world. The dance is more or less same; what's changed is the nationality of the dancers. Every year, fewer Egyptians dance *raqs sharqi.* In the cabarets you'll find belly dancers from Lebanon, belly dancers from Moscow, belly dancers from Rio, and at least three belly dancers who hail from America. The most famous, Leila, grew up on a Native American reservation in Washington State. Another, Diana, supposedly graduated from Harvard. The most recent arrival is a native of Los Angeles, the granddaughter of Mexican immigrants, a brunette with an hourglass figure named Alegra Pena.

I call Alegra and inquire about her class. I haven't a clue what belly dancing entails, but decide to find out. I warn Alegra that I've never done any Middle Eastern dancing. Fairer warning would be that I lived in Cuba and can't dance salsa, that I lived in the Dominican Republic and can't dance meringue, that bouncing around barefoot at an Indian wedding is the closest I've come to picking up a foreign dance. She assures me walk-ins are most welcome.

Alegra stands before a wall of mirrors, dressed in skin-tight black plants that flare at the ankle. I stand off to her left and notice some key differences in our reflections. I'm new to Cairo and look it. My t-shirt reaches the base of my neck; my pants are loose and full-length; I have chosen to bare no belly. I'm in what one American journalist in Cairo called "the dowdy phase," sacking my physique under scarves and peasant blouses and shawls as vast as blankets. I doubt Alegra ever went through such a dowdy phase. She seems more comfortable in her body in Cairo than I've ever been in America. Her abs, by no means a washboard, are the focal point of this class. We watch them, expecting to learn.

Alegra demonstrates how to puff out our bellies, like kids do, when pretending to be fat. Next, she leads us in a "figure-eight," winding her hips through space, squatting low to the ground and sticking her butt out impossibly far, the whole time watching her reflection, as though agreeing with the Egyptian who once told Alegra she had "the perfect body for Cairo."

Another friend, a Jordanian, had already planted the seed. They were out at a club in New York City, and Alegra began playfully imitating her friend's moves on the dance floor. He promised she'd have no trouble mastering belly dancing, with hips and rhythm and confidence like that. At the time, Alegra's career had nothing to do with dance, nor had she given serious thought to living abroad. She loved to dance, felt instantly happy doing it, but was raised to go after money. Alegra describes her father as a man in perpetual search of the next "get-rich" scheme. She inherited her father's habit of juggling a dozen ventures at once. She flipped properties, sold used guitars on ebay, exported electronics to Lebanon—at one point needing fifteen credit cards to manage it all. On the side, she had a pastime she also credits her father with: self-help retreats. Dad was a seminar junkie.

"Life Directions" was the retreat that shifted everything for Alegra. She was given a hypothetical question and time alone to answer it: if she had all the money in the world, what would she be doing? She thought hard. She'd been chasing money for many years. Erase that carrot, forget the jackpot on the horizon, and what did she see? Two dreams became clear. The first was to host the Oprah Winfrey show. Ruling this unrealistic, she moved along to dream two: dancing in Cairo.

First, though, she had to extricate herself from life in America. Alegra owned three properties and two cats. She had a car loan and a blasé relationship. Doubtful they'd ever marry, she also doubted they'd ever break up. Life had become so tangled with drama and debts that a close friend theorized she'd done this on purpose—tangled her own web, that is, so that one day she'd yearn to escape. She admits this could be true: that she created prime conditions for her own clean break.

The linoleum floor of Alegra's apartment is cool beneath my bare feet. She tells us to assume a plié, the starting position of ballet, and reaches over to correct my uneven squat. I've heard Egyptian belly dancing described as "the anti-ballet." While the ballerina stands straight—as tall as pointe shoes let her stretch—the belly dancer performs barefoot, crouching on the floor and rolling around it, her moves sensual and earthy. Ballerinas look angular, almost porcelain; belly dancers appear fertile and fleshy. Staring at my teacher in the mirror, I notice another key difference: facial expression. Alegra, smiling broadly, could not look any more delighted to dance this dance—even its basic steps, even among beginners.

The only beginner in the wall of mirrors is me. I try to put that out of my mind by watching Alegra. I'm a stick figure, imitating a serpent. Alegra's left arm winds one way, while the right arm takes the reverse course, with gorgeous fluidity. Her hip, meanwhile, lifts to its own sure beat, like a metronome set to slow. This woman has a metronome in her hip, and I'm supposed to dance like her. *Tick . . . tick . . . tick:* her hip, without any help from either leg, rises straight up. That lifting—when done right, when neither leg cheats, when the rest of the body remains still—is about as sexy as a single gesture can be.

I wish she weren't so good a teacher. Alegra nitpicks, corrects my hip tick, continues to push my legs into a plié. I'm looking forward to the point in class when she gives up on me. And she will; it's just a matter of time. It'd be nice to save her that time, all that teacherly concern and sweat, because there are talented dancers in the room. Behind me is a Norwegian who came to Cairo with a coughing toddler for this chance to dance. I'm thinking hard about quitting—for everyone's sake, just bowing out and hitting the couch—when Alegra quits correcting and spends the rest of class dancing in silence.

She dances at her own reflection, sultry and admiring, running her fingers through her loose brown hair and lifting it up over her head. I think of the Egyptian man who told me it was fine to wear Western clothes in Cairo, "as long as they're not seducing," as I watch this American seduce her own reflection. There are, I've learned, many ways a Western woman can respond to all the rules that govern Cairo, all the gazes that enforce them. She can cover up and hurry up. She can cease to read the periphery of her vision. She can toughen and harden.

Alegra, though, does none of the above. Her smile is soft, her appearance feminine, the way she moves through space is nothing if not sensual. She's made a career for herself out of celebrating her body in a place where showing skin is taboo. As tough as it is to imitate her aura, her moves, her undulations, I do enjoy playing Alegra. We close the weeknight class with a series of hip lifts, advancing in unison toward the mirror, looking coordinated, brassy, unstoppable, hot— the very opposite of how we'll appear disbanding down separate streets as night falls in Egypt.

Alegra and I live in two different Cairos. I learn this when I try to make plans with her. "Nothing happens in Cairo before noon!" she practically yells when I propose meeting in the morning. Alegra blames the city for hibernating half the day, giving her zero reason to get out of bed.

My apartment is next to a mosque. I have no choice but to hear the predawn wailings of the call to prayer. By five A.M., when the muezzin leaks across the Nile, you can already hear the whirr of taxis and trucks along the Corniche. By a quarter to nine, you can't board a subway car without pushing.

I don't mention early-bird Cairo to Alegra and instead just meet her for breakfast at four o'clock. I order crepes; she orders burritos, helping herself to my crepes, too. The owner, a good friend of Alegra's, keeps coming over to our table to chat and dote. He calls her Aleya, the easier-to-pronounce, Egypt-friendly version of her name, which she tells everyone, including me, to call her.

Thinking this is my chance to compliment Alegra—
Aleya—I ask the restaurant owner whether he's seen her dance.
Right away, I know I've done something wrong. Aleya fidgets
and answers his questions curtly. She'd never told him what she
teaches (that's not, she later explains, the sort of thing a woman
publicizes in Cairo). I feel awful, but Aleya doesn't seem at all
mad. This woman may have skipped the dowdy phase, but
she was once as green to Cairo's codes as I am. Before moving to Egypt, she'd heard that belly dancing was stigmatized,
but didn't know the extent of it until she arrived. The extent
of it, I'm just beginning to grasp: lying about your profession to
make friends.

Lacking a real life of my own in Cairo, I'm free to pass
in and out of everyone else's. Staying just one month, I can
say yes, yes, yes. People invite me to things, and I go. People
tell me where they live, and I give the address to the cabbie.
A club advertises a meeting and I show up. I tell people I'm
open; I make myself an easy bring-along. All Cairo asks is that
I stay awake, and really: could Cairo make it any easier to?
Cairo honks; Cairo never closes; Cairo wails like an old man
dying promptly at five each morning.

Only after fourteen straight days of rising with the faith-
ful, shadowing the journalists, and stalking the Egyptologists
does my frenetic study of the American expat take a toll. I
notice a numbness in my legs. I notice my eyes looking like
caves. I notice the empty jar of instant coffee and know who
did that. I did that. I'm an engine that runs on Nescafe. And
wouldn't you know: Aleya calls, just as the engine sputters, to
invite me out on the town. Her belly-dancer friends are getting together at midnight.

"Midnight?" I repeat the hour aloud, hoping she'll modify
it. I was awake and typing before sunrise today, kneeling in
a church pew at eight A.M., making crafts by noon, dodging
trucks and taxis in-between, all of which was supposed to

draw to a close over a dinner with a tireless foreign correspondent at ten P.M.

"Midnight," she repeats.

I try dressing up, dolling up, chugging one of my roommate's Diet Cokes. Still, I want nothing more than to collapse. I'm *right* on the line. I'm wearing lipstick and leaning back on a bed. I'm clutching a purse and closing my eyes to consider this choice under the heavy lids of heavy eyes that just need time slipping down—

"I'm awake!" I say to the phone on my bed that vibrates. "I'm awake," I promise again, like it's Cairo calling, testing my end of the deal. Aleya tells me to get in a cab. It's midnight and also a miracle: I'm refreshed. Just refreshed enough to make it over the line, past the stroke of midnight, and into the other Cairo.

The show is on stage but everyone's watching one table. Even the singer, the man holding the microphone, is transfixed by a group of Saudi men seated front and center. An Egyptian beside me, looking disgusted but not away, mutters, "I wouldn't be surprised if there's a prince at that table."

If there's a prince at that table, he must be the one who climbs on stage, unbidden, stomping to the beat, then spinning in a circle with arms akimbo, like a kid trying to make himself dizzy. Reaching dizzy, he slows and slows then stomps again, stomps to find and squash that beat.

Princely indeed: the thick-necked one in the black velvet cowboy hat. His court sits below, clapping high over their heads, ready to cheer if he falls right off the stage. When at last the prince snatches the microphone from the singer and lets out a battle cry (AY-YI-YI-YI-YI!), then a WOOF, I know he is, in fact, aware of us: his audience.

My roommate, Sid, was the first person to tell me about Gulf Arabs in Cairo. He pointed out the window at a huge apartment complex, just beyond ours, and told me that's where the Saudis live—not now, but in summer. Egypt, with milder rules and milder weather, has a long tradition as the playground of the region. Arabs who come to play nowadays bring petroleum money to burn. Sid says there are nightclubs in Cairo where Emiratis drop thousands of dollars in a night.

I'm pretty sure I'm at one of those nightclubs. The prince holds in his hand a wad of cash the size of a brick and flings it high in the air so it sprays like confetti over a thirty-man band. A pair of teenage boys appear from nowhere and start gathering the money in quick snatches, keeping low to the ground; they've had practice.

The men who bang tambourines watch the princes who twirl in circles near prostitutes who drift onto stage into the view of old men slumped in chairs who smoke water pipes and gaze stonily at the princes who neither watch money flying nor hookers drifting nor the thirty-some men who make this music so deafening.

Every time I look up I catch at least one band member staring down at our table, watching tonight's show in the mirror of the nearest eyes. The same skinny harpist tries to read my gaze as I wonder what makes some prostitutes look so enthralling and others so repugnant and what it will take for a prince and a prostitute to look right at each other? Why is everything about eye contact in Cairo? Why do I always feel like power rests in the right to look? Because I lost that right?

Not even the belly dancer gets to look. Aleya climbs up on stage, looking just as mirthful as she did in her private class— same wide grin—but she might as well be dancing alone in her bedroom, the only mirror in her mind's eye. I watch, mesmerized by Aleya, nervous for Aleya, smiling with Aleya. I can't watch her dance without a grin, without wondering how the attention of this cabaret feels. If she's affected, she doesn't let on. *Raqs sharqi* is danced as though alone; belly dancers occupy a false vacuum, a snow globe no one can see in, blurred by squalls of cash. Everyone who climbs on stage—even the showoffs, even the women for sale—succeeds in making it look like a dance for themselves alone, leaving us free to stare through the flying money at bare flesh.

Money falls in our laps, on our heads, in the folds of our clothes. More often, it scatters under our chairs and tables. I see now why the money-collectors are boys; they climb under our tables like monkeys, reaching and snatching without a peep, without a bump. Only late in the morning, when the fruit platters and nut bowls on our table have all been buried at least twice in cash (and I have to remind myself that snacking on guava slices and cashews is sort of like licking ten pound notes by now, so how about we stop) am I more or less accustomed to it.

Outside the cabaret, in the gray light of a new day that we'll go home to sleep through, an Egyptian looks down and sees a ten pound note in the lip of her boot. There it is: proof. That flutter in the dark, that mess on the floor was not an illusion after all. Those were bills; those were princes; this is Cairo—a land not endowed with fields of oil but positioned by history and geography to host the barons, the overnight princes, men with throwaway wealth. Cairo throws the party. Cairo cleans up. Cairo has staff enough to collect, to count, to turn confetti back into bricks.

The Egyptian who finds oil money in her boot gives it back to a doorman who nods appreciatively and runs it back inside. People keep telling me that Cairo is not as chaotic as it first appears. "There are patterns for things that seem patternless," Leila, the most famous American belly dancer, tells me. In the back rooms of these cabarets, the detritus of another late night goes back into currency, back into the hands of people who use pounds to buy bread and ride cabs and pay rents.

I pay a few hundred dollars rent for a room with a tiny glimpse of the Nile River. My sliver view from the eleventh floor will never look the same to me. Now, rather than see river—that car-and-a-half's-length of glimmer—I notice instead the concrete building blocking the way, where lights never come on, where Saudis only summer. I imagine my way into all those empty flats, stealing a glimpse of their full-river view.

The city has been called to prayer by the time I get home from the cabaret. If I thought I could sneak back into my apartment, dart unnoticed between Cairo's night and Cairo's day, I was mistaken. Already, the shopkeepers on Nawal Street are unlocking gates; hulking men sit outside the Agouza police station. As my cab slows, a familiar dread rises: I don't want to get out.

I'm dressed modestly enough—in the same giant shawl I wrapped around me like a cocoon all night—but clearly, I've been out. There's indecency in the hour of my arrival, and perhaps my company too. Sitting in shotgun is a gay man in a trench coat who designs costumes for belly dancers: sweet, soft-spoken Mamdou. I owe him my thanks for seeing me home and want to express it sincerely. I reach into the front seat and give his shoulder a squeeze. Who sees this squeeze? What does it mean? Are the men who watch the same every day? How will I know if I never look? How can you discern without the right to look?

Women I meet in Cairo seem to be telling me—in their own stories, in self-styled advice—that my life here will get immeasurably easier as soon as I stop seeing Cairo see me. I've listened, all the while doubting I'd ever fog over the mirror in my mind. But I do feel like I've crossed some sort of line tonight, followed Aleya beyond a boundary I won't step back behind. I'm going to bed and won't open my eyes until two in the afternoon. I'll start the new day in cowboy boots and skinny jeans and some shirt whose neckline I don't stare at hard in the mirror. I'll walk through this same parking lot of quiet stares, with a laser gaze of my own—fixed, distant, hot, asking zero permission and begging no pardon.

Colleen Kinder has written essays and articles for The New Republic, Salon, National Geographic Traveler, The New York Times, *Gadling, Atlantic.com,* The Wall Street Journal, Ninth Letter, A Public Space, The New York Times Magazine*, and* Creative Nonfiction*. She is the author of* Delaying the Real World *and currently teaches travel writing at Yale.*

❧ ❧ ❧

That Time I Got Married at Burning Man

In a matter of hours, he would be her husband.

*L*ate one morning, on my way back from the hug deli at 8:30 & Dandelion, I looked up to see a black ring of smoke rising slowly above the dusty horizon. I got off my bike, dismounted with the clunk of silver combat boots against the hard-packed playa, and leaned against a pink PVC-pipe jungle gym.

I was too distracted by the sky to notice him at first, a barefoot, shirtless boy in low-slung orange Thai fisherman pants. He was lanky, lean, with a mess of brown hair and full, chapped lips. A streak of thick white paint stretched from his shoulder down to the crease where his thigh met his hip. He stood next to me, our shoulders touching.

"Crazy, isn't it?"

I wondered if he was talking about this place, where mornings blend into evenings into afternoons and midnights, or about those strange smoke rings.

He pointed. "I think they're coming from an art car, or that tiny movie theater way out there in deep playa. I went last night, watched *Singing in the Rain* and found a box of Red Vines under the seat."

We sat down on the couch in the middle of the road. A procession of bicycles, tricycles, unicycles, steampunk octopus-mobiles, girls with furry boots and top hats, scarves, and hula hoops passed by. Fire dancers lit their torches; a couple held hands and skipped backwards.

He told me his philosophy on life, on death, on happiness, and success, about his childhood in Chicago and his move to Dallas, about his Labrador named Bo Dacious, and his thoughts on global warming, before I even knew his name—Henry.

Three hours passed, then four. He kissed me as the chill of another desert night descended. Later, we ventured out onto the playa together.

At Opulent Temple, we danced to deep bass music, surrounded by fire and hundreds of ecstatic bodies covered in glitter, sweat, fur, and sticky spilled playa rum. He borrowed juggling balls from a freckled blond boy in a tiger suit, spinning and tossing them in the air. I laughed, free and easy.

We found a trampoline off the main drag. My legs were shaking, but we jumped anyway. Henry took my hand, and we just kept jumping until we both collapsed under the weight of the heat and the long day. I straddled him right there on the trampoline, nestled my head into his neck, and breathed in the smell of sweat and alkaline dust. He wrapped his lanky, tanned arms around my waist. We lay there sleeping until the sun began to rise.

Next door, a margarita bar turned on Jimmy Buffet. Zed, the bartender, had purple hair and wore a broken coconut bra. I unclipped my tin drinking cup from its backpack carabiner and he poured me a strawberry daiquiri. Henry had a shot of straight tequila. We sat in the hammock next to the bar and yelled compliments at passersby.

A couple holding hands ran by, dressed all in white. I shouted, "You make a beautiful couple!" They smiled and turned around.

The woman had a streak of faded blue glitter running through her long blonde braid. Grinning, she asked, "Would you like to come with us to the Elvis chapel down the way? We're on our honeymoon and want to get remarried on the playa! Come be our witnesses!"

The ceremony was brief, lovely. We gathered in the tiny canvas and wood-beamed chapel as Lady Elvis had them recite their vows, all Blue Suede Shoes and dusty tears. I held Henry's hand tight, sticky palms and all. We cheered as the man kissed his already-bride.

Flushed, she turned to us. "Why don't you get married? It seems as if you've been together a lifetime."

It felt like we had.

When we signed our names in the guestbook, I saw he had written "Henry Blietz."

I poked him, shot a teasing grin. "That's very sweet of you to take my name already," I said, "but you spelled it wrong!"

He looked confused. I suddenly realized I hadn't told him my full name. I leaned over and right under his name wrote slowly, deliberately, "Carly Blitz."

If there was ever a time to trust fate, it seemed to me, this was it: under the dry, hazy skies of Black Rock City, with this mysterious boy whose name was almost mine.

Two drag queens pulled me into the back, where dresses, hats, and veils were draped on a pop-up rack. They pulled a rough pink tulle ball gown over my head and spun me around; the dress was missing a sleeve, and my breath became shallow. Unzip. One of them helped me step into another dress, while the other held up an old wrought-iron mirror.

This one was cream, fully lace, with cap sleeves and a mer-maid tail. It fit perfectly over my hips, cinching at my waist, dipping off my shoulders. I brushed off the dust, and glitter exploded from the seams. The drag queens hovered a long shredded veil over my hair; I fixed my feather earring and wiped clean the smudged turquoise war paint still clinging to my cheeks from when I had left camp twenty hours ago.

I walked into the chapel from the front, a drag queen on each arm. The keyboardist began to play "Only Fools Rush In." Henry was standing at the far end of the chapel next to Burning Man Elvis. I took three purposeful, if slightly tipsy, steps—and was at his side.

"We are gathered here today . . ." Elvis began.

Everything was cloaked in a thin layer of ethereal dust. I wondered if this was a dream, lowered my eyes under the veil.

"Do you, Carly, take this cool cat, Henry, as your hubby (*uh huh-uh huh*)?"

I glimpsed Henry's hazy eyes through the tulle, kept my gaze steady. He looked back at me with his tilted top hat and crooked grin.

Is this where my love story would begin? How strange.

"I do."

He did. We kissed, and my hands were shaking again.

Everyone danced, piling out of the chapel into the early morning light of the playa, laughing and hugging.

Henry and I returned to his camp with the hopeful enthusiasm of real newlyweds, crept into his tent and fumbled with leather vests and rigid boots. He was unsure, gentle, so I pulled him down to me with clenched fists and pressed my lips onto his, hard.

Two days later, we broke down camp, said our goodbyes. Exchanging numbers seemed strange, as if neither of us had thought about this moment, the end of our time together on the playa. And in truth, we hadn't. Each moment out there in the desert seems to last forever, the future constantly hazy with swirling dust.

Back in the default world we pretended, at first, to go through the motions of a long-distance relationship. I lived by the phone, waited for the melodic bell of my text messages. *Hubby*, I would joke. *Wife*, he would respond. We played a version of across-the-country house, but there were no trampolines and margarita bars, no fire-breathing octopus or impromptu Elvis chapels. I booked a flight to visit him in Dallas.

I packed lace lingerie, had visions of days talking, playing in bed, cooking chocolate-chip pancakes, and mixing Bloody Marys in the morning. As it happened, he had to work most of the weekend, didn't care much for lingerie. In his fridge were two lone Red Bulls, a jar of pickles, and a frozen deep-dish pepperoni pizza from Chicago. I went out that day while he was at work, bought steaks, giant peaches, and burrata cheese from the farmers market. I explored Dallas, felt disoriented and sticky. That night, he sat at the computer, distracted, while I made us dinner. I perched on his lap, arm draped across his neck.

"I'm glad you're home, Hubby," I said to his ear, with a coy smile.

He jumped up abruptly, knocking me to the floor.

"Let's go out to the bars and drink," he said, grabbing his keys.

We held hands walking through Deep Ellum. Henry half-heartedly swatted my ass after a few beers. I giggled, but it caught in my throat. At the bar, he began a high-speed tangent I couldn't follow, something about LSD, Al Gore, and the Chicago Bears—I nodded assiduously. We got drunk and fell asleep on the couch that night, facing opposite directions.

I went home to Colorado early the next morning. Over time, the texts and late-night phone calls began to taper, the deep knot in my stomach began to unravel, and dreams of Burning Man began to fade, until they were so faint I began to wonder if it ever really happened at all.

❧ ❧ ❧

Carly Blitz is a backpacking, bacon-loving, bourbon-drinking, hopelessly nomadic freelance writer. Her work has appeared in Every Day with Rachael Ray, *on popular traveler's hub Matador Network, and most often, on her parents' fridge. She believes in the Oxford comma, dancing barefoot, and the kindness of strangers. Currently, she is working on a collection of nonfiction essays tentatively titled* The Little Book of Short Relationships. *For more about Carly, please visit cargocollective.com/carlyblitz.*

ℬ ℬ ℬ

Incoming

A hard landing in Afghanistan.

*T*he flyer on the door explained what to do in case of a rocket attack, but I didn't pay much attention to it. I had more important things on my mind. Like a nap.

I'd just flown halfway around the world, to Afghanistan, and had arrived in Kabul that morning. It was my first embed with the U.S. military, and I was here to write a story about some women Marines. After a quick jaunt into town to borrow a helmet and body armor from a friend of a friend (the military doesn't ask much of journalists—they'll house you, feed you, and move you about the country, but they do insist that you bring your own protective gear), it was midday before I'd made it to the NATO base where I'd start my trip. And since the C-130 I was scheduled to take to Helmand wasn't leaving until later that night, I had plenty of time to catch up on sleep.

Gray winter skies hung low over the base, which was tucked between the Kabul airfield and the mountains surrounding the city. Twenty-foot-high blast walls segmented the place into quasi-blocks and stood guard around structures where any sizeable number of people were likely to gather: the gym, the recreation center, the dining hall. Soldiers from a dozen different nations promenaded along the main road, while white SUVs zipped between huge gun-turreted combat trucks. Rows of Quonset-hut-shaped tents made out of beige vinyl sat on one side of the road, peppered by loudspeakers, chin-up bars, and latrine trailers. On the other side, next to the runway, stood a large concrete building that housed the military air terminal.

A public affairs officer took me inside and got me permission to use the "female transient" tent, where they housed all women visitors, both military and civilian. The soldier manning the billeting desk gave me directions and handed me the combination to the cipher lock on the tent's door (sexual assault is, regrettably, a nut the deployed military has yet to crack). The public affairs officer dropped me off at my temporary home and bid me good luck as I stepped inside.

The place was empty. A loud hum rattled throughout the tent as an industrial heater pumped in warm air. Rows of bunk beds lined each side, bearing mattresses that had clearly seen a lot of use. A few of the bunks had already been commandeered, sleeping bags stretched out on the lower beds and duffels tossed onto the uppers. The two bunks at the back had sheets draped around them, presumably by soldiers who, temporarily assigned to this base, had grabbed the choice real estate and tried to establish some semblance of privacy.

The flyer on the door, the one about the rockets, showed a picture of a soldier lying face down on the ground, in flak jacket and helmet, as if they were inventing a new, militarized yoga pose or were simply passed out from a night on the town. Truthfully, I hadn't thought about rockets much. When it came to threats in Afghanistan, I'd focused exclusively on roadside bombs, which were killing and maiming U.S. soldiers on a weekly, if not daily, basis.

The insurgents had very logically concluded that full frontal attacks on Americans were a losing proposition. U.S.

troops came wrapped in body armor and drove around in monster trucks rigorously designed to withstand everything from bullets to RPGs. The insurgents, in comparison, came off more like ragamuffins. In fact, as impolitic as it might be to point out, the robotic-looking U.S. troops, with their giant helmets, wraparound sunglasses, gloved hands, and kneepads, looked more like Empire storm troopers from *Star Wars*, and the insurgents, with their long tunics and flowing pants, more like the Rebel Alliance, minus the Ewoks.

In any case, given the asymmetry in capabilities, the insurgents had mastered the art of attacking from afar. Their weapon of choice was the makeshift land mine—also known in militarese as an "improvised explosive device" or IED. They planted large ones in roads to blow up vehicles and small ones on paths and in buildings to knock out soldiers on foot. As such, I was not looking forward to the prospect of eventually getting into a combat vehicle and rolling out overland. Riding in the back of a truck and waiting for it to go boom made you feel helpless. I wasn't as worried about foot patrols. At least then, you could delude yourself into believing you had some control over your fate.

In an earlier life, I'd been a TV news producer based in Jerusalem. The first time I went out into the field with a camera crew, I'd ended up in the middle of a clash. We'd been filming stone-throwing Palestinians when an Israeli army bus rolled up. I remember an Israeli soldier stepping out of the vehicle and raising his rifle directly at us. One minute I was in the middle of the street, the next I was crouched behind a wall—but without any recollection of how I'd gotten there. "Good instincts," one of the cameramen had said. I didn't know if those instincts would prove useful on the ground in Afghanistan. If you found yourself in the middle of a firefight and launched yourself into a gully for cover, you could just as easily land on a mine. But still, I worked well in denial.

Rockets, however, were something I hadn't considered. And despite the warning on the door, it didn't occur to me to start doing so now. I was in Kabul. There was the occasional attack on a hotel or shopping center, but I'd never heard of an attack on a base in Kabul. I turned my focus instead to the more pressing matter of a nap. I'd been up for two days. It was time to lie down.

I grabbed a bunk halfway down the tent and set myself up. My duffels and daypack went up top, along with the body armor. I pulled off my sneakers and changed from my travel clothes—nice top and tailored jeans—into my embed wear—functional t-shirt and cargo pants. I took out my contacts and set my alarm for sometime before the end of the evening meal service. Then I tossed back a sleeping pill, climbed into my sleeping bag, and prepared to sink into a deep sleep.

I couldn't have been out for more than an hour before a siren invaded my slumber. My sleep-deprived brain resisted it. I was on a military base, after all. Surely sirens were commonplace. I turned over, determined to let it waft over me.

Then the voice of a cultured British woman came over the loudspeaker. "Rocket attack," she declared. "Rocket attack."

Now I was awake. *You have got to be fucking kidding me*, I thought, not moving. *I just got here. Things like this* never *happen. The day I arrive is the day the Taliban decide to attack?*

I crawled out of bed and arranged myself on the floor as the flyer had demonstrated, immediately regretting, of course, not having given it the attention it clearly deserved. *Was anyone else in the tent?* They'd probably know what to do next. I surveyed the floor. No dice. *Maybe in one of the beds?* I popped my head up, but it was too dim to tell if any of the sleeping bags contained human forms. And if they were breathing or shifting around, I couldn't hear it over the rattle of the heating unit.

I assumed I was on my own and tried to assess how big of a mess I was in. I'd been rocketed before. Or, more precisely, missiled. It was in Jerusalem during the first Gulf War, when Iraq had rained Scuds on Israel. Throughout the war, our correspondents would do live shots, sometimes alone or sometimes with correspondents stationed in Saudi Arabia, which also got its share of Scuds. Every now and then, either in Israel or in Saudi, a live shot was interrupted by a siren warning of incoming missiles. Instead of taking cover, our reporters would usually tough it out on camera. Once, an anchor back in the States asked the three reporters he was interviewing—one in Israel and two in Saudi—why they didn't heave off to the bunkers. Two of them, younger reporters and new to war, blustered something about it being their responsibility to stay out and report, and that they were paid handsomely to take risks like these. The third, the one in Israel, was an old warhorse who put it more simply. "It's a very big world," he said, "and they're very small missiles." Which, in a sense, was true. Scuds are quite large. But if you're standing in the middle of a city and Saddam Hussein lobs a missile at you, the probability it's going to hit your building isn't particularly high.

I didn't know much about rockets in Afghanistan. Back in Israel, the Palestinians had used Katyushas. I decided that whatever the Taliban had, it probably approximated Katyushas. So while they weren't small rockets, it was a big base. The likelihood of any one rocket hitting my particular tent was small. I'd stay put for now. Still, I inched my way under the bed for good measure.

About ninety seconds passed. Or so it seemed—my brain was addled from a cocktail of Ambien, deep sleep, and raging adrenaline, so my grasp of time could have been off. Then another siren sounded. The British lady came back over the loudspeaker: "Terrorist inside," she said. "Terrorist inside."

I was dumbfounded. It wasn't just that insurgents had somehow managed to breach the perimeter and were now on the base, which was already inconceivable; I had a hard time processing the fact that NATO was calling insurgents "terrorists." I mean, after all, it was *their* country. Technically, it was the NATO troops who were the interlopers. If local insurgents chose to do battle against foreign soldiers, it seemed a bit overreaching to call them terrorists.

Still, my pulse kicked into high gear as my primordial lizard brain processed the new information: an insurgent, or several, had entered the base, presumably armed. My status as a journalist probably wouldn't carry much weight with them. *What did I need to do to protect myself?*

I strained again, over the rattle of the heater, to hear sounds from behind the draped sheets. If anyone was back there, they weren't moving. My brain careered between taking this seriously and not wanting to overreact. Should I put on my body armor? I certainly didn't want to be the idiot who got shot because she decided not to pay attention to the nice lady on the loudspeaker. But it also wouldn't make the best first impression if a soldier *did* emerge from behind the sheets, all casual-like, only to discover a civilian cowering on the floor, fully encased in combat gear.

I decided to err on the side of staying alive. My brain cycled through the potential scenarios: *What if one of the attackers, while running around the base, tried to hide in this tent?* There would be nobody here to defend me. But then I remembered the cipher lock. They wouldn't be able to get in. (Not so for the male tents next door, but they were soldiers, so they could probably take care of themselves.) *But what about bullets?* The walls were fabric. If shooting erupted near the tent, the bullets would go straight through. *And grenades?* Also no protection. *How long would I be stuck here?* The hunt for the insurgents would involve a massive game of hide-and-seek. *How would the NATO troops even* know *how many insurgents had gotten onto the base?* This could go on for hours. Maybe longer.

It seemed a good idea to be ready to move quickly. I didn't want a soldier bursting in and telling me to get moving, only to have me stare back blankly because I didn't have any shoes on. I pulled myself back up onto the bed and stuffed my feet into my sneakers. My hands shook as I tried to shove my contacts back into my eyes. I silently unleashed a violent stream of cusswords. I still couldn't get over the fact this was happening on the very day I arrived. Give a girl a chance to get her sea legs, I argued to no one in particular.

Another siren came on. "Mass casualties. Mass casualties," the nice British lady said.

Mass casualties? That could only mean a rocket had made it over a blast wall and into some building with a lot of people in it. I pictured bodies strewn hither and thither. Rescuers racing to the site to evacuate the wounded. The base hospital filling up with stretchers. I thought about my family. They'd been nervous about my coming here. I'd assured them I'd be nowhere near any action. I'd been, how shall we put this, flexible with the truth. It's what you do. Now I was desperately hoping they wouldn't hear about the attack before I could get online and tell them I was safe.

But wait, it suddenly occurred to me: *Where were these mass casualties?* I mentally ticked off all the sites where there'd be enough people all in one place. *The gym?* That was right next to me, but I hadn't heard any booms. *The rec center?* Also near me. *The dining hall?* Also nearby. All these places were near me, and yet I hadn't heard a thing. No thump from a round hitting. No running around. No yelling for help. No screeching of tires or gunning of engines. In fact, the whole place seemed eerily quiet for a base under siege. It was my first experience with combat of this kind, but even I could see something wasn't adding up.

Another siren. "Exercise. Exercise," the nice British lady announced. Then, a brief pause and: "All clear. All clear."

It took a while to process her words. My brain understood them, of course, but the chemicals coursing through my body still had me primed for a fight. *Would it have killed you*, I silently asked the nice British lady, *to have announced the "exercise" bit* at the beginning?

And then I realized she probably had. She'd probably said something to that effect before the first siren went off, but I'd been unconscious.

It would be two years before I'd experience a rocket attack for real, on another reporting trip to Afghanistan. I'd be on a different base then, one dubbed a "rocket city" because of the frequency of attacks. That base would get hit almost every day, sometimes several times. The troops I'd embed with would brief me the minute I arrived: When the siren goes off, hit the deck; when the siren stops (which means the round has hit), run for a bunker and stay there until the "All Clear" announcement, in case there are more incoming.

In fact, throughout my time with the military in Afghanistan, rockets would be more of a factor than roadside bombs, perhaps because much more of my time would be spent on bases than out on roads. I'd learn to take them seriously, and I'd become adept at hitting the ground quickly. As for insurgents breaching a perimeter, I'd never be on a base that was overrun, though I'd be on several that trained for it. And in fact, this NATO base, where my heart was still thumping, would actually come under attack a couple of years later. But according to news reports, the insurgents would make little headway, and they'd all be taken out.

For now, though, the base was quiet. Nothing was left but the hum from the heater. My brain was still spinning, trying to catch up with all that had happened. But it soon relaxed into more mundane matters. There were still a few hours left before dinner, and I was exhausted. I pulled off my sneakers and took out my contacts. I double-checked my alarm. Then I popped another sleeping pill, rolled back into my sleeping bag, and slowly drifted off to sleep.

 ✍ ✍ ✍

E. B. Boyd ("Liza") lived in France as a child and spent vacations camping with her family throughout Europe. After college, she worked as a producer for CNN in the Jerusalem bureau. She first went to Afghanistan in 2011 to report on women Marines working with combat units. She returned in 2013, twice, once to do stories about American military advisers working with the Afghan army and another time about the end of the U.S. war there. She has also reported from China, Haiti, and the Dominican Republic. Her work has appeared in Elle, Fast Company, San Francisco, *the* San Francisco Chronicle, *and* Reuters. *She loves to explore, the more off-the-beaten-path the better, and she will always happily hop on a plane for the far reaches of the planet with little more than a map and a camera.*

❧ ❧ ❧

Travels with Carly

Love in the time of travel.

"I'm pregnant," Carly said. It was only seven A.M. in Australia and her voice was still raspy. In my Skype box, she looked tired but happy—and totally unruffled—as she followed one confounding statement with another. "And I'm getting married."

"You're joking," I said. "I mean . . . you're not serious. Are you serious? You can't be serious."

Even after she assured me this wasn't an elaborate ruse designed to prey on my American gullibility, I couldn't properly absorb the news. Marriage? A baby? No way. Not Carly, my fiercely independent travel mate who acquired countries with the ease others amassed expensive shoes or clichéd life philosophies.

"Were you using protection?" I indelicately interrogated.

"No," she said.

"So you got pregnant on purpose?"

"No."

"I don't understand."

"Sometimes these things just happen."

"You do know how babies are made, right?" I asked.

Eventually, I managed to sputter out my congratulations, but I was grateful my old laptop lacked a webcam to broadcast my slack-jawed expression.

Carly and I have been friends for ten years. We met in Galway, Ireland, when we were both twenty. She was on her first round-the-world trip, and I was spending the summer before my final year of college alone in a foreign country to avoid living with either of my newly remarried parents and their respective spouses, a prospect I considered a Dantean form of torture reserved especially for children of divorce. After responding to an ad posted on the wall of an Internet café, I moved into a beat-up apartment near the river with Carly, a guy from Basque country on the dole, and a Spaniard who always dragged his chair closer to mine after a few drinks to not-at-all subtly expound on the particular talents of Spanish lovers.

Most mornings, hungover and heavy-limbed, the boys and I scrambled eggs, too hazy to notice the bits of shell mixed in. As we ate, I'd admonish them for forgetting in the previous night's reverie our house rule about stubbing out cigarettes on dinner plates. It made everything taste like ash, no matter how hard we scrubbed. Carly would already be at work by then. She waitressed at a local café where the owner only hired foreigners paid off the books. I took late-night shifts at student bars and seedy clubs, tottering around the latter in tight tops and uncomfortable heels while drunken Irishmen leered at my exposed midriff.

The first few weeks we lived together, Carly ignored me. We slept in the same small room, side by side in twin beds with scratchy comforters (doonas, she called them), but we barely spoke. It was only after she sliced her hand at work tossing a glass-filled garbage bag into the dumpster and couldn't waitress for a while that our schedules aligned and her icy indifference melted. I like to think it was my convincing impression of Steve Irwin the crocodile hunter, or my vast knowledge of Galway's best happy hours that won her over, but she might simply have been in a sunnier mood from not having to trudge to work at dawn every morning—not to mention the boon of weekly unemployment checks.

That summer I fretted nonstop about the postgraduate plans my friends were all making, while I had none.

"What's the rush?" Carly asked. All that mattered to her was seeing the world, and she had easily abandoned any trappings of conventional adulthood that might slow her in this pursuit. "Stay in Europe and go see some other countries," she counseled. "The longer you have student status, the better the travel discounts."

A professor's daughter, I had never considered higher education a means to secure cheap train tickets and two-for-one drink specials, and I'll admit the sacrilegious thought thrilled me.

Yet at summer's end I returned as planned to the U.S. to finish college. I was too afraid of disappointing my parents, whose happiness had long been intertwined with my academic achievements, and school still felt like the safest place to be. I'd always thrived on its comforting routine and carefully delineated work/reward system. Take this class. Write this paper. Live in this dorm. Simple. I was moving dangerously close to a world outside campus where I'd have to make up my own mind about my life, and I didn't feel ready for that leap.

I hoped to be bestowed with a sense of direction along with my diploma that rainy May graduation day, but of course no answers were forthcoming. Even my diploma itself was a blank piece of paper—the real document would be mailed in a few weeks. The English major in me appreciated the overt symbolism, but even symbols didn't satisfy me the way they once had, when I was a peppy freshman hopped up on James Joyce and Judith Butler.

"What do I do now?" I asked Carly a few weeks later.

"Come to Australia," she commanded.

It was a far more coherent plan than any I'd conjured. And though I wasn't yet brave enough to admit I wanted to keep traveling, I knew if I turned to Carly she'd give me the push and permission I needed.

After saving up waitressing tips for four months in Philadelphia, I moved in with Carly's family in Sydney, taking over her brother's bedroom while he was off backpacking in Europe for the year. Now half a world away, my parents' concerns for my future temporarily sated by the fact that my college degree was in hand, I gave myself over wholly to Carly's no-rush-no-worries philosophy. Australian time stretched and expanded like the Silly Putty I loved digging my thumbs into as a kid. I spent a few days a week working in a cafe where I butchered the coffee orders of Aussies whose accents didn't translate. The rest of the time Carly and I explored Sydney or swam in the ocean or gorged on mangoes in her kitchen while throwing around names of faraway cities we longed to explore: Istanbul, Prague, Calcutta, Buenos Aires.

Over breakfast one day, Carly announced that I should quit my job to travel up the coast the following week. "It'll be too hot soon," she said. I called my manager that morning. Quitting anything would have mortified the dutiful girl I had been mere weeks before, but I barely recognized her now. In Australia, far from societal and parental expectations, I had turned into a wild thing—or maybe just discovered I'd always been one.

After four months in Australia, Carly and I strapped on backpacks and took off for South America, looping from Argentina through Bolivia and Peru and back down through Chile.

There we let ourselves disappear for weeks at a time—still easy to do when reliable Internet was a rare species.

In South America, Carly convinced me to go skydiving and bungee jumping, white water rafting and paragliding. She instigated a seventeen-hour bus trip down Bolivia's "death road" and a swim in the piranha-infested Amazon with pink dolphins nipping our toes below murky waters. She was the reason I didn't go home after I got robbed in La Paz or even after a man with dark eyebrows and dirty fingernails put a purposeful hand between my legs and grabbed me hard midday on a crowded street. With Carly, I was a braver version of myself.

My parents remained an ever-present "no" voice in the back of my head: *don't get on that motorcycle, don't eat that street meat, don't stay in that sleazy Peruvian motel* (they were right about that last one, unless you believe coming-of-age adventures require bed bugs). But Carly's voice was the new "yes" counterpoint my early-twenties self needed to slough off the sheltered suburban girl I'd always been. *Do that. Eat this. Stay there.* It said other words I needed to hear, though sometimes I hated those hard lessons. *Toughen up. The world is not a fair place. You're not entitled to anything. No one can make the difficult choices for you.*

A few weeks after Carly's surprise announcements, I called with one of my own.

"My marriage is over."

"Come to Australia," she commanded, just like she had when we were twenty-two.

"I don't know. . . ." I wanted her to convince me and knew she would.

"How else are you going to get some perspective? You need space and time. You need the *ocean*." A week later, I depleted my meager savings account and booked a ticket to Sydney.

A child of divorce, I was cynical about marriage and had never intended to marry young. But while traveling in Peru, I'd fallen hard for a robustly bearded New Zealander. We quickly tired of long-distance courtship, and although I was only twenty-four, I refused to surrender the best relationship I'd ever had over an obstacle as trivial as geography. I had found a man who was smart and funny and sexy and, most intoxicatingly, loyal.

In what will be a familiar tale to anyone who has had the displeasure of ending a relationship in Manhattan without a trust fund or job in finance, I continued living in our one-bedroom apartment after we decided to split up. Our high-ceilinged, six-hundred-square-foot flat in Murray Hill had felt palatial when we moved in nine months earlier, gleefully fleeing our Upper East Side studio. That long last month, though, I felt overwhelmed by claustrophobia, boxed in tight with my husband and all our sadness. But I was too broke to rent anywhere on my own. My freelance writing income was unpredictable and unimpressive, and I was shell-shocked by the idea of losing all that our new appliances and exposed brick symbolized: that we were finally ascending in the world, though that's not something I realized even mattered to me until I was descending. At month's end, we both agreed I had to go, so I packed a bag and alighted on various friends' couches, depositing thank-you bottles of cheap sparkling wine like the Prosecco fairy in one kitchen after another.

I knew I wouldn't last through summer in New York like this. At the very least, I'd be unable to tolerate the relentless wall of heat that descends on the city in July and August. I also worried I wouldn't be able to see my way fully out of my marriage if I didn't do something geographically drastic.

Then there was the anger I could feel creeping in toward the city itself. When you're happy, Manhattan is wondrous. You feel buoyed by its beauty and spectacle. But being broke and vulnerable in Manhattan is like moving in with a socio-path. You can look for sympathy but you'll get none. Man-hattan doesn't care where you stay or who you have sex with or how much you drink. It doesn't even care if you move to one of those flyover states where your parents live. In fact, you probably should, to make way for someone tougher or younger or more successful. The city has no room for wrecks, despite the fact that it's teeming with them.

When I first moved to Manhattan, newly married, Carly came to visit for a month. I'd just sold a book, a travel memoir that focused on our friendship. I thought of it as akin to *On the Road* or *The Motorcycle Diaries*, though my agent pitched it as the next *Eat, Pray, Love*. During the days, I worked as an editorial assistant. At night, Carly and I lounged in bars, and she helped me work through scenes. Sometimes I wanted her to corroborate memories for me. Did you really say this? Did we really do that? Mostly I just wanted to write with her near me in order to capture that heady sense of freedom we'd felt traveling together.

Because as much as I desired the stability that marriage seemed to promise, I couldn't shake a feeling of confinement. Almost the moment after I said my vows, an internal tighten-ing had taken hold, like suddenly my lungs couldn't take in all the necessary air. It quickly became clear that my husband and I had incompatible notions about our relationship. What he saw as compromise I viewed as sacrifice, and often vice versa.

For a girl who once craved definition and order, traveling post-college had quickly hooked me on its opposite. I worried I'd never stop feeling restless, that my love for my husband was no match for my love of the limitless freedom I glimpsed, always, just beyond the horizon.

*   *   *

While I had spent my late twenties sinking deeper into my New York life and marriage, Carly had continued storming the world. She eventually wound up in a small Colombian town doing volunteer work. Her job was to accompany human rights organizations around the country, helping ensure no activists got hurt or disappeared—or both.

"So you're basically a human shield?" I said.

"That's putting it a bit dramatically," she assured me.

She was fluent in Spanish now, not like when we struggled through mimed exchanges in South America at twenty-two. When I called her in Colombia, I heard her switch effortlessly between languages when her colleagues shouted that dinner was ready or it was time for a meeting. I was proud but envious of the deep relationship she had developed with Latin America. I'd remained a more mercenary traveler, staying for short bursts in many different countries, never committing to one.

I knew Carly was dating someone named Deybi in Colombia, but she had never used the word "love," much less "baby" or "marriage." I assumed the relationship would end when she left the country, as all her previous ones had.

I wanted to feel happy for her, but I couldn't. For starters, I thought she was being foolish. It took my ex-husband years to rebuild his career and social network in the U.S. And the pressure it put on us—me always worrying if he was O.K., him missing home, both of us feeling like we had to stay together no matter what because it had taken so much work to *be* together—eventually took its toll. And now, in the wake of my relationship's demise, it was almost a personal affront that Carly had fallen in love with a foreigner who was leaving his country to live in hers.

I was also disappointed. Carly was my nomadic role model. While I'd traded adventure for domesticity, she had stayed wild. Now that I was cutting myself loose again at thirty, I wanted my travel mate back.

In my blackest moods, it all felt terribly unfair. Part of the reason Carly traveled so much, I always told myself, was pathological. She was addicted to being somewhere new. You didn't get the husband and baby if you were indulging an affair with the world. Yet here she was, having it all, and I resented that she could.

In the month leading up to my trip to Australia, I got myself so worked up about Carly's choices that I was almost angry at her when I landed, not to mention the grudge I was holding against her buzzkill baby. But my self-absorbed stance crumbled the moment she hugged me in the Arrivals Hall.

"I'm really happy you're here, mate," she said, as intense a sober expression of emotion as I'd ever witnessed from her.

We decided to drive downtown for dinner. My arrival coincided with the last few days of the Sydney Vivid Lights festival. Various landmarks around the waterfront were spectacularly lit up, and there seemed no better way to be reintroduced to the city than when it was aglow. We walked to the edge of the water and stared at the Opera House for a long time that first night. On its white sail-like appendages was a mesmerizing projected image of a woman performing slow acrobatics, her suspended body twisting and rolling along the grand structure.

We wanted to head to a less populated neighborhood to eat, but a few blocks into the walk Carly declared she was too tired to go much farther. A former competitive speed walker (with the middle-school medals to prove it), pregnant Carly moved at a much slower place. As we ambled up a small hill to the closest restaurants, she put her hand on my arm and breathed a little heavier. I thought back to the oxygen-deprived weeks we spent in high-altitude Bolivia in our twenties, how we sometimes just sat on the side of the road to rest, halfway to wherever we were lazily headed.

At dinner, Carly asked to smell my wine. "I don't miss the taste," she said. "But all of a sudden it smells *so* amazing." She took another deep inhalation and pushed the glass back.

"How is it being home?" I asked.

She shrugged and stared at her menu. "It's strange. I haven't felt like doing much. I miss Deybi. We try to Skype every day, but sometimes it's impossible for him to get to an Internet café. And Mum seems angry at me, like I've ruined her and Dad's retirement."

Carly's parents had recently sold their four-bedroom home and purchased a lovely little condo in Collaroy, a breezy beach town in the northern suburbs of Sydney whose main drag consisted of an ancient cinema and a few restaurants and shops. Now Carly was occupying their spare bedroom while saving money teaching English and waiting for her fiancé's months-long immigration issues to resolve themselves. It was obvious I hadn't been summoned to Australia only to escape my own life; Carly needed the distraction, too.

Still, a few days later, after she seemed sufficiently perked up by our new regimen of movies and long walks, I couldn't help peppering her with questions about her future, which struck me as precarious.

"How is Deybi planning to make a living in Australia?" I asked.

"He'll learn English. Then he'll work."

"What will he do?"

"Anything he can," she said. "Landscaping, maybe. Or construction."

"Where will you live?"

"In Sydney for a few years, and then we'll go back to Colombia and buy some land." At which point her father, pretending to read the newspaper, turned a shade of pale not normally seen on sun-weathered Australians.

"How are you going to keep traveling?"

"People travel with kids all the time," she said.

And then, without prompting, like she had known all along the question I really wanted to ask, she said, "I'm still going to be *me*, Rachel."

It was difficult to believe her, since I had recently failed so spectacularly at being "me" in my own marriage. Not that I was even certain who "me" was when I first got married, which was undoubtedly part of the problem. It had taken me five years to realize I didn't want to be someone's wife, or someone's mother. Not now, maybe, terrifyingly, not ever. And if *I* didn't want these traditional roles, how could Carly, who seemed born to defy convention, desire them?

Carly's fiancé's visa was approved halfway through my seven-week trip, and he arrived in Australia five days later. Although I was happy their separation was over, I worried about being an unwanted third wheel, but Deybi absorbed me into their little unit like we were old friends. He was intelligent and good-natured and totally in love with my friend. I watched as they started putting down the roots I had always assumed Carly eschewed. They rented a ramshackle house with a lemon tree in the front yard. They planned their beach wedding. And, of course, they prepared for and wondered about the baby on his way.

In the evenings, Carly curled into Deybi on the couch, his hands stroking her growing belly, her fingers crocheting a tiny yellow sweater. Watching this intimate ritual night after night, I finally understood Carly's choices. Deybi made her happy. Their baby made her happy. The house with the lemon tree made her happy. That this insta-family had not been planned didn't faze her. She put no stock in plans— never had—only in desire and action.

*   *   *

Once, after I had sent the final draft of my book to Carly, she called me up to complain about my portrayal of her in a certain chapter.

"You make me sound bossy," she said.

"Ummm. You are bossy," I said.

"No one has ever told me I'm bossy before."

"I'm sorry," I said, not knowing any other way to respond, worried both that I'd upset her and that she was going to ask me to change the scene.

A long silence held between us, during which I wondered if she was considering how dumb and unfair it was that I got to go around telling the story of our friendship, a version where she was a sidekick along for the ride of my self-evolution.

"Well, fuck it," she finally said, laughing into my ear.

I've spent much of my career writing about Carly. I seem to return endlessly to our friendship as a touchstone for understanding my own place in the world. In story after story, she functions as my foil. Everything from her blonde hair to her boldness contrasts with me.

Defining yourself in opposition to someone is a decent literary strategy, but a lousy life one. I've been unfair, expecting her to stay the same forever. I've been unfair to myself, too, for the same reasons. Carly craved more stability than she initially realized. I needed more freedom than I accounted for. Simple as that. Well, complicated as that.

Maybe in another five years our lives will be completely different. We'll want another career or country or person. Soaking up the winter sun one lazy afternoon, two days before my flight back to New York, I expressed to Carly how unnerving I found this uncertainty. She shrugged in her typical no-worries way: "That's life."

"Gee, thanks," I said. "Very helpful."

She chuckled, her now supremely pregnant belly shaking a little. "Sorry," she said. "That's all I've got."

ॐ ॐ ॐ

Rachel Friedman is the author of The Good Girl's Guide to Getting Lost: A Memoir of Three Continents, Two Friends, and One Unexpected Adventure. *It was selected by Goodreads' readers as one of the best travel books of 2011. She's written for* The New York Times, National Geographic Traveler, New York, BUST, Bitch, Creative Nonfiction, The Chronicle of Higher Education, Bon Appetit, *and* Nerve, *among others. She's a contributor to* The McSweeney's Book of Politics and Musicals *and* The Best Women's Travel Writing, Volume 9. *Her essay "Discovery" is listed as a notable piece in* The Best American Travel Writing 2013.

჻ ჻ ჻

The Grease Devil Is Not Real

The war may have been over, but the terror wasn't.

During my first two days on Sri Lanka's Jaffna Peninsula, I heard about the Grease Man from everyone who spoke English. He smeared his naked body in oil to evade capture, the villagers told me, and then snuck into homes to commit random acts of violence. Most people said he sexually assaulted women or bit their necks and breasts. One boy told me he had knives for fingers, which he used to cut out people's organs while they were sleeping. He hid in trees, the villagers believed, waiting for the right moment to pounce upon his victims—women drawing well water or children using the outhouse. One man thought Grease Men were just common thieves, profiting from the rumors to take advantage of a cowed populace. But most people spoke of him in the singular, as if he were a mythical demon. What everyone agreed on was that the Grease Man was either protected by government soldiers or was a soldier himself.

During Sri Lanka's thirty-year civil war between the Sinhalese Buddhist majority and the mainly Hindu Tamil minority, Jaffna was the unofficial capital of the separatist Tamil Tigers. The LTTE, as the Tigers are known in Sri Lanka, was vanquished in 2009 in a no-holds-barred offensive that killed tens of thousands of civilians in five months. Since then, the Sri Lankan Army has occupied the Tamil-dominated areas of the North and East. Shortly before I arrived in Sri Lanka last August, the government had lifted restrictions on travel to the formerly contested Northern Province. I had backpacked throughout Sri Lanka before and was eager to see a new part of the country I loved.

A few days after I got to Jaffna, I spent an afternoon in an Internet café, trying to make sense of these Grease Man rumors. "Grease Devils" had been sighted in Muslim and Tamil areas throughout Sri Lanka. Several women claimed they'd been followed or attacked. Facing police apathy, villagers had armed themselves with clubs and machetes. At least two suspected Grease Men were hacked to death. Police had arrested dozens of men for vigilante attacks. The defense secretary issued a warning that vigilantism was "akin to terrorism" and would receive "the maximum punishment." But even as authorities denied the existence of a Grease Devil threat, Sri Lankan TV was continually airing a terrifying photo of a teenager vaguely identified as a "suspect." Covered in white face paint, he bared his reddened teeth and flared his nostrils; fake blood poured from his mouth. Absurdly, the terrifying photo accompanied the message: "The Grease Devil is not real."

A young man interrupted my Internet reading to welcome me to his city. Wide-faced with thick black curls, he spoke the best English I'd heard anywhere in Sri Lanka. Kumar used to be a translator for NGOs and now worked as an English teacher. His pudgy cheeks and flawless skin made him look much younger than twenty-eight. He asked me what I thought of Jaffna.

I had spent the morning wandering the city center, thick with noise and motion. Autorickshaws swerved around women carrying baskets of chilies and mangoes on their heads.

Trucks blared their horns at bicyclists. A soldier stood on the edge of a field where boys played cricket. He would be there all day, sweating in his leather boots, shifting his rifle from one shoulder to the other. I turned down a narrow road that led to the sea, and the landscape shifted so dramatically that I found myself standing still, one hand over my open mouth. The fruit stands and tea shops and brick houses gave way to a warscape of bullet-riddled walls with no roofs, the ruins of former homes. Babies' cries rang out from behind old sheets that covered holes in the walls.

Kumar looked at me expectantly. "I'm very happy to be in your city," I said.

He invited me to his home for dinner, and I hopped on the back of his motorbike. "Thank you for trusting me," he said. It hadn't occurred to me that this was a matter of trust.

His parents' two-room brick house was shuttered and locked, but the curtains were backlit by the green glow of the TV. Kumar banged on the door, calling out his name. "My mother is afraid of the Grease Man," he said. He grinned, but he sounded apologetic. Kumar's mother opened the door. Kumar introduced me in Tamil. His mother took my hands and beamed. We effused in our respective languages. Kumar's brother clapped his hands and pronounced his joy to meet an American lady. Rajesh was twenty. He had large, attentive eyes and a sudden, raucous laugh, and he wanted to be a famous singer. In the meantime, he worked as a public health inspector. While their mother prepared rice and curry, I asked Rajesh and Kumar for their theories on the Grease Man.

"How could he enter the village with a sentry point on every corner? He operates through the blessing of the soldiers," Rajesh said in his elegant but imperfect English. Kumar glanced through the open door to the alley outside their house. It had only taken me a few hours in Jaffna to become familiar with the habitual furtiveness of discussions about the war and the current occupation.

"Do you think it's possible the Grease Man is just a rumor the government started?" I asked. "A way to keep Tamils under control since the emergency laws ended?"

A few days before I got to Jaffna, President Rajapaksa had acquiesced to international pressure to end emergency laws, which had allowed the government to displace residents, detain people without trial, and operate secret prisons. The government stood to benefit from the Grease Man rumor. People who are afraid are less likely to organize or to make demands. Most of Jaffna stayed home after dark, locking themselves in their sweltering brick houses, each family separate and afraid.

"They want to scare us, yes," Rajesh said. "But the Grease Man is real." Outside, a stray dog lay in the rectangle of smoky light cast by the doorway. He sat in the empty road, picking at fleas.

This was during the annual Nallur festival, honoring the god Murugan, protector of the Tamil people. Every morning and evening, nearly all of Jaffna crowded into the sandy grounds around the Nallur Kandaswamy Kovil, a garish temple surrounding a holy pool that has cleansed Hindu pilgrims for centuries.

One evening, I joined Kumar among the throngs of worshippers. Women wore heavy gold jewelry and brilliant silk saris. Men in red *dhotis* clashed cymbals and beat handheld drums as they belted out devotional songs, so enrapt that their faces registered grief. Toddlers on their fathers' shoulders stared wide-eyed at the statue that had been erected for the festival, a three-story-high replica of a temple, affixed with hundreds of light bulbs. The huge triangle of white light began to move, seeming to float through the crowd. It took me a moment to realize that it was attached to a rope, pulled by dozens of laughing, groaning boys. I was carried by the tide of the crowd as the tower of fluorescent light bore down on us. Somehow being packed inside a mass of quickly moving strangers was freeing rather than claustrophobic. With perfect, mysterious synchronization, the crowd would occasionally raise their hands and cry out, "*Haro Hara!*"

"When everyone looks at the god together, it gives him power," Kumar said. "And then that power comes back to us."

The next morning, I walked into town for breakfast. A squat man with slick salt-and-pepper hair fell in step beside me. "With whom did you travel to Jaffna?" he asked in stilted English. He was an engineer and had lived in Jaffna since riots, in 1983, forced him out of Colombo. In reprisal for the Tamil Tigers' first attack—an ambush that killed thirteen Sinhalese soldiers—Sinhalese mobs rampaged through the capital, beating, crucifying, and burning Tamils alive. "The mobs were not average people," the engineer said. "They were antisocial elements. The government used them for its own ends." He escaped Colombo with the help of Sinhalese friends.

I asked the engineer if he believed the government was using the Grease Man for its own ends. "Of course!" he said. "About a year ago, it was the white vans. Black windows, no identity plates. They abducted people. Sometimes hurt them and let them go. Sometimes gone. The authorities say it is a mystery. But to the people it is no mystery." He glanced around and lowered his voice. "The people are missing the LTTE. They had their minus points, but at least we had some bargaining power. But we have much hope the Americans will save us. We love Hillary Clinton." He hoped she would pressure the government to house internally displaced Tamils and abolish the Prevention of Terrorism Act, which authorizes indefinite detention.

"Do you know that we have the same law in our country?" I explained that several laws passed since 9/11 empowered the president to arrest and jail non-U.S. citizens without charging them with a crime. The engineer was shocked. He had never heard of Guantanamo.

On our way to the temple one morning, Kumar and I passed a lorry with a makeshift wooden crane attached to the roof. A man in a loincloth hung from the crane, suspended from four thick hooks that pierced the skin of his calves and upper back. Another man, also clad in a loincloth, stood atop the crane, pulling up on a rope attached to the hooks. The hooked man waved palm fronds—slowly, methodically—as he bounced. His face was utterly impassive, as if he were withstanding the experience by willfully vacating it. "He is in a trance," Kumar said admiringly.

We took off our shoes and left them beneath the carved arches at the entrance. Women prostrated themselves before the statues, touching their heads to the cold stone floor and gazing at the gaudy wooden deities. I sat on the limestone steps that led down to the holy pool. Shadows of clouds moved across the surface of the water. Slow drumbeats sounded outside the temple.

"Can we sit here for a little while?" I asked.

"Why not?" Kumar said. "It is our temple."

On my way out of my guesthouse to meet Kumar one day, I passed four teenage boys standing in the shade of a tamarind tree. They called after me in Tamil, jeering tones followed by hollow laughter. Kumar was across the street, straddling his bike with the motor running. He handed me my helmet before he even said hello. "Those boys are gangsters," he said after we'd begun moving. "Do not talk to them, O.K.?"

He was taking me to the Dutch fort, which was a battleground during the war, oscillating between LTTE and army control. The government was now reconstructing the star-shaped, colonial relic as a tourist attraction. Inside the arched gateway, jagged hunks of limestone were piled nearly two stories high. "You see how strong the bombs were," Kumar said.

At the upper level of the fort, an upturned tree grew parallel to the earth, its roots gripping the remains of a stone wall.

"With LTTE, we had no gangsters," Kumar said. "It was so safe. But it was also too strict." Thieves and gangsters were beaten or shot. Women had to keep their legs covered and mostly stay at home. American movies and music were forbidden. "Because if you enjoy the life, you don't want to fight. But I listened anyway. With the computer, you can get everything. You like Michael Jackson?"

I shrugged.

"I could not live without Michael. He taught me English. You know 'Man in the Mirror'?"

We sang the chorus together. Kumar lifted his fist into the air at the climax. I felt a brief, stupid pride in my country.

I asked if it was worse when the LTTE was in control.

"I'd say fifty-fifty badness. The worst is when there's fighting. As long as one group is in control, it's O.K."

Kumar said that his uncles had been repairmen, so the LTTE ordered them to build barracks. Not wanting to get mixed up with the Tigers, they paid a fisherman to row them the fifty miles to India. They worked odd jobs for years, until they had enough money to get to Europe. Now they are in Germany. One is an engineer, the other a businessman. When I told my Sinhalese friend that I was going to Jaffna, she said, "You can meet all the Tamils who are mistreated by the Sinhalese." She rolled her eyes. When I started to argue, she said, "Don't feel sorry for them. They are all rich. So many Tamils living abroad are sending money."

The far end of the fort was grassy and empty. A bird landed on the parapet and cawed at us. "We should go back," Kumar said. "There are no people here."

"Is it dangerous?"

"It's just—we try always not to be in an empty place. This is army land, right? They have control. So if it's me against four or five guys—we don't want to find out." He laughed and started walking back toward the entrance.

While Kumar's mother taught me to make *pittu*—a steamed mash of roasted flour and coconut—Rajesh climbed up and down trees in their backyard, gathering fruit for me to taste. It was early morning. Kumar had offered to take me to the beach after breakfast.

I was stupidly happy on the back of his motorbike, hurtling toward a place I could never find on my own. We rode over a flat, paved bridge that led to one of the tiny, inhabited islands off Jaffna's coast. Fish nets tied to wooden stakes jutted out of the shallow sea. Silver fish jumped out of the water and hurled themselves against the netting, so pretty as their breath drained away. On the island, Kumar's bike was the only vehicle in sight, flying through a field of tall, dry sea grass interrupted by piles of colorful rubbish and the concrete foundations of former homes.

"There's so much land out here," I shouted over the bike's rattling engine. "It's awful to think of all those people living in refugee camps when they could be building houses here." Hundreds of thousands of civilians displaced by the war had yet to be returned home. And most of the people who had been "resettled" were given no government assistance; they lived with family or in one of the bombed-out houses.

"There is land here, yes," Kumar said. "But the army is here. So if they want, they will take." He spoke just loudly enough to be heard over the wind. There was no anger in his voice.

We passed two checkpoints as we approached the beach. Kumar showed his I.D. I stared at the ground while the soldiers stared at me. The beach had white sand, tall palm trees, emerald water. It was easy to imagine planting a resort there, Europeans in tanning oil drinking rum out of coconuts. A resort would mean that Sri Lanka was O.K. at last; Jaffna had gone through hell and come out on the other side. For now, a couple of families splashed in the glassy water, the women in cotton saris and the men in jeans. It wasn't as weird to swim in my clothes as I imagined it would be. My beige skirt clung to my legs when we left the ocean. Sand burning my feet, I ran on tiptoe to a palm tree and bought a mango from a boy who looked about seven. As he sliced it into neat strips, three more boys flocked to my side, shaking bags of palmyrah bark and oranges. I bought one bag from each boy, even though I hated thinking of their parents sending them to hawk fruits on the beach.

"Boyfriend?" the boys asked, grinning and pointing to Kumar.

"No, no. We are friends."

I'd never been friends with a man in Sri Lanka before. There was no reason to speak to them, no good that could come from it. Heterosexual friendships did not exist here. Men and women were either relatives or suitors. But Kumar was a one-way glass panel, allowing me to glimpse Sri Lanka's violent history without ever feeling threatened myself.

We sat at the base of the tree, taking bites of bright orange flesh. "You know, in the U.S.," I said, "it's totally normal for men and women to be just friends. Like we are."

"I know. Here it is so strict." Kumar's index finger traced circles in the sand near my foot. I finished the mango and suggested we head back to town.

At Kumar's house that night, Rajesh was irate about an attack in a village called Navanthurai. "Some Grease Devils try to get a woman and she calls for help," he told me. "The villagers chase the Grease Devils, and the Devils run inside the army camp. So the Grease Men are hiding in the army camp and the villagers are saying, 'Let us catch them,' and they throw rocks toward the camp. And then that night the soldiers go into the homes and they take all the men out from the beds and beat the men and take them to the jail." He was nearly shouting. "They must pass the night in jail with these brutal injuries. In the morning, the magistrate sees the men and orders they go to hospital."

"How do you know all this?" I asked. It was hard to have faith in someone so indignant, no matter how inclined I was to trust. Rajesh fetched a newspaper and turned to a spread of photos of men with bandaged heads and limbs, some of them in wheelchairs. "After I read this, I go to the hospital. I see this with my eyes." He jabbed the air with his finger.

Kumar opened a large bottle of lager. "Do you want beer?" I never drank in Sri Lanka, out of respect for the gendered cultural prohibitions. But this time I nodded yes.

"I know there are some good Sinhalese," Rajesh said, sitting back down. He sounded magnanimous, the same tone my Sinhalese friend took when she spoke of Tamils. She would not hate a whole race, even if her only association with them was bomb scares, just as the only Sinhalese people Rajesh knew were soldiers. The ethnic rivalry seemed to become more entrenched with each generation.

"Do you have any Sinhalese friends?" I asked Kumar.

He lived in Colombo for a little while after he finished his studies, working at KFC. He had Sinhalese friends there. He liked living in the capital, but every time there was a bomb scare, the police arrested Tamils indiscriminately. So he moved back to Jaffna, like almost all Tamils. Or they went abroad if they could. "One time, I was going to a restaurant with my friend," he said, "but then I decided I was tired and went home. My friend went to the restaurant and the police were there and they got him. So I was saved by not eating." He took a sip of beer and patted the mound of his lower stomach. "Maybe if I stayed in Colombo, I wouldn't have this rice belly."

His laugh was interrupted by the eerie whistle of ammunition arcing through the air and exploding nearby. I looked at Kumar, my eyes wide. "Shelling," he said.

"You still hear that? Why?"

"Probably soldiers training. They must train, right?" He shrugged.

When he dropped me off at my guesthouse, Kumar told me about some videos he saw on the Internet. "It must have been soldiers who took the videos. Some soldiers who felt bad. Because even someone who would participate in these things, he must have some humanity. The principal of my school told me to watch them. He said, 'Before I was not pro-LTTE. But since I watched these videos, I support LTTE.'" Kumar's whisper was barely audible. "I thought, this is what happened to my people. So I watched. It is more horrible than you can imagine. It took me two hours to come back to normal after watching. The most brutal thing one human being can do to another." Wind rustled the thick banana leaves.

"Please don't tell me." My voice was too loud.

"These videos should not exist," Kumar continued. "It just makes Tamils hate. We must forget. Because we cannot fight. We will not win." I opened my mouth to argue that the victims of war crimes deserve for the truth to be known. Kumar spoke first. "Of course," he said, "if it was my brother in those videos, I would have to revenge. I would have no choice." I shut my mouth.

The next day, after breakfast in town, I walked two dusty miles to the newspaper office. In a neighborhood of jewelry and liquor stores, the office was down a narrow alleyway and up a dark flight of stairs. A life-size cardboard cutout of Gandhi marked the entrance. A lanky man with a pockmarked face walked up to me and stared intently. I asked if he could tell me about the attack in Navanthurai. He motioned to an empty chair at a table and sat down opposite me. He wore a plaid shirt missing a button and smelled faintly of women's perfume. His name was Sanjeev and he was the editor in chief. All of the imprisoned men from Navanthurai had been released on bail, he said. No one knew what happened to the suspected Grease Devils.

"How did you get here?" he asked. His eye contact was steady.

"I walked. From town."

"They know you're here."

"The security forces?"

"They will notice an American woman here. You should know. Be a little careful."

"Do they constantly watch your office?"

"Of course. We have the harassment, the abductions. Last month, one of my colleagues was beaten. Right outside his home. He is getting better day by day but he will not write again. He has a family. When are you leaving Sri Lanka?"

"In a week."

"Good." He nodded once. I thought of the red-eyed men outside the liquor stores who would stare at me as I walked out of the office.

"The people are missing the LTTE," the editor said tonelessly.

"But weren't they really strict—shooting people in the street and torturing—"

"With the LTTE, there was no theft, no rape. Immediate punishment for such crimes. Rape has increased much since the war ended. Widows are not safe."

"Didn't they recruit children? Didn't they force people to fight?"

"That was the only mistake they made, in the last months of the war. Because they didn't have help. We should have helped. We were enjoying the life while our brothers were sacrificing." Turning away from Sanjeev's small, intense eyes, I said that I was hoping to write an article about the Grease Man. Could he connect me with people who had been attacked?

"Of course I will help you. The international media is our only hope." He told me to call him in the morning. He would take me to Navanthurai.

But the next day Sanjeev never answered his mobile phone. When I showed up at his office, a nervous, well-dressed young man told me Sanjeev was busy today; please could I return tomorrow? I walked to another newspaper. The rotund editor in chief invited me in to his office. His secretary served us tea and chili doughnuts. The editor clapped his hands in joy when he learned that an American lady was writing about the Grease Devil. I asked him to tell me everything he knew about the army raid in Navanthurai. He repeated the story I'd heard from Rajesh, adding that one of his reporters believed two girls had been raped. I asked if he could connect me with some of the villagers. "Oh no. The people will not give a statement. Because if they give a statement, tomorrow they will be nowhere." He reached into his desk and retrieved a camera. With no warning, he snapped two photos of me. "To remember my American colleague," he said, beaming. He walked me to the door. I asked if he knew of anyone in Jaffna who'd seen a Grease Devil, if any of the journalists on his staff had ever been beaten or disappeared. "I have much work," he said, and left me standing alone in his gravel yard.

I found a pay phone and called Kumar. "Would it be dumb of me to go to the Security Forces office?" I asked, referring to the public relations unit of the Sri Lankan Army. "I just wonder what they would tell a foreigner about the Grease Man."

"Do not go to the Security Forces, Hannah," he said slowly and evenly, as if explaining the obvious to a child. "Your plane leaves soon, and I think you want to be on it."

*   *   *

I spent the next five mornings fruitlessly harassing the staff
of Jaffna's four newspapers. I spent the next five afternoons
waiting for hours to meet with local government officials (all
Tamil), each of whom directed me to another official who
would be sure to answer my basic questions about security
zones and landmines and displaced people. No one, including
Kumar, would help me meet someone who had witnessed a
Grease Devil attack. The day before I was to leave Jaffna, I
returned yet again to Sanjeev's office and begged his young
employee to let me speak with him; I needed some basic facts
if I was to have a story at all. The young man listened, nodded, and disappeared into the office's only room with a door.
He returned several minutes later. "I am sorry, but our editor
cannot see you," he said. "He is sleeping."

It seemed that even the man with the most rebellious job in
town believed Jaffna's only hope for normalcy was to pretend
that everything was normal.

On my last night in Jaffna, I went to the *Kovil* with Kumar. We
got jostled among well-groomed women making coconut offerings and shirtless men rolling in the sand around the perimeter,
moving so fast Kumar promised they would vomit when they
stood up. A baby girl with holy ash smeared on her forehead
giggled atop her father's shoulders. The Grease Man felt like a
stupid horror movie playing in the background of a party.

The silence of the thick, black air was unsettling on the
ride back. I gripped the seatback as Kumar leaned into sharp
turns and swerved around a stray dog curled in the middle
of the road. Kumar picked up speed as we passed the neighborhood of bombed-out houses. Through a doorless doorway,
a woman's legs jutted out beside a flickering oil lamp. Her
face was in darkness. Kumar started to slow down. Slivers

of silvered light in the center of the road resolved themselves into stop signs, held aloft by soldiers. As Kumar eased off the gas, five soldiers fanned out across the street, blocking our way. One shined a flashlight in our faces. His gun was wider than his thigh. This is when it happens, I thought. I felt the helmet on my head, the hot space between its hard dome and my scalp. The bike stopped. Kumar touched his feet down to steady us. We were less than ten yards from the entrance to my guesthouse. They followed me home from the newspaper. They would punish Kumar for my interest in the Grease Man attack, my compulsion to carry a war story back home.

The soldiers formed a semicircle around the bike. The man with the flashlight walked up to us. He planted his feet in an awkwardly wide stance and crossed his arms over his chest. Kumar reached into his back pocket and handed the soldier a small plastic rectangle. The soldier glanced at the I.D., handed it back. He stepped away from the bike and waved us through. The soldiers gathered on the side of the road to let us pass. Kumar thanked them in English, their common language. I looked at the lead soldier's face as we drove away. He looked sheepish, almost deferential.

My heart was still pounding as I stood at the gate to my guesthouse. "Are you O.K.?" I asked Kumar.

"Fine. No problem." He waved his hand through the air, unconsciously imitating the soldier's gesture of release. A porch light flicked on. My guesthouse owner walked out and stared menacingly at the source of our voices. Kumar said he would miss me. His eyes were huge and teary. "I'll miss you, too," I said with false cheeriness. "Please tell your family thank you and goodbye." I walked up to my rented room, taking the steps two at a time.

A few weeks after I returned home, Kumar sent an email to tell me about his brother's new job and the play he was

directing in his English class. There was a postscript saying
that the police had taken two Grease Men into custody; the
threat was over, for now. A few months later, Sri Lankan
media mentioned the incident for probably the last time.
Forensic experts, funded partly by the state, had pronounced
the Grease Devil phenomenon nothing more than mass hys-
teria. After interviewing six supposed victims of Grease Man
attacks, the doctors concluded that their injuries were either
self-inflicted or caused by "a friendly hand."

Hannah Tennant-Moore writes for The New Republic, n+1,
and New York Times *book reviews. Her work also appears
in such places as* Los Angeles Review of Books, The Paris
Review Daily, *and* Tin House, *and received an honorable mention in* The Best American Travel Writing 2011. (Names in
this story have been changed.)

❧ ❧ ❧

Balloons Over Burma

Warmly Welcome and Take Care of Tourists.

I was eighteen when I attended my first festival in a brown field seventy miles south of Toronto. Waiting three hours on the highway in my friend Stephanie's Suburban to get in, I resorted to changing my tampon in a bush, the entire parade of cars cheering me on. I danced for two days without changing my clothes or eating solid food and found the live-for-the-moment experience a cure-all for the pains of teenaged life.

Fourteen years and countless festivals later, I see no end.

After a three-hour-delayed flight on a dubious airline owned by drug traffickers (yes, I feel guilty, but it was that or the sixteen-hour bus) plus an overpriced hour-long cab ride, Deano and I arrive in Nyaungshwe, a touristy but welcoming town on Inle Lake's northern tip in Myanmar. We trek the dusty streets past orderly rows of child monks and bicycling grandpas with benevolent smiles, and when I catch sight of a paper sign that reads, "Shared taxis to Taunggyi Fire Balloon Fest," I squeeze Deano's hand—we're in.

It can be awkward, looking for a party in a strange town. A week later, I will show up in Baguio, Philippines for a tribal dance festival that doesn't exist. I will swear to Jose at the tourism board that it's right on his company website, but he'll just laugh and suggest strawberry picking instead. So this paper sign, scrawled in sharpie and posted on the wall of a corner "travel agency" (or let's be honest, man with phone), is merciful validation. I book a driver for the next day, trying not to wince at the seventy USD price tag, check into our hotel and marvel at the lengths I'm willing to go, *still*, for a good time.

Egging me on now is Deano, who loves festivals at least as much as I do. It was the first thing we bonded over as new Craigslist roommates, painting his room in dodgy swathes of white. Two months later, he'd utter his first "I love you," during the Fatboy Slim set at Coachella. Two months after that, we were flying to England for Glastonbury, where, four years later he'd propose, terrified of dropping the one-of-a-kind Art Deco ring in the mud.

Along with the significant, festivals are also about the fleeting, random moments. A high-five with a stranger in an Indian headdress. An impromptu conga line. A power station of dancing hippos in the middle of a crowd. The ritual of getting loose en masse exists in many cultures, but the ways in which to do it are infinite, and I intend to experience them all. Even the slightly dangerous ones, like Taunggyi.

"Don't go near the balloons."

That's PK, our hotel porter. Fanning his fingers between us, the shocking whites of his eyes popping against the velvet night, he mimics the cry of a failed balloon with a sharp, "POW!"

Later, over a traditional Shan meal of tomato and tofu salads, restaurant owner Susu is so frenzied in her descriptions, the whimsical bow in her hair band quivers with excitement.

"Big explosion!" Susu cries.

"Do people get hurt?" I ask.

"Oh yes, yes," she admits, "Every year at least a few."

Two hundred people in fact, going back to 2009. As for other years, records are scarce. But every festival has its risks, I reason. You could get trampled, arrested, so high you never come back. Never mind the discomfort—crowds that move like drying cement; hot, stinking loos; the chance of getting sloshed by a flying cup of piss. Still, if I'm honest with myself, I must concede: Taunggyi Fire Balloon Festival is some next-level shit.

Spanning a week in mid-November in the sunflower-fringed Shan Hills, this Buddhist tradition aims to keep evil spirits at bay by offering elaborate, fire-powered balloons to sky-dwelling "devas" or superhuman beings. There are three types: brightly colored animal-shaped balloons; elegant candlelit balloons called *Seinnaban;* and the explosive balloons, *Nya Mie Gyi,* whose minutes-long spectacles and sometimes catastrophic misfirings are what make the festival so notorious. Indeed, *The Myanmar Times* has called Taunggyi Fire Balloon Festival a "raucous pyromaniac's playground."

The next morning, at an hour and fifteen minutes past our eleven o'clock pick up time, our driver, Kon Sai finally appears and ushers us into a shiny white sedan. A twenty-year-old bleached blond in skinny jeans, he conducts himself in hipster silence. About halfway into our hour-long drive, we begin our ascent of the Shan Hills, the scenery shifting from flat and soggy to steep and dry. We pass ferns and wildflowers, a skyscraper-tall waterfall thin and sharp as an icicle, and a winery with white-haired Europeans crowding the entrance. Soon we're rounding a traffic circle in Taunggyi, past a conspicuous blue sign reading, "Warmly Welcome and Take Care of Tourists."

Parting ways with Kon Sai, we resist setting a meeting time. Who knows how we'll feel in five, ten hours? Instead, we take down his number, trust in Burmese goodwill (and cell phone reception) and say something like: "Oh look, there's a green and red parrot on fire!"

We arrive at the action as the exploded five-meter-tall parrot hits the ground, a small team of men rushing to the scene to douse its flaming wooden ribs. How quickly a puffed up parrot becomes a steaming parrot carcass. And a jungle gym for the kids.

Next up, a fat grayish dove, held aloft by a team of about twenty. I attempt to make friends with some of them, posing generic questions like, *So how long did it take to make this? What's your team called? What's this supposed to be?* but quickly learn from a dapper attendee in a long black coat that at six weeks' preparation and an investment of three thousand U.S. dollars for some of the more elaborate balloons (or ten times the average local's salary), launching time is no time to kibbitz.

A makeshift band spurs on Team Gray Dove with crashing cymbals and bamboo sticks taped with golden trails of ribbon. Three or four team members with torches huddle in the balloon's gaping underbelly, gingerly lighting its giant "flame stick."

"This is what makes it go," explains my dapper new friend.

"But what's to keep the balloon from catching fire?" I wonder.

"Ah," he answers, "The paper."

This special Shan paper is dipped in oil and wax for several days. And sure enough, when the wick has been sufficiently torched and the team breaks into a sprint, giving the balloon momentum, it is the fiery center that powers Gray Dove's lift-off, fast and hillwards, above a transfixed crowd.

The cymbal crashing and bamboo thwacking intensify as the team erupts in cheer, parading a gold tinfoil reindeer above their heads, like a winning football team with their star player. The chubby gray dove ascends quickly until it's barely a scratch on the gray sky.

But most balloons are failures. A horned bird has a hasty start, its head exploding in a tailspin of char. A pink hoofed beast is caught in a wind current, swiftly crashing into a mercifully vacant snack stand. A green dragon puffs smoke from its jagged red mouth but fails to launch. As it down-grades to a raging fire with woefully atrophied limbs, the fickle crowd moves on, leaving dejected team members to beat their failed entry with a stick.

With each launch (or non-launch), a judge appears at the scene in a curiously flammable straw hat. He marks down three key results in a notebook—quickest to launch, height reached, and aesthetic appeal. I ask him who's winning and get shooed away like an errant moth.

I pose for a man with a smartphone camera and telltale red teeth of a betel nut fiend. I pose for another who grins mani-cally, asking if I'm "happy."

"Of course!" I respond, as only a girl amongst exploding balloons, roughly eight thousand miles from home, can.

The rain politely waits for the daytime portion of the pro-gram to finish, then comes down hard. We buy two large, true-to-name Dagon Extra Strongs and take refuge in a noodle booth. Beer becomes our stopgap between the day and evening balloons (with a necessary switch to the lighter "Myanmar" brand). We had hoped for live music, especially since Burmese music is so alluring, all shimmery psychedelic waves coasting on a bed of dirty, syncopated rhythms. But with the exception of "Gangnam Style" blaring from some of the vendor booths and a taped 1990-ish performance of what looks like the Asian Spice Girls, tunes are surprisingly scarce.

We will later learn from a guide named Win Win that there typically *is* music. It was banned this year in reaction to the recent bombings that injured an American woman in Yangon and killed three. That live music might spark further tragedy over say, explosive-laced balloons, themselves a sort of sanctioned bomb, is to us an interesting perspective.

But we don't dwell on the tunelessness for long. Beyond the barred fence of our crowd-facing lounge are two teenaged girls, studying me like keen primatologists. One is pale skinned, round faced and, though she can't know it yet, pop-star beautiful. The other is darker and thin with a more tomboyish look, her chin-length hair hanging casually from a wool cap. When I finally catch their eye through the bars, they are gleefully startled, erupting in a mountain of giggles. So begins our game of peek-a-boo, back and forth until Deano says, "Look, they're calling you over."

I lean over the fence, dazed, as Pop Star presses a folded something into my hand. Go back to my table. Open it. Blush.

A vital warmth spreads through my body (or is that just the beer?). It's not the first time I'm touched by the unbridled sweetness of Burmese locals. To encounter people without agenda, people genuinely thrilled to have visitors in their midst, can be for the Westerner like refocusing a lens and seeing possibility where once you saw doom. Entering Myanmar for the first time, I was prepared for a certain solemnity. I'd heard much about the joie de vivre of the people, about the country's "authentic," "lost in time" ambience. Still, nothing could lift the cloak my brain had placed over the country with two names (and many more opinions on which is correct, and why). Years of reading about human rights abuses as repressive and savagely violent as anything the world has seen, of following the plight of housebound political prisoner Aung San Suu Kyi and watching gruesome documentaries like *Burma VJ* in which the Yangon River flows with fresh monk's blood, it was impossible to approach this trip with the same giddiness I'd have for say, well . . . Glastonbury. And while the two-year-old quasi-democracy has brought significant, even miraculous improvements, minority villages are still lynched, a genocide rages on, and the longstanding fear that anyone can disappear at any time is not easily shrugged. It is against this backdrop that I prepared for solemnity. Yet what I've gotten so far is joy.

I look up from the note to see the girls steadying each other against their convulsive laughter. Wave. In half a beer, we'll be friends.

We shimmy onto a blanket with Lwin Htwe (pop star) and Ya Ya (tomboy), and bowls of soup and popcorn are thrust excitedly into our hands. The girls are fifteen and "sisters," though with their very different looks, I may have misunderstood. There is also Mom, chatty and radiant, an older sister strapped with a baby, a pretty twenty-something cousin, and her fine-boned husband. Between them, they have about twelve words of English to my two words of Burmese, so we communicate with charades and laughter. Lots of laughter, though I'd be lying if I said what about. I just know we feel instantly absorbed by this family, untroubled with personal space, free to tug at shirtsleeves and tease Mom.

They have endless questions: *how do you like Myanmar* (love it!), *what is your age* (old) and *where do you come from* (a distant outcrop called *Cal-i-fornia*). We throw our arms around each other for photos, and they coo over the results beaming from Deano's DSLR screen. I get the feeling this joyful encounter is one of those random, fleeting festival moments that become emblems of my festival-going career. This simple act of strangers from strange lands acknowledging each other's humanity is like live music or explosive balloons, an attraction in itself.

Darkness falls around us like a lowering tarp, the nighttime activities sparking to life. There's a distant Ferris wheel, and we wonder if it's human-powered, like the one we saw on Anthony Bourdain.

"Go, go!" urges Ya Ya with carpe-diem urgency.

"You sure?" I ask.

"Go!"

So we go, vowing to return. The Ferris wheel is in a lively carnival section of whirring attractions studded with colored bulbs and a fever-pitch devotion to "Gangnam Style." The crowd has thickened since daytime, the grounds have muddied. Jostling my way to the wheel, I lament my choice of pastel blue shoes.

The Ferris wheel is indeed human-powered, a large handful of very lean boys working together to create and curb momentum. Some climb the ascending side, pumping the wheel with their arms, then hang on, legs dangling as it rushes around, jumping off just before they're toast. One stands directly under the wheel's path—as cabins hurtle toward him, he uses both arms and the weight of his meager body to thrust them onward, knees bent so deeply his tailbone hits the ground each time. The boys call giddily to each other, flashing grins.

A wildly swinging compartment slows to a stop, and in a flurry of excited shouting and skinny limbs, two of the boys usher us inside (but not before I walk flat into a wooden Ferris wheel spoke). We smile at our cabin mate, a twenty-something monk with the classic smooth head and loose scarlet robe. He's far from chatty, but he makes up for it in rising excitement, revealing blackened teeth in a wide, boyish grin as we creakily ascend. Suddenly we're rushing forward in the fastest Ferris wheel ride of my life. (And oldest. And most prone to collapse.) As the ride operators clamber around us and I hear snatches of "Gangnam Style" plus the *ding* of carnival games and the monk's shrieks of terror with every drop and jerk, and see him ghoulishly rolling his eyes, I feel we have fused with Taunggyi Fire Balloon Festival. I wave with abandon at the cabin next to us and they erupt in cheers.

At 8:30, the first night balloon appears. We're halfway up a hill on a potato sack, procured from a roaming vendor for fifty cents. We tried to rejoin our family, but the dense crowd overwhelmed us. Plus, reflecting on their close proximity to the action, we suddenly took yesterday's warnings to heart.

We're too far to see the preparation, only the balloon's sudden, orange rise from the dark pit of the crowd. It's big as a Volkswagen Beetle, smoothly swelling with fire, graphically painted with Corinthian-style ornamentals and red polka dots. Inside a thick blue border is the team name in curvy Burmese script.

The crowd emits a soft gasp as the balloon achieves liftoff, trailing a cloud of smoke. But the journey is short-lived. About fifteen feet up, there's a clear *pop,* and the balloon is shooting back down. The surrounding revelers shriek with both terror and joy, breaking from the landing zone in what looks from our vantage point like the Red Sea parting. In their wake are a handful of stalwarts, too spellbound to budge. When the balloon reaches eye level, it explodes into horizontal fireworks a football field wide. Now people are running for their lives, hitting the muddy ground as fire trails blast overhead.

"I don't understand this," Deano says over and over.

In a few short seconds, the balloon is a flaming cage on the ground. We crane our necks for signs of casualties, but there are no sirens, and no one is carted off. How? An entire Fourth of July program rained down on human heads. As a silhouetted team rushes forward to douse the fire, I feel like an accomplice to something masochistic—and like I don't understand Taunggyi Fire Balloon Festival at all.

But merriment rages around us, dwarfing our concern. A woman sells quail eggs from a bamboo platter on her head. A psychedelic disco train weaves through the crowd, led by a towering effigy with cartoonishly big hands. Before I know it, Balloon Number Two is aloft, flickering with the light of hundreds of cellophane-wrapped candles forming a crouched rabbit on one side and a peacock on the other, framed in a fan of diamond-tipped feathers. Both are enclosed stamp-like in a circular red border, and dangling below them is a candle-laden lattice of several meters, showcasing a glittering red duck. I watch it float ominously above the crowd, flinching as it sparks, then realize the sparks are hundreds of little red and gold parachutes, spreading across the sky like shooting stars in slow motion.

The next few balloons launch seamlessly, slowly turning in flight to reveal intricate Buddhist graphics and abstract patterns. But the interludes are long, and by Balloon Number Four, I'm cranky from being on my feet, ill-fed, dehydrated, and up since four A.M. We decide to reunite with our family for one last launch.

We ply the festival's perimeter, now clogged with drunk, sweaty men, some setting off fireworks of their own. There are randomly placed barbecue stands spitting hot oil into the crowd, and we make startled stops for the odd motorcycle blazing recklessly through. We weave in and out of tented noodleries, clear a jagged fence, apply the limits of our own body weight to fist-tight crowds. Finally, triumphantly, we reunite with Lwin Htwe, Ya Ya, and family.

"Closer, closer!" say the girls, scooting back to make space for us on the blanket. Only when we are snug as a game of Tetris do Lwin Htwe and Ya Ya feel we've sufficiently settled. We catch up on the last hours with bug-eyed signing, the family showing zero distress from the earlier explosion, a mere couple hundred yards away. Could there really have been no casualties?

The thrill of reunion soon wears as we realize our proximity to the next launch. It's not spitting distance, but maybe throwing distance (if I was an elite-level discus thrower). Certainly close enough to see the preparations. First a pickup truck backs into the crowd, nearly flattening a baby in the process. Materials are offloaded from the truck, starting with the balloon, deflated, folded, waxed and white. Under deft hands, unfurling its several unwieldy meters, the balloon spreads, peaking above the crowd like a snowcap. I catch glints of metallic blue on its surface but can't yet discern the design.

Next comes a cage of six notched ribs, visible through a film of cellophane. As it's hoisted above the crowd, I see the notches are in fact thousands of cilia-like white tubes, a few inches long and pointed outward like miniature cannons. The bottom rib is stacked with much larger cracker-style fireworks, ringed and streaming with shiny blue ribbon. The cage is attached to a wider square base, its bottom so completely covered with ribbon-laced firecrackers it could be sprouting Astroturf.

I brace myself—this is an explosive balloon.

Lwin Htwe and Ya Ya delight in our apprehension, chanting "*Dan-ger, dan-ger, dan-ger.*" Like little boys in mock battle, they make searing explosion sounds, punctuated by puffed cheeks and jazz hands. Meanwhile, Older Sister's husband, joined in our absence, is the kind of charitable Burmese we had hoped for. Over and over, he tries our driver's cell phone; when he redials for the seventeenth time, we assure him he can stop.

Blazing torches bob around the balloon, each bowing to kiss the flame stick inside. At the first lick of heat, the balloon stirs like an awakening beast, tugging the single rope that tethers it to the crowd. Older Sister jumps abruptly to her feet, shielding her be-slinged baby as they duck behind a vendor booth. A rush of hands keep the balloon from tearing away, the tension mounting over several seconds until, at the last possible moment, it is released.

The balloon wavers slightly, sending a *swish* of sharp breaths through the crowd and then it's a steady, shiny ascent. It comes at us on a diagonal, looking oddly like an overturned speedball. The metallic blue glints from earlier reveal themselves as a pattern of interlocking tiles, interrupted only by the team name. It's not the most elaborate design we've seen, but then come the fireworks.

They are bright, arcing red and silver starbursts, shooting toward the crowd before dispersing to sparky dust. They're the kind of languid, drippy fireworks you get lost in, like looped animation, each round an exact replica of the last. The kind of fireworks you get lost in, until you realize they're coming for you.

"Deano?"

"It's all right babe," he says uncertainly, "it's aaalll-right."

Within seconds, the fireworks are almost directly over our heads. The energy of the crowd has shifted to that of sprinters on the block, ready for action at the sound of the gun. Even Lwin Htwe and Ya Ya have gone silent.

"Deano?"

Sensing our moments together are numbered, Lwin Htwe turns to us, her thickly lashed doe eyes brimming with hope.

"Myanmar 2014?" she asks.

"I don't know," I admit, breathless. "Expensive."

She nods. I stay with her and Ya Ya and the family until I feel like my face is open to raining fire. Until my neck is craned back so far the mass of molten molecules rocketing down will surely singe my eyes. When people start to flee, I know our time has come.

"Run, babe!"

I pull Ya Ya, the closest, into a violent hug, frantically waving at the rest.

"Goodbye!" I holler, already part of the masses, my view of our family obscured by the bodies closing in. We run with the crowd, hissing fireworks overhead, surely seconds from our heads.

"Where, Deano?"

"Anywhere. Just run!"

We push toward the parking lot, dodging bonfires and babies, the rude squish of mud beneath our feet. And then, no more than twenty yards into escape, the crowd settles around us and we stop. I look down at my pastel blue shoes, spattered brown. Above us, the balloon safely ascends, alighting the sky with minutes upon minutes of winning displays until it's a single spark and then gone.

By some Buddhist miracle, in the middle of the jammed, baby-littered, traffic conductor-free parking lot, we find Kon Sai almost immediately and are swiftly ushered into the white sedan and on our way. As we drive by the festival outskirts of chock-a-block arcades and a disco roller rink, Deano and I marvel at the miserable hours spent in the staffed, far more "organized" lots of Glastonbury and Coachella. It's impressive, the kind of can-do spirit that exists in places like Myanmar, where people have little in the way of governments or systems to lean on.

We sleep most of the way home, and the next day, over coffee milkshakes at The French Touch Café in Nyaungshwe, wonder if human-powered Ferris wheels, killer balloons, and a handwritten note from two giggling strangers were part of some accidental opium trip. Which reminds me.

I pull the note from my purse, the one that was passed over the barred fence of the crowd-facing lounge and into my heart. The one that reaffirmed why I festival, and why the little things are often as memorable as the main events. On a lined sheet of mini notebook paper, in girlish scrawl, it reads:

You are beautiful. Welcome to Myanmar.
Lwin Htwe and Ya Ya.

Becky Hutner is a Canadian writer and editor of various media including documentary film, television, digital, and print. She holds a BFA in Screenwriting from the University of Southern California and lives in the gentrified-but-still-respectably-bohemian enclave of Venice Beach.

✿ ✿ ✿

Free Range

Learning to let go, under the African sun.

Months before our trip to Tanzania, first on safari in the Selous Game Reserve and then to the beaches of Zanzibar, I began my campaign to keep our daughters, aged thirteen and fifteen, from peril.

I made sure the girls had booster shots up to date and received jabs against yellow fever. One by one, I lined up bottles of 50+ sunscreen and 50 percent DEET bug repellent, pocket-sized dispensers of hand sanitizer, and LED flashlights, like ready soldiers, on a shelf in my closet. I purchased new sneakers, pairs of tube socks, and long-sleeved lightweight blouses.

I ordered duffels in impenetrable material, then hovered over the girls' efforts at filling them, although—having grown up mostly as expats because of my husband's work as a human rights lawyer, and having traveled often—they were used to packing. Because our weight allowance was small for the prop-plane flights we'd be taking once in Tanzania, but also to limit the possibility of loss or theft, anything of monetary or personal value—other than cameras and my younger daughter's totemic baby blanket—was deemed verboten.

For safari clothing, Internet forums advised against black (too hot), dark blue (attracts tse-tse flies), bright (scares the

animals), and white (too many problems to enumerate) clothing. Bare legs and shoulders would be no-nos on Zanzibar
(about 96 percent Muslim). Oscillating between the girls' bags,
I nixed and naysayed.

"You do realize," my older daughter finally said, "you
aren't leaving many options."

I moved on to my husband. His employer, the U.N., pro-
vides him with an emergency first aid kit; I insisted he empty
it onto our bed and explain each item so I'd know what to
shop for. After, I raided our medicine cabinet and made a trip
back to the pharmacy, buying Norfloxacin and Azithromy-
cin, Loperamide, paracetamol, a topical antihistamine, an oral
antihistamine, water-purifying tablets, rehydration salts, an
antiseptic gel, a thermometer, bandages, and a small mountain of Malarone, the pricy but side-effect-free anti-malarial
prophylactic.

Had I thought of everything?

"Remember," I told the girls, "these are *wild* animals."
I ran through a litany of behaviors they mustn't exhibit on
safari, finishing with, "And at all times, you do what the guide
tells you."

The night before our departure, we watched a biopic about
Bethany Hamilton, the champion surfer girl who lost an arm
to a shark attack at the age of thirteen. When my younger
daughter asked, during the closing credits, "Are there *sharks*
around Zanzibar?" the better, saner parent inside me realized
I might have freaked out the children.

"Honey," I said with a laugh, "don't you worry about it."

Then I went straight to my office and googled "sharks"
and "Zanzibar." (Note: offshore, there are reef sharks, tiger
sharks, lemon and white and whale sharks, and hammer-
heads. Stingrays and barracuda are also known to Zanzibar's
deeper waters.)

I traveled far and wide as a journalist, usually alone, before
getting married and becoming a parent, and I can remember

feeling real fear only once. As largely expat parents, my husband and I are set up for giving our daughters broad and varied experiences of the world. It's something I deeply want for them. I just don't want any of those experiences to leave them hurt or unhappy.

I am not a tiger mother. I am a lion mother. I do not fight with my children, but—from the moment I insisted one be born by Caesarean, rather than forced to turn in my womb, and the other be nestled, against all local convention, in my French hospital room as a newborn—I've fought for them.

As my kids were growing up, there were times when some people told me I was being overprotective. Maybe there were times when I was.

We set off for East Africa.

Over five days in the Selous Reserve, we came eye to eye with lions, elephants, buffalos, warthogs, wildebeest, hyenas, zebras, giraffes, monkeys, baboons, crocodiles, hippos, and impalas. I was having the time of my life—except for that moment when a crocodile slithered directly beneath us as we putt-putted along the silty Rufiji River in our flat-bottomed boat. Or, when one daughter absent-mindedly stood up in the back seat of our Jeep to get a better view of a group of seven young male lions— about six feet from us. (In fairness, this was the only time I saw our usually calm guide also lose his cool. "*Get down,*" he hissed.)

Slowly, I began to trust in the experience. In potentially hazardous situations, I saw my daughters learn fast and listen carefully. Like the heat, it sunk in. By the last day of our stay in the game reserve, I had relaxed enough to leave the girls to their own devices while my husband and I joined an armed ranger on a walking safari, proscribed to kids sixteen and under. They hung around the camp reading, watching hippos in the adjacent river, and swimming in the little pool. They had a good time. And amongst giraffes and whistling thorn trees, the dusty soil and scrub under our feet and hot dry breeze on our backs, so did my husband and I.

We left the next day for Zanzibar exuberant and unscathed. I thought the most perilous part of our trip was finished.

Somewhere over the dusty red expanse between the Selous and Dar es Salaam, our flippety-floppety twelve-seater prop plane hit turbulence. Miles above the wide earth, we were flung up and down like puppets. It hadn't escaped my notice that of the two "pilots" onboard, the one actually flying the plane was receiving instruction from the other.

"Look," I said, pointing out the window, while gripping my seat. "There's the Rufiji!"

As I successfully diverted both the kids' and my own attention from worrying about falling out of the sky to appreciating the beauty of the river snaking its limpid brown way through the acacia-dotted landscape beneath us, I thought: Maybe I'm finally becoming a cool mother.

At our hotel in northern Zanzibar, there was a problem with the reservation. Sleeping quarters were located in two small whitewashed structures, separated by a thatched-roof reception area. Despite having booked adjoining rooms, my husband and I were put in one building; the girls in the other.

My mouth dropped. "*No* way."

"We *like* our room," the girls said.

"We don't have anything else," the reservationist said.

"They'll be fine," my husband said, patting my shoulder.

By the time we were ready to move on to Kizimkazi in the south of Zanzibar, my family was laughing at my fussing, and I was laughing a little at myself.

In Kizimkazi, placid monkeys played around thatched-roof villas of the resort where we were staying, sheltered by huge gnarly baobab trees. Green-blue water glistened just steps from our villa's patio. The feeling of peace was as soft and sultry as the weather.

When the girls asked to go surfing off a reef in open sea at sunrise, I personally zipped up their wetsuits and waved as their little boat disappeared toward the lightening horizon.

And that's when it happened.

Halfway through lunch, with my daughters back on land, the thirteen-year-old announced, "I think housekeeping took my blanket while I was out surfing."

Since her birth, this daughter had slept entwined in a soft white cotton blanket with a turquoise trim, bestowed upon her by a doting aunt in America. That blanket had been every-where; every move we made, every journey, every overnight visit. I'd turned whole houses upside down searching for it, a baby perched on my hip, small trusting hands clutching my shoulder. In a life with a lot of transiency, that blanket was a constant. There was no coincidence in it having been the only object of personal value either of the girls was allowed to bring on this holiday.

An investigation was launched. After discussing strategy with the hotel owner, I joined my thirteen-year-old by the pool, where she was sipping passion fruit juice over *Jane Eyre*, her blue-painted toenails dangling in the water.

"They're going to look for it," I said, keeping my voice level.

"O.K." She smiled. She went back to her reading.

"O.K.?" I searched her face, ready to offer comfort and assurance.

"O.K."

A few hours later, the owner had news: Yes, housekeeping had taken the blanket. They would wash it then leave it in my daughter's room.

At dinner, my daughter said, "My blanket's back." She added, with a wry expression, "I think it was used for cleaning."

Back at our villa, she showed me the once snowy-white blanket. It was now gray, threadbare in places to the point of being almost transparent. Swathes of the satin trim hung loose from the cotton. The housekeepers must have washed down the whole resort with it.

I gathered what was left of the blanket and gingerly tucked it into a plastic bag. "I'll fix it up as soon as we get home," I promised. "I'll bleach it and patch it, and I'll make it O.K. again."

"Great," my daughter said, serenely. "Thank you."

All that night, I churned under my bed's swirling mosquito netting. There was no one to blame—mistaking the blanket for a cleaning rag had been a careless but innocent error by housekeeping. Still, I knew no matter how I sewed or patched, I would never be able to turn that blanket back into the pristine unbroken white square with continuous green-blue border it had been for thirteen years.

The more I thought it over, the more upset I became. And the more upset I became, the more I began to wonder. Of all the things to go wrong—this was something I'd never even thought about. Was my daughter more upset than she was showing? Was she less upset because she trusted me to be able to make the blanket all right again?

As the eastern skyline turned from periwinkle to pink to bright blue, and quiet *dhow* fishing boats appeared on the wide expanse of the Indian Ocean, the truth dawned on me.

I was more upset than she was.

During the years I'd been busy trying to give my daughters the world at the same time as shielding them from it, a curious thing had happened. Even my baby daughter had grown older.

The blanket sits on a shelf in my office cupboard now. When we returned home, I bleached it white again but didn't try to patch it. I decided, instead, to see what would happen. Sure enough, my daughter never asked for it.

I catch a glimpse of what's left of the blanket sometimes, when I'm looking for a new printer cartridge. I know my daughter sees it too, because she keeps things in that cupboard. A little part of her surely misses her old blanket and would like to see it whole again, but not enough to ask me about it.

She's dealt with the loss in her own way, just as I'm learning to deal with it in mine. Allowing your kids to grow up is a slow letting go that continues all through their teenage years. First, they go out the door to travel to school on their own. Eventually, they go out the door to make new lives on their own.

"Don't worry," my younger daughter remarked recently to me, as I was marveling over how she and her sister now tower over me. "We will always need you."

And they will. And they won't. As I learned in an unexpected way, under the shade of baobabs and at the feet of lions.

Anne Korkeakivi is the author of the novel, An Unexpected Guest. *Her short fiction has been published by* The Atlantic, The Yale Review, The Bellevue Literary Review, Consequence, *and others. Her nonfiction has appeared in* The New York Times, Wall Street Journal, Times (UK), Travel & Leisure, Islands, *and on* The Millions. *She, her husband, and their daughters currently divide their time between Geneva, Switzerland, her hometown of New York City, and wherever their travels may take them.*

∽ ∽ ∽

Sea Change

Can a gypsy settle down without settling?

I knew a man had died. On our boat ride from the mainland of southwest Thailand to Koh Surin Tai, one of five small islands comprising the Surin Islands archipelago, my translator Nui shared the news with me. Over the roar of the outboard motor behind us, she told me that his name was Wylip, he had died from tuberculosis, and he was only thirty years old.

In the village that night, I heard them drinking and dancing, the group of men and women and children keeping Wylip's body company until the burial. On the way to the toilet, which was set back a short distance in the forest, I passed the house where they were gathered. They danced outside, within the sphere of light cast by a single hanging bulb, while generators hummed and music pulsed from a table full of speakers. I asked Nui if we could join them, to get a closer look at their death ritual, but she said no. She didn't feel comfortable joining them herself.

It wasn't until breakfast the next morning, as Nui and I sat on the porch dunking Hobnobs into our cups of instant coffee, that six men suddenly appeared carrying a long plywood crate on their shoulders. Three stood on either side of the coffin, over which had been placed a blue and orange plaid cloth. They moved quickly through the rows of stilted, thatched-roof houses, toward the longtail boats moored along the sandy beach.

Nui was sitting across from me, with her back to the village, so I was the first to see the men. In my haste to alert her, I tipped over my coffee, the last of it draining through the uneven bamboo floor onto the sand below. By the time I looked back up, they had slid the coffin across the bench seats of a boat and pushed off.

Breakfast came to an abrupt end; this time, Nui said, we would join them. Within minutes we were in the final boat to leave. As we headed to the neighboring island where they bury their deceased, I was transfixed by the sea. Near the shallow shores of Koh Surin Tai, the water was as clear as glass and a mesmerizing blue—the blue of icebergs and glaciers, of sulfur lakes and blue lace agate. But the farther we moved away from the coast, the more the water darkened, losing its tropical colors. It shifted in shade from jade to slate to sapphire, the depths below imbued with a certain opacity. Had the water itself changed, I wondered, or was it merely reflecting its environment? I slipped my hand over the side of the boat, letting the sea pass through my fingers.

When I first heard about the village of sea gypsies on Koh Surin Tai, I had assumed we were talking about pirates. I knew nothing of the Moken—as they call themselves, a name that means, "diving into the sea"—nor of their traditionally nomadic past, nor of their current struggle to attain full citizenship from the Thai government.

The two hundred or so Moken living on the Surin Islands are part of a larger ethnic group spread out across the Mergui Archipelago off the coasts of Burma and Thailand. Following a tradition of maritime nomadism in the region, the Moken had shifted from island to island for centuries, subsisting on what they gathered underwater, along the foreshore, and from the forest. While other related people groups were semi-nomadic and formed coastal communities, the Moken considered themselves true nomads of the sea. Their lives revolved around their dugout wooden boats, known as *kabangs*, which have distinctive notches carved out of their prow and stern that function as steps into the boat from the water. These boats were their homes, in which they lived, worked, cooked, gave birth, raised their families, and died. Only in the monsoon season would they construct temporary huts from pandanus leaves, repair their boats, and wait out the rain.

The Thai have two names for the Moken—*chao ley*, people of the sea, and *chao nam*, people of the water—and when you take into account the ease with which they inhabit the ocean, free dive to depths of fifty feet or more, hold their breath for minutes, hunt for turtles, shells, and sea cucumbers, and navigate between distant islands, led only by instinct, both names are equally fitting. And so it is problematic that in recent years, the Thai and Burmese governments have been requiring them to settle down, to stay in one place, to stop moving.

In 1981, the Surin Islands were declared Thailand's twenty-ninth national park. After the 2004 tsunami devastated the region, park officials brought the several Moken settlements present there together on the same beach on Koh Surin Tai. "Easier to manage that way," Nui told me, even though it would lead to overcrowding. All of their homes and boats were destroyed in the storm. Although organizations such as Reuters donated new Thai longtail boats to the village, one boat per two families, nothing could replace the *kabangs* they had lost.

But the biggest human rights concern has been that of the Moken's identity—the question of where they belong. Obtaining citizenship hasn't been an easy process, and for those who do have a Thai ID card, there's yet another issue at play. Every ID card has an identity number, but if the number starts with zero, the holder of that card is not allowed to travel outside his or her province. Half of the Moken living in the Surin Islands have an identity number beginning with zero.

There's a government-sponsored primary school in the village now, as well as a small clinic run by a Thai nurse. During the dry season, many of the men are employed by the national park, manning the boats used for snorkeling trips, and the women weave mats and baskets from pandanus leaves to sell to the tourists who visit their beach every day. As Nui explained to me, by earning these small amounts of money, they no longer need to dive as often for goods to trade, which can be dangerous for their health. Today their children have the possibility of attending university, and medical care is available both in the village and on the mainland. The changes being implemented are sometimes practical, but at what cost to their culture?

"Before, they moved everywhere," Nui said. "It was not fixed."

I learned by chance about the Moken from family friends who lived in Bangkok. They were connected to a Thai NGO working in the Surin Islands and arranged for me to stay in the village on Koh Surin Tai for a week.

What my friends didn't know was that I was also in a transition; that I had recently brought my own nomadic way of life into question. After nearly five years of traveling and living overseas since my college graduation, I was beginning to long for things incompatible with my lifestyle—a relationship, stable community of friends, home—and I was considering returning to the States to set up a more permanent base. It was an idea that crawled into my head one morning in Delhi, where I was living at the time, and the idea hadn't left.

The question I kept asking was: Could I give it up? It being the freedom and flow of a life lived untethered from traditional responsibilities—a life without roots, deracinated. A friend had once described my wandering existence as "fluid," and though it hadn't felt like a compliment at the time, I'd held on to this fluidity as though it were my most prized possession. I loved that plans could change within a moment's notice; that a single email could have my course heading in a new direction. And perhaps like the Moken's own affinity with the sea, whose depths were as familiar to them as its vast surface, I loved that getting to know the world continually brought me to a deeper understanding of myself.

But even as changing my address every six months was losing its appeal, I still wondered if one could truly settle down without settling. I sensed this chapter in my life closing, an era nearing its end, and to find myself about to spend a week with people facing the same dilemma—albeit with much greater consequences—seemed no accident.

Nui met me in the seaside town of Khuraburi, where we boarded a speedboat to the Surin Islands, located thirty miles off the Thai coast. The journey took an hour and a half, and as we clipped across the choppy waves, pale shadows of land grew ever darker on the horizon. We stopped first at the largest island in the archipelago, Koh Surin Nua, home to the national park's headquarters and two sites of bungalows and tents available for tourists to rent. Already I was struck by the lack of openness in the Surin Islands. Their rugged terrain betrayed nothing, with undulating ridges rising sharply from the sea. Draped in vines and thick vegetation, the hills permitted only the narrowest of beaches along their periphery. They seemed to hold a mystery as inscrutable as the clotted branches of their mangroves.

Koh Surin Tai is the second largest in the group, another oddly shaped amoeba of land. As we proceeded around a bend and into an opening in the island's jungled coastline, I suddenly leaned forward on my hard bench. There, at the far end of the cove, situated on a fringe of sand between verdant hills and an iridescent bay, lay the Moken village.

There were some fifty or sixty small square houses built along the shore, each a few feet from its neighbor. They sat above the ground on stilts, like flamingos balanced on impossibly thin legs. Their roofs were made of overlapping pandanus leaves, their walls from another kind of dried leaf—both of which, Nui told me, had to be replaced every few years. Nui led me to the house where we'd be staying for the week. Inside, there was no furniture; no chairs or beds, no nightstands or tables—only a few tall cabinets and shelving units placed against the walls, the slatted wooden floor swept bare. "Every Moken home is like this," she told me. "They keep the center clean—maybe because that's how it was in the boats. They would cook in the middle, then push everything to the sides so they could sleep."

That night, I slept uneasily in a hammock strung between two posts on the porch. A light rain fell, waves brushed up below the house, and something one of the Moken women had said earlier in the day circled in my head. "If you stay in the same house, to stay long time is boring. We want to move, to change environment. We move to see new things."

I knew exactly what she meant.

In the days after I arrived, the Moken largely kept to themselves, my greetings of *Sawadee ka* often going unreturned. I read, took notes, chatted with Nui, swung in the hammock, but never felt like anything more than an observer. One afternoon, I sat sketching on the porch, my feet balanced on a rung of the wooden ladder leading up to the house. As a black kitten competed with my sketchbook for lap space, I noticed a girl sitting on the ground by a neighboring home. She held a thin stick in her hand and was drawing with it in the sand, bringing a flower to life petal by grainy petal. The key I had been looking for—my key to connecting with the Moken—was right in front of me.

I climbed down the ladder and approached the girl, who looked to be ten or twelve at most. I tore a sheet from my sketchbook and placed it in front of her with a pen on top. She made no move toward them, but two other girls playing nearby saw what was going on and swooped in to join us. I offered them each pen and paper and then sat back to watch. They both drew a wavy horizontal line across the page. Above the line, trees were drawn, as were flowers, hills, clouds, butterflies, a few people, and a round sun in the center. It was a scene any child might create. However, a vastly different world soon appeared below the line. The girls drew fish—not the kind I had drawn growing up, with just an oval body and triangle tail, but fish with gills and fins and scales. Fish that actually belonged underwater. They sketched squiggly seaweed and sea anemones and jellyfish with symmetrical tentacles; they sketched tiny spiraled conch shells lined up on brown boulders. Their world below the surface was equally alive and brimming with detail as their world above it.

This continued every day while I was with them, and every day our assembly of young artists grew in number. My sketchbook was slowly emptied of paper, but no matter how many sheets I gave them, they drew the same thing each time—one scene on land and another underwater, either on a page that had been divided into halves or on opposite sides of the same piece of paper. In their lives as in their sketches, the children seemed to exist between land and sea, equally at home in both worlds.

They say old habits die hard, and the more time I spent on Koh Surin Tai, the more I saw this to be true for the Moken.

Every evening I watched an elderly couple, Sunai and his wife Pa Do, depart from the village in their weathered boat, not to return again until the next day. One morning, Nui called out to them and asked where they'd been. "She said they sleep better in the boat," Nui explained, cradling her hands and rocking them, to evoke the motion they were so accustomed to after a lifetime of being swayed to sleep by the waves.

She also told me that every year, some families on the island switch homes with each other—perhaps enough of a change to sate their innate need for movement—and that when the village was rebuilt after the tsunami, officials had instructed the Moken to set their homes as far back from the shore as possible. But over the last decade, they've been inching closer and closer to the tide. It was almost comical to imagine—that whenever the national park turned its head, the houses would gather up their skirts and tiptoe a few more meters forward, until they were back, as Moken researcher Jacques Ivanoff once described it, with their "feet in the water."

I had come to the Surin Islands expecting to find a culture on its way out, but what I discovered was more adaptation than destruction. The Moken were at the mercy of a changing world, one in which there were no easy answers for their assimilation, but I sensed that no matter what the answers might prove to be, their lives would continue to rotate around the same axis—a fixed fulcrum of identity at the center of their ever-shifting universe. Girls would look for shells just as their grandmothers did generations before them, boys would help bail out the rain from their fathers' boats every morning, and the shoreline would never be empty of naked children laughing, swimming, and doing handstands in the surf. They might not have grown up on the water as their parents had, but the sea would still be a part of them, and they a part of it.

At the same time, I sought to discern the point around which my own transition would pivot. What had drawn me to my wandering life, and why was it so hard to relinquish? Over the five years in which I'd called England, New Zealand, and India home, I had come to believe that as long as I was moving through the world, I was moving forward in life. Starting over in new countries kept me from becoming too comfortable; it kept my routines from becoming ruts. Never before had I felt so alive in my daily existence—never had I lived with such an awareness of the people, places, and possibilities around me. Like the Moken, who have no tradition of saving what they earn or catch today for tomorrow, I had stopped fixating on the future. It was only through travel that I'd learned to stay present in each moment of my life.

But what if I didn't let go of this presence? What if I kept moving forward, even as I learned to stay still? In watching Sunai and Pa Do go off to sleep on their boat each night, in seeing how the Moken belonged to one another—if to no one else—I believed I could finally summon the courage to do just that. To take the fluidity I'd so prized and let it guide me to more solid ground.

On my final afternoon in the village, a group of visiting filmmakers invited me to go snorkeling with them in the waters just beyond the Moken's beach. I was delighted to join them, to plunge below the surface of this place. I had only just begun to take in the dazzling array of life on the reef—the bright orange clown anemone fish, neon-striped sweet lips, feeding frenzies of parrotfish—when I followed the direction of someone's pointed finger and spotted an octopus, the first I'd ever come across in the wild. I instantly stopped moving to watch him steal across the floor of the sea. He wasn't big, but he struck me as beautiful, his pliant arms unfurling with poise. And when he changed colors, I knew I would never see anything as astonishing again. His skin flushed from pale blue to beige to a dappled gray, taking on the tone of every piece of coral and rock he encountered. Only the octopus himself never changed.

Along with the filmmakers, who were Norwegian, two other people had returned to the village: twenty-something Moken brothers named Ngui and Hook— "like Captain Hook," he said when we were introduced. While Ngui had followed a rather traditional path in life—he was married, had three children, and it was his house I'd been staying in— Hook felt more tension between life in the village and life on the Thai mainland. He had spent a season in the busy resort town of Phuket, driving a tour boat, and the decisions he was working through were actually the subject of the film crew's documentary. "He's a man between worlds," the cinematographer had told me during our snorkeling trip that afternoon. While the other Moken men I'd met alternated between sarongs and swim trunks, Hook had arrived wearing a stylish sweater and fitted jean shorts that were cuffed at the hem; while the rest of the village rolled their own cigarettes, he smoked store-bought packets. His thick dark hair was as shaggy and disheveled as a rock star's, which was exactly the impression he gave.

That night, Hook, Ngui, and I sat on the bare living room floor of the house and talked about their trip to Norway the year before to kick off the documentary—their first time on a plane—which led to a discussion about flying and flight times and distance. I drew a wobbly-shaped world map in my notebook, with arcs connecting Bangkok and Delhi, Oslo and London, and my hometown near Washington D.C., so that it began to resemble an airline's route map.

They told me they'd needed to get their passports for the journey, and then asked, "You want to see them?" We happily exchanged books, and as I flipped through their passports and they through mine, I was reminded of what these objects—and their pages, and the colorful stamps inside—had always represented for me: expanding worlds and boundless possibilities. A life whose comfort zone is forever being challenged and redefined. Through travel, I had fallen in love with the thrill of the new, with the untested border. The call before me now was to live out the promise of these tangible objects that Hook, Ngui, and I were comparing on a more symbolic level—to greet the contours of my everyday world with the same expectations of discovery.

After handing back their passports, I asked Hook what kind of life he'd like to lead.

"Phuket too many people, too many cars," he said, telling me that he still enjoys coming back to the village for part of the year. "I want to live half-half."

The two words hit me like lightning. All week I had seen the idea played out in the children's sketches, as they created worlds that were half land and half sea. For the first time, this dichotomy was more than a picture—it was Hook's reality.

I was discovering that the tension the Moken faced—especially forward-thinking Moken such as Hook—and the tension I myself was experiencing could perhaps find resolution in a delicate balance. It isn't giving up one world for the other; it's uniting the two halves—new and old, land and sea, home and away. It's borrowing from both realms and then forging our own. We make our own home, our own country, our own world.

In the weeks and months after my departure from the Moken, one image stayed with me above all others, following me from Thailand back to India, and ultimately the U.S. I often replayed in my mind the burial I witnessed that first morning in the village.

My translator Nui and I had stood on the beach, which was heavily sheltered by trees and undergrowth, while men took turns digging thirty-year-old Wylip's grave. They sang as they dug, their tuneless songs keeping time to the beat of a cooking pot drum. I could almost taste the freshly turned soil and cigarette smoke, sharp from the unfiltered tobacco they used. When they rested, they sat on the plywood crate as though it were a coffee table, not a coffin.

Roots covered the earth, some thick as a man's leg. They were long, too, spanning the entire length of the intended grave. The men wrangled with the roots, twisting them back and forth, up and down, like sailors battling a sea monster. They swung their hoes and knives high above their heads, chanting "*Oi, oi, oi,*" with each strike. When the bigger roots were defeated, the whole group cheered.

It took six men to lower the crate into the ground. Before everyone returned to their boats, they each tossed two handfuls of sand onto the narrow mound of soil. And then, when only one woman was left, she brought over two tree seedlings, little green shoots with just a couple of leaves on them. She planted one at the head of the grave, and the other at the foot.

Never before had I seen the answer I sought made so visceral—the call to grow, to adapt, to move through life's myriad evolutions with soul intact. We dig up roots, wrestling with the habits and patterns we've established, only to put down new roots. We change environments, change countries and jobs, change homes, but our essence is immutable.

We change, but we stay the same—just like water, just like an octopus, just like the Moken.

✥ ✥ ✥

Candace Rose Rardon is a writer and sketch artist originally from Virginia, although she has also called England, New Zealand, India, and a cozy yurt in rural Canada home. In addition to running her travel blog, The Great Affair, which has been featured in The New York Times, *her stories and sketches have appeared on and in outlets such as BBC Travel, AOL Travel, World Hum, National Geographic Traveler's Intelligent Travel blog, and Selamta Magazine. A favorite moment from her time with the sea nomads in Thailand was being lent a traditional floral sarong to wear and called "Moken Candace"—but only after tripping face-first down a ladder, catching the hem of her skirt on a rung, and nearly flashing the village.*

ᴣᴧ ᴣᴧ ᴣᴧ

Pretty Red

She wondered if her Irish roots
went deeper than those on her head.

Carrot Top. Rusty. Ginger. Pippi Longstocking.

"How original. I've never heard that one before," I want to respond.

"Connect the dots with my freckles?" Forehead smack. "What a clever idea."

"Yes, that's right, someone did leave me outside in the rain, and my hair rusted."

As a redhead, I've heard all the jokes and jeers.

The only tag that never made me wince was the one my grandfather coined. "How's my Pretty Red?" I can still hear his sonorous voice ask, employing the tender name he'd used for me all my life. It was always *my* Pretty Red. I was always *his*.

I'm the sole redhead on a family tree of dark-haired relatives (including a twin brother) whose roots sink four generations deep in American soil. Beyond that, the branches are forgotten or unnoted. I'm often asked where my red hair comes from and whether I'm Irish. "I don't think so," is my normal response.

But on a recent trip to the Emerald Isle, I began to wonder if a homeland could only be defined by ancestral roots. Could feeling at home tether me to the land too?

Growing up in Los Angeles, I felt there was a certain circus-freak fascination with my hair. *Step right up, folks, and get your tickets to see The Bearded Lady, test your arm-wrestling skills against The World's Strongest Man, and don't forget to feed a nickname to The Redhead before you go!*

The authenticity of my hair color—a nutmeg/cinnamon/ginger blend—also provoked prolific questioning throughout the years, an inquiry my mother says would send her into orbit when strangers asked whether her infant daughter's locks were "natural."

"Why would I dye a baby's hair?" was her frustrated response.

I spent my teens rubbing lemon juice onto my tresses to lighten them up, and in an attempt to obliterate my freckles, I slathered "fade out" cream on my face, hoping the dots, and the attention to them, would abate. Dating was hell, especially in L.A., where blondes were bombshells, brunettes were sultry, and redheads had "great personalities," the kiss of death in courting jargon.

I remember during college, a friend set me up with her boyfriend's roommate. On the night of the double date, while we primped at her place, the guy left a message on the answering machine.

"I'm looking forward to meeting your friend. She's cute, right? Not some red-haired, freckle-faced girl. Ha ha ha . . ."

I went on the date anyway, but the remark stung.

When I was a kid, my mom or grandmother tended to my wounds, braiding my hair with ribbons and soothing me with verbal Band-Aids like "special" and "unique."

As I got older, however, it was my grandfather's advice that got me through. "Pretty Red," he said during one of our yearly visits, "pay no attention to boys who are color blind."

My grandfather had been doling out life lessons since I could remember.

When I was about nine, my mom drove my brother and me to Pismo Beach to meet my grandparents for a long weekend. My grandfather had planned to teach me to fly a kite, and at seven A.M. on a damp Saturday morning we trudged across the dunes, my hand in his, to the shoreline. The rainbow-colored wing was stretched over a balsa-wood skeleton that was tied off by white string that wound around a red plastic spool with two posts on either side, like bike handlebars. My grandfather laid the kite on the sand and backed up down the beach, letting out the line slowly. I kept step with him until we were about twenty feet away.

He began to run as he talked, jerking at the spool.

"Pretty Red, flying a kite is a lot like life," he said, yanking at the kite. "You need some runway and wind to get it going, and it can get a little tricky at times. . . ."

The kite fluttered and lurched side to side, and the fragile frame flexed against the air. I ran alongside my grandfather, and when we heard the whoosh of the wind catch the colored fabric and lift it skyward, we turned and watched.

". . . but it's up to us to make it soar."

My grandfather steadied the kite then handed me the spool, and I took the two posts in my hands. The strength of the wind dragged me a few inches across the sand.

My first visit to Ireland was more than thirty years later. I was in my early forties, and once there, I wished I had visited decades earlier. Though still a minority, redheads are found in higher concentration there than anywhere else in the world—reportedly making up an estimated 10 percent of the population. At social events back home I often felt like a zebra at the horse farm, but in Ireland three or more members of my homogeneous herd were always roaming about.

Being a redhead anywhere is like being in a club whose secret handshake blazes atop your head. In a hotel, at a restaurant, on the street, whenever I cross paths with another redhead, there's an unspoken connection forged by recessive genes and shared experience—an eye lock I always perceive to mean, "Yeah, I know what it's like." In Ireland, at times, that bond was a little stronger than expected.

At a pub in Belfast, I somehow ended up pseudo-Riverdancing with a blue-eyed, auburn-haired girl about ten years younger than I. We hooked arms and carved figure eights around the dance floor, kicking our knees and feet. When the music ended, she put her speckled nose up to mine and kissed me on the lips. "I love Irish girls," she said in her sexy brogue. Too stunned to break the probably-very-obvious news that I was not a real Riverdancer, nor Irish, I let her disappear into the bar's crowded thicket, preferring to savor the souvenir of my first and only kiss as an Irish girl, with an Irish girl.

On a more recent trip, it was instant kinship with redheaded Olive, whose pale skin, carved cheekbones, and fiery spirit seemed cut from quintessentially Irish literary-heroine cloth. I'd met her on the vast and idyllic Liss Ard Estate in the countryside near Skibbereen, County Cork, and when I saw her at our communal dinner table, I immediately planted myself next to her. She told me something I didn't expect to hear: "Even though redheads are more popular here in Ireland, we're still made to feel different and awkward." Garfield, Marmalade Head, Freckles, and Ginger Nut were all names hurled her way.

I thought red hair would surely be more celebrated in a land where the trait is embedded in common Irish surnames such as Flannery, meaning "descendant of the red warrior," and Flynn, "son of red-haired man." Someone took a photo of me with Olive, and when I viewed it later I thought we looked like sisters. In a way we are, connected by recessive genes and shared experiences.

As redheads do, Olive and I eventually moved on to discuss curious superstitions linked to our kind. "Ya know, some of my cousins were involved in building the Dunbrody replica ship moored in New Ross [the homestead of John F. Kennedy]," Olive said. "They told me they had heard stories that red-haired women should not be allowed near the ship when it takes her maiden voyage. Bad luck."

Another Irish woman told me it's considered bad luck if the first person to enter a house on New Year's Day is a redhead.

And still more. During the Middle Ages, people with red hair were sometimes thought to be witches, and even Shakespeare, I'd heard, used red wigs on his most dastardly characters. The list goes on.

During the two weeks of my most recent visit to Ireland, I'd been quizzing redheads and non alike to see if I could turn up any charms or folklore beyond banal nicknames and typical omens of bad luck, witchery, and hellfire and brimstone. I wasn't sure what I was looking for, but in Ireland, there's a good chance you'll find an answer—or at least have a late-night epiphany—at the local pub.

Pubs are the epicenter and social glue of any Irish town—and certainly they are in tiny Portmagee, a Crayola-colored fishing village on a rocky stretch of coast in southwest Ireland, where I'd landed for a night. Its pint-sized bar with beer-sticky floors was packed with young and old, couples and singles, working and retired, all of whom had gathered like members of an extended family. Cheers and backslaps greeted new arrivals, while local musicians sat on wooden stools in the corner and jammed on odd-looking instruments. I'd struck up a conversation with the fleshy-faced, red-bearded man next to me who belted out spirited lyrics of cultural anthems I wanted to know. During a lull, I acknowledged our shared gingerness and asked him what wacky stories and names he'd heard all his life.

"Ay, don't ya worry about dat," he said, tugging on the ends of my hair. "I always tell people that red is the color of lust and sensuality, of power, of candied apples and strawberries, of wine and of love. All things we enjoy and can't resist."

Forehead smack. I had really never heard *that* one before.

And until that moment, I'd forgotten something else my grandfather had once said: "Pretty Red, you'll spend your school years trying to fit in—and the rest of your life trying to stand out. Consider your hair a head start."

He was right. The whole freckle-faced, carrot-top thing works a little like the ugly duckling story. At a certain point in my late twenties, I, like most redheads, began to feel more like the swan. The splintered debris of a taunted youth eventually transformed into thick protective plumes, billowed by confidence and teeth-grit determination. And eventually, like most redheads, I learned to love my fiery hair and embrace the attention and distinctness I had once shunned.

In a taxi on the way to the airport on my final day in Ireland, the chatty driver studied me in the rearview mirror.

"I can hear ya are American, but ya must have a little Irish in ya there, eh, Pretty Red?"

There's something about the Irish lilt that makes my knees weak and my eyes pinwheel. It took away some of the sting of hearing the beloved nickname I hadn't heard for a while.

My grandfather had died the November before my last trip to Ireland. I sat with him on the couch, holding his fragile hand; the same hand that had helped me fly a kite; the same hand that two decades later led me down the aisle; the hand I'd always felt on the small of my back urging me forward and supporting me when I stumbled.

I was teary-eyed, anticipating the goodbye.

"Well, Pretty Red, it looks like I won't make it until Thanksgiving," he said.

He didn't.

But in Ireland, surrounded by a coterie of Carrot Tops, Marmalade Heads, and Ginger Nuts, I felt like I belonged. And I felt my grandfather near, his hand on mine again.

I felt like *his* Pretty Red.

ॐ   ॐ   ॐ

Kimberley Lovato is a freelance writer and author whose travel, lifestyle, and food articles have appeared in print and online media including National Geographic Traveler, American Way, Delta Sky, AFAR, Australian Voyeur, Marin Magazine, *travelandleisure.com, bbc.com, and more. Her culinary travel book,* Walnut Wine & Truffle Groves, *won the 2012 Gold Lowell Thomas Award given by the Society of American Travel Writers Foundation, while her essay "Lost and Liberated" received the 2012 Bronze Lowell Thomas Award as well as a Solas Award from Travelers' Tales, and appeared in* The Best Women's Travel Writing, Volume 9. *Her essay "City of Beginnings" appeared in* The Best Women's Travel Writing, Volume 9, *and won a silver Solas Award in 2013. www.kimberleylovato.com*

✿ ✿ ✿

Leader of the Pack

It was the year of weathering extremes.

Nico, a sharp-eyed, deeply dimpled thirty-four-year-old Swiss man, peered at me. "Will you take an ice bath?" he asked expectantly.

I'd just traveled for two days from California to Finland's slice of the Arctic Circle, lugging my suitcase the last quarter mile through snowdrifts and subzero temperatures. This was to be my last night in civilization—a cozy inn—before a five-day dogsledding journey through Pallas-Yllästunturi National Park. After that I'd be sharing a one-room cabin, lacking heat and running water, with seven strangers, including Nico and his perpetually amused wife, Michaela. The weather report predicted record cold. An ice bath—whatever that was—was the last thing on my to-do list.

"After the sauna," Nico persisted in clipped, Swiss-German-accented English. "Will you take a bath in a hole in the ice in the lake?"

Michaela laughed. "He's joking," she said.

Nico only nodded. "I will dig a hole, and you will see," he said. "You will take an ice bath."

* * *

Six months earlier, I had weathered a different sort of extreme: lying in an intensive care unit recovering from a mastectomy after a return of breast cancer. I had first been diagnosed and treated at age thirty-five; by fifty, recurrence-free, I figured I had it beat. Then one evening my fingers grazed a small, hard knot under my lumpectomy scar. Just like that, my passport to the land of the healthy was revoked. In most cases, you can't have radiation to the same body part twice, so though my tumor was low grade and small and I would almost surely survive it, the whole breast had to go. My doc sculpted a new one out of my abdominal fat, essentially giving me a tummy tuck in the process (now aren't you jealous?). The downside was a grueling double surgery—eight hours under the knife—followed by a long, slow recovery. A month after leaving the hospital, I couldn't stand up straight. Two months after, a walk around the block left me gasping for breath. The idea of dogsledding in the Arctic Circle seemed preposterous; it was also, on my darkest days—when my energy ran low and my terror ran high—a hope I could cling to.

Markku and Mari Rauhala, the owners of Pallas Husky, gathered our group after breakfast: There were Nico and Michaela; a pair of twenty-seven-year-old German Ph.D. candidates in physics (whose habit of explaining the mechanics of virtually everything earned them the nickname "the Einstein brothers"); a photographer in his late thirties based in Los Angeles; and an Australian architect in his fifties. There was also Margarete, another German, who was seventy. *At least*, I thought selfishly, *I won't be the weakest on the trip.*

In my woolen long underwear, fleece pants and hoodie, down jacket, two pairs of socks, gloves, scarf, neoprene balaclava and goggles, I looked like the love child of a ninja warrior and the Pillsbury Doughboy. Yet I could already feel the cold seeping in. At the Rauhalas' farm we added bib overalls, anoraks, fur-lined caps with earflaps, clunky polar boots, and leather driving mittens that looked like oven mitts. When I stepped outside again, the day felt almost balmy. I recalled my childhood in Minnesota, with a climate not unlike Finland's—one, incidentally, I'd eagerly left behind—when my mom bundled me in so many layers that I was red-faced and sweating by the time I left the house. Dressed like that, I could play in the snow for hours. And I did, making forts, snowmen, stockpiles of snowballs, and fields of angels.

Markku showed us our sleds, simple birch contraptions with boatlike prows and runners about two-thirds the width of my boots. There were two foot-operated brakes: a metal bar with claws that dug into the snow, stopping the dogs immediately, and a flat pan we could step on to slow them down. We'd each have our own team of five. Everything else, Markku said, we could pick up as we went along. "Um," someone asked, "how do we steer?" Finnish is an uninflected language that makes anything Finns say in English sound vaguely ironic. So it was unclear to me whether Markku intended to be quite so deadpan when he answered, "You don't."

I'd expected sled dogs to have a touch of the wolf in them, but my lead pooch, Bambi, looked at me with the melting brown eyes of her namesake and immediately tried to crawl into my lap. Her daughter, Ninni (named after a character in a Finnish children's book), was equally sweet. All the dogs were, instantly forgiving me for jamming their harnesses on upside down or mercilessly torquing their paws as I tried to hook them to the sled. The howling of some forty dogs eager to run spiraled from din to pandemonium. They didn't even sound like dogs: they screamed like monkeys, yowled like cats, shrieked like parrots. Their energy built like fizz in a fast-shaken can of soda. I began to worry about what would happen when it was released.

At last I stood on my runners, one foot planted on the main brake. Markku took off first, followed by Margarete and one of the Einstein brothers. I was next. Mari, standing a short distance from me, called out one last piece of advice in that laconic Finnish intonation: "Hold on with both hands!"

For years I had thought of myself as a Weeble, one of those roly-poly children's toys that "wobble but they don't fall down." I had, after all, survived breast cancer in my thirties, an age when it tends to be especially deadly; after three miscarriages and six years of infertility, I got pregnant in my forties with my daughter. There were other crises, too, of the heart and the head as well as the body—how could there not be after five decades of living?—but they didn't define me. I'd always popped up fine. Yet lately, incrementally, I had begun to feel defective, emotionally diminished rather than strengthened by trauma, in danger of becoming the sum of my pain. Had that happened after this latest bout of cancer or before? I couldn't say. But I felt cleaved, a word that also means its opposite: cleaved to this body, whether I liked it or not, and from it by its many betrayals. I wanted to bounce back, but this time I just couldn't.

My dogs lunged forward. The sled tipped left, listed right; I felt myself start to tumble. Then I stomped on the pan brake with one foot, and magically the team slowed. My whole body thrummed, but I stayed on the sled. The barking had stopped the second the dogs took off. Now it was quiet, the only sounds their rhythmic panting, the creak of the wooden sled, the scrape and skitter of the pan brake along the powder. I relaxed my death grip on the handlebar and looked around: at spruce trees whose needles were individually etched in crystals of ice, at birches laden so heavily with snow that they'd bent into arches over the trail. We sledded through crystallized snow and powder snow, compacted layers and snow as granular as salt.

I zoomed over moguls, catching air and momentarily taking flight. In truth, we averaged about seven miles an hour and covered up to nineteen miles a day, but when you're balanced on two thin wooden planks, trust me, that is blazing. One of my dogs, Harald, lifted his leg to pee whenever I rode the brake or neglected to help on hills by pushing with one foot. Maybe it was my imagination, but his gesture felt personal.

Too soon we pulled into our camp for the week: a cabin on a snow-covered lake with an outhouse, a wood-burning sauna and a *kota*—a traditional hexagonal cottage with a conical roof and a central fire pit—in which we'd eat our meals. Although we'd been out in the cold for hours, pausing only for a lunch of sausages roasted over an open fire, we now tended to the dogs' comfort before our own. I stroked shoulders and cradled paws, cuddled Bambi, gave Ninni a belly rub. I chained each one to a little straw-filled house where they built their nightly nest. Mari, meanwhile, pulled around a sled weighed down with kibble and a barrel of broth studded with animal fat and parts I preferred not to contemplate.

Nico spied a volunteer staffer heading toward the sauna with an ice pick. There was a hole in the ice of a stream there, just wide enough for the bucket. The staffer cut it open twice a day to haul water for washing dishes and sluicing ourselves in the sauna (the nearest we'd get to bathing). Nico offered to take over, plotting to enlarge the hole so he could fit through it. The ice was nearly two feet thick. Michaela laughed at him. The rest of us did, too. Even Nico laughed. But he kept chipping away.

"Now we have soup," Mari said when the dogs were settled, as if this were normal, as if the whole world took a soup break around five o'clock. Maybe they should: It turns out there is nothing so comforting or convivial. On successive days we warmed to steamy bowls of cream of mushroom, potato-leek, tomato, vegetable and ginger-carrot accompanied by tea, bread, white Finnish cheese, and a little cake. We laughed and shared stories from the trail, holding our hands and stocking feet out to the fire.

When Mari said it was sauna time, I hesitated. Finnish women used to give birth in saunas. There is an entire wing devoted to saunas in the country's Parliament House. And an estimated two million private homes in a country of about five million people have them. There is even a sauna about 4,600 feet below sea level, in a Finnish mine. Taking a sauna was virtually obligatory for a visitor, but this would be the first time since my surgery that I'd disrobe in front of anyone besides my husband and my daughter.

Dressed, I looked fine—better than fine: My new breast passed for natural, and my stomach was flatter than it had been since puberty. I may have felt lousy about myself, but I looked great. Beneath my clothes, however, a jagged purple scar slashed from hip to hip. My reconstructed belly button was ringed by scars, and another scar cupped the underside of my breast. They were the price of staying alive, and I was grateful for them, but I didn't want to discuss them. Not even with other women. Still, I couldn't skip such an integral part of the experience. Besides, I was *freezing*. On our way to the sauna building, I told Michaela and Margarete as briefly and casually as I could, precluding any pity. They were sympathetic, but that wasn't the point: I was here to transcend the identity of illness, not confess it.

Here is what you are supposed to do in a Finnish sauna: sit on a wooden bench until the sweat cascades off you, until you are flushed and slimy and so hot that you can't bear it any longer. So hot that you will do this mad thing: You will run outside, stark naked, and fling yourself in the snow. It is not something I imagined I would ever do—*could* ever do—yet with the others urging me on, I dashed outside, screaming, and flung myself face-first into a snowdrift. It was cold. *Burning* cold. And the snow was the texture of sandpaper. I stood up, turning toward the sauna, but Margarete stopped me. "Now on the back!" she said. So I threw myself backward, tush first. Then, laughing and still whooping, living nowhere but that moment, I returned to the heat.

That night I dreamed my dogs were pulling my sled without harnesses—no ropes, no clips. We simply floated together, a unit, through the snowy nights and days. There was no cold. There was no heat. There was just being.

By morning the cup of water I'd left on the windowsill for toothbrushing had frozen solid. So had my toothpaste. So had my contact lenses. My camera would also freeze, as would the ink in my pens. I shimmied into an extra layer of long underwear inside my sleeping bag, then climbed out to check the thermometer; it was nine degrees in the cabin and twenty-seven below outside. And although I had been trying to drink as little as possible, I had to pee. I steeled myself for the task by piling on pants, a jacket, a hat, mittens, socks, and boots.

The outhouse was a short jaunt down a snowy path: a deceptively quaint, snow-covered log structure with diamond cutouts in the door and back wall for ventilation. A Styrofoam seat covered a wooden hole—it wasn't cold to the touch, exactly, but neither was it warm, and an Arctic breeze whooshed up from below. On my way back to the cabin, I passed Margarete, who waved cheerfully. She was wearing an undershirt and leggings—no jacket, nothing on her head or hands. I glanced down: Her feet were bare, in flip-flops.

That second day, my sled shot out from under me; I hung suspended in midair, flailing like a cartoon character, then was dumped headfirst into the snow. The dogs kept going, until Markku grabbed them. Everyone waited while, in the musher's walk of shame, I struggled through the snow to fetch them back. I'd go down three times before realizing that mushing was in the legs: The trick was to go with the motion, not fight it—to dance with your dogs.

We burst onto a snow-covered lake, a glittering expanse under a crystalline sky. It was spectacular, that emptiness, a vista of frozen potential. I took a deep breath. Northern Finland has some of the cleanest air in Europe; every inhale felt like a sip of spring water, delicious and pure. I'd assumed that we'd sled the same terrain every day and that, while lovely, it would get a little dull. Now we circled upward to the top of a fell—a small Finnish mountain—stopping at the edge of the tree line. Moisture in the air had condensed on the branches in layers, forming wild, Seussian phantasms: child fishing, queen in white fur cape, flying dragons, sentinels. I would say it felt like another planet, but it didn't, not at all. It felt, at last, as if we were in the Arctic.

My nostalgia for Rudolph aside, I'd been excited about trying reindeer meat, common in the Finnish diet, but it proved less succulent than I'd imagined. It's a little chewy, like a lesser cut of beef, but Mari cooked it into a tasty stew. For dessert there were sour lingonberries she had picked and frozen over the summer, topped with yogurt and caramel sauce.

Afterward, we duly donned our Arctic gear and trudged into the moonless night, walking single file along the trail (to avoid sinking into the snow) until we reached the lake. A faint green stripe fanned across the horizon, then changed direction and shot straight up. The northern lights. The Einstein brothers began to natter on about the science—something about collisions of gaseous particles—but I turned away. I preferred the Finnish explanation: The lights are sparks swept from the snow by the tail of a magical fox as it runs across the fells. I gazed up at the firmament, at stars brighter than any I might ever see again. There were Orion, the Big and Little Dippers. There were the Pleiades and Cassiopeia. There was the bright North Star, glittering like an icy gem, leading lost travelers home.

We mushed uphill all the next morning. On the steepest slopes I jogged behind my sled, pushing until the crest, then hopping back on before the dogs could pull off without me. I sweated through my many layers, that fresh Finnish air now searing my lungs. My arm ached from the dogs' yanking. Harald lifted his leg. A lot. *I can't do this.* It was too soon. I was too weak. I would have to quit. I focused on Margarete, straight and sinewy, two teams ahead of me. Hanging on to the pretense of youth mattered to her not at all. Her hair was white, clipped short for ease, not style; her face was lined; her teeth were yellowed. Yet she was tougher than the rest of us: the first one up every morning, the last one inside at night. Her beauty ran deep, a product of spirit, not cosmetics. And if she could do this, dang it, I could, too.

Nico's ice bath was ready on our last afternoon at camp. Michaela snapped pictures as he streaked to the hole. Somehow he persuaded the other men, one by one, to follow his lead. They returned to the cabin pink and swaggering, urging us ladies to give it a try.

"*Anyone* can roll in snow," Nico announced. "*This* is special."

It was twenty-two degrees below zero outside, but I am a sucker for a dare. So I sat in the sauna until I thought my eyeballs would blister. Then, before rationality could set in, I sprinted, naked and steaming, to the hole's icy ledge, slipping and sliding my way in. The water was surprisingly gentle on the skin, less scratchy than snow. I dunked to my armpits, grinning crazily, desperate to get out, loving that I was in.

Back in the sauna, I felt as shining and phosphorescent as the aurora itself. For months my body's limits had defined me, but not anymore. It wasn't that I felt invulnerable— those days are gone. But I was resilient. And in the end, isn't that better?

ॐ ॐ ॐ

Peggy Orenstein is the author of The New York Times *bestsellers* Cinderella Ate My Daughter: Dispatches from the Front Lines of the New Girlie-Girl Culture *and* Waiting for Daisy, *a memoir. Her previous books include the classic* Schoolgirls: Young Women, Self-Esteem, and the Confidence Gap *and* Flux: Women on Sex, Work, Kids, Love and Life in a Half-Changed World. *A contributing writer for* The New York Times Magazine, *Peggy dreams of running the Iditarod.*

*T*his year's edition of *The Best Women's Travel Writing* marks the tenth in the annual series, so I want to take this opportunity to extend my sincere congratulations and gratitude to Travelers' Tales for a decade of offering countless women a superb outlet in which to publish travel narratives. In the field of writing, women are seriously underrepresented (Google "VIDA count" if there's any doubt), and in the field of travel writing, it's even worse. Travelers' Tales is one major exception to this rule, with a long and impressive commitment to publishing women. So I wholeheartedly salute the gentlemen pioneers of Travelers' Tales—James O'Reilly, Larry Habegger, and Sean O'Reilly—for the hard work and tremendous dedication you've poured into creating and sustaining this phenomenal series, and for the publishing opportunities you've provided to hundreds of women, through this and many, many other books. Thank you for using your powers for good!

On a more personal note, James, Larry, and Sean, you guys rule. As I finish working on this, my fifth book with you, I'm filled more than ever with admiration and respect for what you do, and I *adore* working with you. Thanks, a million times over, for allowing me to be part of your superstar editorial team—it has truly changed my life. (James: coffee this week? You free Wednesday?)

Enormous thanks to the friends and colleagues who helped with this book in myriad ways, from providing editorial guidance to spreading the word and nominating stories, to offering moral support, to dragging me out for a glass of wine when I was going cross-eyed. A million thanks to Dolly Spalding (the Dolly Mama herself): lifelong cheerleader and editorial sidekick and the reason I have this life that I cherish. Dan Prothero, you are the world's best husband, and I cannot thank you enough times for delivering to me—every single morning—the perfect cup of coffee, without which this anthology would not have happened.

I have to thank Laurie Weed twice, once for last year and once for this year. Thank you, and thank you. And thank you again. (A third time for good measure and future blunders.) *Un grand merci beaucoup* to Kimberley Lovato and Marcia DeSanctis for moral support and writerly assistance, and to Don George, Jim Benning, David Miller, Susan Orlean, Sarah Menkedick, Julia Cosgrove, Derk Richardson, and David Farley, who nominated stories and/or helped spread the word about submissions. And Susan Brady deserves not just a thank-you but a trophy for pulling this off in time. Thanks to the San Francisco Writers' Grotto for providing a truly inspiring and supportive workspace.

Erin Melcher: What can I say? Thank you for letting me ride shotgun through life with you.

Finally, my appreciation to the hundreds and hundreds of adventurous women who took the leap and dared to hit "send" and submitted stories. You never cease to amaze and inspire and entertain me. This book belongs to you.

Editor Lavinia Spalding is the author of two books: Writing Away: A Creative Guide to Awakening the Journal-Writing Traveler, *and* With a Measure of Grace, the Story and Recipes of a Small Town Restaurant, *and she introduced the reissued e-book edition of Edith Wharton's classic travelogue,* A Motor-Flight Through France. *Her writing has appeared in many print and online publications, as well as in tattered, coffee-stained journals around the world. She lives in San Francisco, where she's a resident of the Writers' Grotto and co-founder of the award-winning monthly travel reading series Weekday Wanderlust.*